A BOX SEAT
TO THE
END TIMES

RON TEED

A BOX SEAT
TO THE
END TIMES

A COMMENTARY OF THE BOOK OF REVELATION
VOLUME 1: GOD'S LETTERS TO THE CHURCHES
SECOND EDITION

TATE PUBLISHING
AND ENTERPRISES, LLC

Published by Tate Publishing & Enterprises, LLC
127 E. Trade Center Terrace | Mustang, Oklahoma 73064 USA
1.888.361.9473 | www.tatepublishing.com

Tate Publishing is committed to excellence in the publishing industry. The company reflects the philosophy established by the founders, based on Psalm 68:11,
"The Lord gave the word and great was the company of those who published it."

Book design copyright © 2016 by Tate Publishing, LLC. All rights reserved.
Cover design by Joana Quilantang
Interior design by Mary Jean Archival

Published in the United States of America

ISBN: 978-1-68270-992-4
1. Religion / Eschatology
2. Religion / Biblical Studies / Prophecy
16.01.13

BIBLE TRANSLATIONS USED AND ABBREVIATIONS

UNLESS OTHERWISE INDICATED all Bible quotations are from the New American Standard Bible, 1995 edition. Scripture taken from the NEW AMERICAN STANDARD BIBLE®,© Copyright 1960, 1962, 1963, 1968, 1971, 1972, 1973, 1975, 1977, 1995 by The Lockman Foundation. Used by permission. www.Lockman.org

Other translations used:

AMP   Scripture quotations taken from the Amplified® Bible, Copyright © 1954, 1958, 1962, 1964, 1965, 1987 by The Lockman Foundation. Used by permission." www. Lockman.org

CEV   Scripture quotations marked (CEV) are from the Contemporary English Version Copyright © 1991, 1992, 1995 by American Bible Society. Used by Permission.

New Testament Commentary—Revelation 1-11. Chicago: Moody Press, 1999; *The MacArthur New Testament Commentary—Revelation 12-22*. Chicago: Moody Press, 2000; and *The Book of Revelation*. Audio Series produced by Grace To You, PO Box 4000, Panorama City, CA are used by permission.

Quotations from *Thru the Bible with J. Vernon McGee*. Nashville, TN: Thomas Nelson, 1983 are used by permission.

DEDICATION

To MY LOVELY wife Betty, without whose help, knowledge, skill, encouragement, and love I could not have produced this work. God has frequently assigned ministry opportunities to a team of two people, and we feel that He has done something very similar in our marriage and relationship.

To my mother and father, the late Alice and Robert Teed, who taught me many valuable lessons.

To my grandchildren: Hannah, Jacob, Zachary, Kelly, and Sarah, who I pray will come to a saving faith in Jesus and join me in the Heavenly City one day.

Acknowledgements

I WISH TO express my gratitude to the thoughtful and sometimes challenging input from the Sunday night Bible study that worked its way through this journey with me. I want to especially acknowledge the comments and input of Scott and Kathy Marshall who asked thoughtful, and sometimes piercing, questions. The input of this group helped me dig even deeper and refine the text of this commentary.

CONTENTS

INTRODUCTION

IF YOU HAVE ever gone on a very special trip or vacation, one that you will never forget, that will give you some idea of the journey we are about to begin together in the book of Revelation. We will travel through time: past, present, and future. We will travel through space, between Heaven and earth, and even under the earth. We will travel the world that John knew and he will tell us what will happen to all the nations of the world when Christ returns at some future time. When we conclude our trip we will have an understanding of the Triune God that we never had before.

Most people think of Heaven as a place with large billowy white clouds with angels sitting on them playing their harps. That description is most definitely a misrepresentation of what the Bible tells us Heaven will be like. You will learn just how wonderful it is actually going to be. However, in spite of all the wonder contained in the book of Revelation, it is probably the most misunderstood and neglected book in the

Bible. It reveals the truth about what is going to happen to people who do not accept Christ as Savior. These people are going to go to Hell according to the teaching of the book of Revelation.

Revelation reveals God's love for each and every human being that He created. It also reveals the perfect judgment and wrath of God toward people who reject His spoken Word in the Bible and the sacrifice His Son made for our salvation. Imagine how God must feel after sending His dearly beloved Son to earth so that the sins of all mankind could be forgiven, only to have people refuse to believe in Jesus' sacrificial death, refuse to believe in what He was willing to do for them. Yet God still loves us and continues to offer us salvation right up until the day we die.

Reference is made to this truth frequently in the Bible. Here are just a couple of examples:

Romans 5:8:

[8] But God demonstrates His own love toward us, in that while we were yet sinners, Christ died for us.

Ephesians 2:1-5, 8-10 (NLT):

Once you were dead because of your disobedience and your many sins. [2] You used to live in sin, just like the rest of the world, obeying the devil—the commander of the powers in the unseen world. He is the spirit at work in the hearts of those who refuse to obey God.

³ All of us used to live that way, following the passionate desires and inclinations of our sinful nature. By our very nature we were subject to God's anger, just like everyone else.4 But God is so rich in mercy, and he loved us so much, 5 that even though we were dead because of our sins, he gave us life when he raised Christ from the dead. (It is only by God's grace that you have been saved!)

8 God saved you by his grace when you believed. And you can't take credit for this; it is a gift from God. 9 Salvation is not a reward for the good things we have done, so none of us can boast about it. 10 For we are God's masterpiece. He has created us anew in Christ Jesus, so we can do the good things he planned for us long ago.

All of the people who have ever lived throughout history are going to live forever. Many people do not understand that. They have a variety of beliefs about what is going to happen to them after they die, but most people do not have facts on which to base that opinion. This book tells us there are only two possible alternatives to where you go after you die: you go either to Heaven or to Hell, and you spend eternity (forever) in one of those two places. If you go to Hell, there is no turning back. There is no purgatory and there is no second chance after you die. Before you die the age of grace is still alive, and those who accept Christ as Savior are going to go to Heaven. Those who reject Him and pursue the evil pleasures of this world are going to go to Hell.

If you choose to follow Christ that does not mean you cannot enjoy life in this world as many people think. You most definitely can and God wants us to enjoy the Christian life abundantly. "*I* [Jesus][1] *came that they may have life, and have it abundantly*" (John 10:10). But you enjoy it by living under God's will, and in so doing you will have enjoyment beyond your wildest expectations. It is the kind of enjoyment that is permanent, not the kind that lasts for only a few minutes, a few hours, and then disappears. Many of us know that those things we think will bring us happiness and satisfaction often bring nothing but pain and grief.

> *Read the book of Revelation,*
> *Do what it says,*
> *And you will receive the blessing of God.*

Revelation is a great book. We all need to understand its message so that we can make our own choice as to where we are going to live for eternity. God makes it very clear in this book that He wants us to know what it teaches. Listen to what the angel tells John in Revelation 22:10: *"Do not seal up the words of the prophecy of this book, for the time is near."* This book describes how we are going to rule and reign with Christ in a perfect place. Yet Revelation is not taught in the greatest majority of churches in this country. Why not? Well, basically because it tells us the truth about Hell and judgment. Remember, these are the words of Jesus and He is giving them to an angel to tell to John. Jesus is the source, the angel

---

1   Brackets mine.

carries the message to John, and John writes it down for all mankind to read. The above verse is a command from Christ Himself that this book be taught to everyone, and those churches and pastors who do not teach it are committing a sin of disobedience against Christ. There is no room for this kind of disobedience in Christ's Church, and we will see this by the warnings that He writes the letters to the churches in chapters two and three.

Further, this is the only book in the Bible that begins and ends with the promise of a blessing from God for those who read it and follow its instructions. Listen to what Jesus says: *"God blesses the one who reads the words of this prophecy to the church, and he blesses all who listen to its message and obey what it says, for the time is near (Revelation 1:3 NLT)."*

Did you get that? Simply read the book or listen to it being taught, do what it says, and you will receive a special blessing from God. What a great promise! But how many of us will take these words off the page and place them in our hearts? Will you? I hope so, or you will miss out on the greatest opportunity of your life. Then in Revelation 22:7 (HCSB), Christ says: *"Look, I am coming quickly! Blessed is the one who keeps the prophetic words of this book."* Here again Jesus affirms the promise He gave us at the very beginning in Revelation 1:3. Blessing is promised at the very beginning and the very end of this book for those who believe it. We need to understand this book because the time of the fulfillment is near. That does not necessarily mean that it is going to happen in the next few days or even within John's lifetime. But it will be the next major event on God's calendar following Christ's death and resurrection. Now *"soon"* or *"near"* in Revelation 1:3 does not mean the same thing to God as it does to us. Scripture tells us that to God a thousand years is like a day (2 Peter 3:8).

We simply need to know that it is coming and that we need to be ready because many people will say, "What makes you think it's so near? We've lived two thousand years since Christ and it hasn't happened yet." Remember that we do not know how God defines "near." Christ told us it is coming and if we do not expect it to happen, it is sure to happen when we least expect it. You may be wondering why Jesus would not tell us exactly when He would return so that all people living in those days would know that they needed to make a decision about Christ by that given date or end up in Hell. Would that not motivate people to want to investigate what the Bible has to say about receiving the gift of salvation and eternal life?

Well, that would be a reasonable question. However, if Jesus had provided a specific date it is the nature of mankind to postpone difficult decisions. If we knew the exact date that Jesus was returning we might repeatedly put off the investigation process, telling ourselves something like this: "I have plenty of time before I have to make a decision, I'll just continue drinking and drugging and cheating on my wife so I might continue to have a good time. I'll put off any religious considerations for a couple of years." Then in a few years, you will probably do the very same thing. You might reason, "I'm so busy working on that new merger that will make me a millionaire, I just don't have time now to worry about Jesus." Such procrastination could go on for ten, twenty, thirty years or more.

But the day finally comes when you know you cannot continue postponing your decision. So on October 3, 2019, you commit to immediately start the process and make a decision by the first of the year. Then as you read and study the Bible and various commentaries, on November 14, 2019 you drop dead. What will happen to you then is the same thing that would happen if Jesus returned. Without having declared your faith in Jesus Christ before you died, accepting His sacrificial death as payment for your sins, you would immediately go to Hell and there would be no second chances. Heed this warning and do not wait another day to believe in Jesus Christ as your Lord and Savior. He is the only One able to wipe away your sin in the eyes of God. All it takes is a sincere confession that you are a sinner in need of a Savior, that you believe in your heart that Jesus is that Savior and that He is alive today in Heaven. That is all it takes for God by His grace to declare you righteous and secure your place with Him on this earth for as long as you live, and then in Heaven with Him for eternity.

"*Near*" in verse 3, as mentioned above, could also refer to our own death as I alluded to above. No one really believes they are going to die today, but some people will. All those things that this book warns about will be just as true on the day of our own death as they will be on the day Christ returns. If we are not ready for both the day Christ returns and the day of our own death, it will be the greatest mistake we ever make. Because at the time either of these events occurs your eternity will be sealed by whether or not you believe in Jesus Christ. If you reject Him, your eternity will be spent in Hell (the Lake of Fire). That will become very clear to you as you progress in this study. You will be able to connect the events that are occurring in our world today with the prophecies that are in the book of Revelation. Some of you will say, *"Well, people have been saying that for hundreds of years."* But I will show you that there are things in this book that could not have happened fifty years ago, or maybe even fifteen years ago, but that can happen now.[2] The clock is ticking and we could be getting very close.

As you read you are going to find that the book of Revelation is very much like a giant jigsaw puzzle. All these pieces are scattered on the table in front of us, and we are to connect all the pieces for the answers to be revealed to us. Adding to the confusion, as you will see as we go through this book, there is really no chronological order. In one verse we can go from Christ's birth to the time of His Second Coming at the end of the Tribulation, and that is a period of time that

---

2   This manuscript was completed in 2015.

at least spans nearly 2,000 years as this commentary is being written. If we look long and hard at this book, we will be able to fit these pieces together to create a pretty good outline of the events leading up to the end of the world and the return of Christ to this earth in glory.

We will find, however, that we run out of pieces to this puzzle before the picture is complete. That is simply because God does not want us to know everything. He tells us right in the book of Revelation that there are some things we are not to know. But He tells us enough to really excite us and get our attention. We see enough to know the truth and to know how magnificent our God is. We see how incredible the home is that He has prepared for us.

Also, we will look at parts of Scripture that promise we will be like Christ when we are in Heaven (1 John 3:2). We will not be God, we will not be deity, but we will have the same kind of perfect physical body and mind as Christ. We will be perfect in mind and body while most likely retaining many of our same physical looks.

Just think, we will not need any meetings to make decisions because we will all know the right thing to do. If you want to know what we will be like, look at Scripture and see what Christ was like. After His resurrection, Christ flew up to Heaven from the earth; Christ walked through walls; and most of us will be delighted to know that Christ ate. The resurrected Christ did all of these things and many more after He rose from the grave. We will be able to do the same things. What a great promise for the believer. What a tragedy for those who choose to miss out on all of this, for those who choose to reject Christ.

About now there may be a few among you who are saying to themselves, "What about all the other religions in the world? Surely he is not going to tell us that faith in Christ alone is the only way to get to Heaven?" We will address this subject in detail later in this study. For now let it be enough to say that in all of the religions that have ever been, among all those who have ever claimed to be God or the Messiah or whatever, there is only one empty grave. There is only one who overcame death and rose from the grave to eternal life. That one person is Christ. That fact alone proves to us that He is the only One through whom we too may overcome death. No one else was God. Yes, God came to earth in a human body (incarnation). No one else could have lived a perfect, sinless life on earth, and for that reason was able to provide the perfect sacrifice that was required for sin. Christ is the only way. Do not be deceived into thinking that there is another way. Christ has the power to give us that same ability to overcome death if we simply accept His free gift of everlasting life through faith in Him and in what He did on the cross.

When we put all the pieces of the puzzle of the book of Revelation together, we see enough to understand clearly what the future holds. I believe you will better understand this entire study if I first take you on a quick overview of the book of Revelation. That will allow us to understand the details better as they unfold.

We have all heard various people make predictions about a specific date that Christ was going to return. Such dates have always come and gone uneventfully. Those predictions were obviously wrong. Such predictions inflict a great deal of damage on the believability of the Gospel message of Christ to the world. The Bible tells us: *"But the exact day and hour? No one knows that, not even heaven's angels, not even the Son. Only the Father"* (Mark 13:32, THE MESSAGE).

The public often sees these people as crackpots who are simply trying to make a name for themselves and stroke their own egos. Unfortunately, if such people claim to be Christians, it suggests that many other Christians may be crackpots as well. Any true Christian who understands the Word of God and the truth of Scripture can tell you that **no one knows the day or hour when Christ will return**. The Bible clearly states again: *"But of that day and hour no one knows, not even the angels of heaven, nor the Son, but the Father alone* (Matthew 24:36)."* This statement was made when Jesus was here on the earth in the body of a human. He did not know at that time because He limited His divine qualities in His humanness (Philippians 2:6-8), but of course He knows now because He is part of the Trinity. But no one other than God the Father, Son, and Holy Spirit know the exact date. No one can possibly gather that information from the Bible because that information is not there. However, we are given many guidelines to indicate what is going to happen just prior to His coming.

Just as an example, there will probably be a new temple in the city of Jerusalem before Christ returns (Revelation 11:1). There is no temple at this time so I do not think He will be returning to earth in the next couple of days. However, such a temple could pop up in the form of a tent or prefabricated building in just a few days. It would not have to be a structure that required ten years to build. But these and other signs are given to us in this book to suggest when the time is getting close. So be vigilant (watchful).

Through His grace, God has given us in the book of Revelation, several indications as to when that day is getting close. Revelation is clear in revealing that the beginning of the end will be signaled by the world moving toward a one-world government. This one-world government will be preceded by a one-world religion. In other words those who have the money and power are going to promote a one-world religion under the spin that this is the only way to solve all the world's problems. Those proposing this plan will suggest that if we can simply all love one another and come together under the umbrella of one religion and one God, then there will be peace and the whole world will be able to live in tranquility. Once that world religion has secured its place throughout the world, there will be a successful movement to establish a world government. We will see this in more detail later.

But this one-world religion will hold out the promise to the world of solving all of its problems. After all, have not most wars in this world been fought over religion? That will be a sure sign that the time of the Tribulation is coming close

Now let me provide a definition of the *"Tribulation"* because we will be encountering this term throughout our journey: This is a seven year period of unparalleled suffering that will come upon the entire earth (Revelation 3:10). Jeremiah called it *"the time of Jacob's distress"* (Jeremiah 30:7). It will be a time of suffering associated with events of the End Time (the end of the world as we know it). It is described as tribulation surpassing any trouble yet experienced in human history (Matthew 24:21). It will also be connected with catastrophic judgments for those inhabitants of the earth who have rejected Jesus and committed acts of wickedness and anti-Semitism.[3] [4]

This one-world religion and one-world government will work together during the first half of the Tribulation in order to have the world under the control of perhaps a few dozen very powerful rulers. There will be a great deal more to be

---

3   Merrill Unger, *The New Unger's Bible Dictionary*, (Chicago: Moody Press, 1957), s.v. ","WORD*search*CROSS e-book.

4   Trent C. Butler, ed., "TRIBULATION," in *Holman Bible Dictionary*, (Nashville, TN: Holman Bible Publishers, 1991), WORD*search* CROSS e-book, under: "TRIBULATION".

said about the world government and Antichrist throughout this study.

Now, what about the **Rapture**, that time when the Church of Jesus Christ is going to be transported from earth to Heaven in the blink of an eye? The Rapture will be an event that takes place between the second hand ticks on a clock. One second you'll be here on earth, the next second believers will be in **Heaven.** All believers that are alive on the earth will be *"beamed up,"* to borrow a term from *Star Trek*, to Heaven. They will find themselves with new resurrection bodies and minds. In the same blink of an eye, all those who have died throughout the history of the Church Age and whose spirits now reside in Heaven will receive their resurrection bodies and minds as well. So, in effect, all believers from the time of Christ until that day will be in Heaven. Old Testament saints will not receive their resurrected bodies until the end of the seven-year Tribulation (more on this later). These new bodies will never wear out and will last throughout eternity, forever and ever and ever. One moment a believer will be sitting in a meeting at work, he or she will blink, and they will be looking into the face of Jesus in Heaven. The Rapture will be discussed in much greater detail in *"Background Information."*

So when we see a world government beginning to take shape, under the promise of solving all the world's problems, it will signal that the beginning of the seven-year Tribulation is very near. When will the Rapture occur? That is a question that I believe cannot be answered with any degree of certainty. There are theologians who have and do believe that the Rapture will occur just before the beginning of the Tribulation. Others maintain it will occur at the midpoint of the Tribulation, and still others at the end of the Tribulation. I have researched this subject extensively and it is my opinion that **the Rapture will occur just prior to the unleashing of God's wrath on the earth**. This would place the time just prior to the seven bowl judgments which probably will occur sometime during the last year of the Tribulation.[5]

Then at the end of that seven-year Tribulation Christ is going to return to this earth to set up His rule for one thousand years. At the end of those thousand years this universe will be destroyed and a new one created. There will be a new Heaven and a new Earth, and the city of Heaven, the New Jerusalem, a cube of fifteen hundred miles in each direction, will be the capital of that new universe. Outside the capital city of Heaven there is going to be an environment of such beauty that our human minds simply can't picture it. We will enjoy every moment of living in this eternal paradise. There may be other planets and stars as there are now but we cannot know for sure. But if there are, we may well be able to travel to them. Imagine being able to fly through the air with a few friends to another planet. There are no limitations to the miracles that Heaven will offer. Please do not miss it. You will not like the alternative.

---

5   Revelation 15:7 and chapter 16.

As the time of the Tribulation begins to unfold we will see that the world government leader, the **Antichrist,** and the world religious leader are going to coexist for the first three-and-a-half years in apparent harmony. At the end of that three-and-a-half years the world government leader is going to overthrow the religious leader (the False Prophet) and declare himself to be the Messiah. He is going to declare himself to be Christ, the savior that the world has been waiting for in one shape or form throughout history.

The world religious leader will then become what the book of Revelation identifies as the False Prophet. He will serve the Antichrist and convince the people of the world to worship the Antichrist. This Antichrist is going to be under the total and complete control of Satan himself.

Before going any further I believe we need to address something head on. Many people become uncomfortable at the mention of Satan. They can somewhat accept the concept of God, but to believe in Satan and his angels is just a little bit too much for them. So we need to have a clear understanding of the existence of Satan and his army of fallen angels or demons. Satan has a whole army of fallen angels numbering in the hundreds of millions. In order to understand the truth of the book of Revelation you must understand and believe this premise. There is continual spiritual warfare occurring 24/7 between the angels of God and the angels of Satan.

Often Satan's angels are referred to as demons. If you are skeptical, please keep an open mind. I am not talking about scary little creatures in red suits that run around frightening people. And Satan is not a fun loving guy with a tail and pitchfork. That is what fiction writers have portrayed to make us think that Satan is really kind of an okay guy who just likes to break a few rules while having a good time. The truth is that Satan and his army have one goal in mind—to create an environment that directs the attention and commitment of people away from God and God's will for their lives.

The purpose of Satan and his demons is to prevent people from seeing the truth of God's Word and accepting Christ as their Savior, the very thing that can give them eternal life in Heaven. Satan's army is composed of people who allow themselves to be corrupted by such things as pornography, homosexuality, fornication, adultery, dishonesty, love of money, and love of fame. They do all these things in search of personal gratification. They are master deceivers and they will draw you into their web by attacking you at your weakest point. But if you are a believer in the atoning death of Christ, if you have confessed that you cannot be perfect on your own and you need a Savior, and invite Him to be that Savior, then you will be protected against the forces of Satan's deceit. You may still be tempted to sin, but when you have the Holy Spirit of God living in you, as all believers do, then you will have the power and ability to resist those temptations. God and Christ are alive in this world. They are not just sitting up in Heaven as spectators wondering how the game is going to turn out. They will work in your life every minute of every day if you only invite them to do so. And if you do, you will have power available to you to do anything within the will of God. That includes resisting the temptations of Satan and his army.

If you cannot accept this truth you are not going to be able to get the full impact of the book of Revelation. We must clearly understand how our lives can be affected by the reality of Satan and Hell as well as God and Heaven. They are all part of this big puzzle that we are putting together. Without a clear understanding of the alternatives we are offered, we may open our eyes immediately after our death and find we have made some horrible choices that have resulted in our being in a place from which we can never escape. So let us do our very best to open our minds to the truth of this book so that we can clearly understand what it has to tell us.

After the establishment of this one world government, which promised to bring a lasting peace to the world, wars are going to begin to break out all over the globe as evil men once again attempt to establish their own power bases. There will be peace for a little while but it is not going to last. Humans may seek after utopia and they may even find it briefly, but it is the nature of people to want what someone else has and that condition will not change until Christ returns.

These wars will continue and become more frequent all the way to the end of the Tribulation when Christ returns. When He returns He is going to defeat all the armies of the world in an instant. But as these wars develop and escalate, a number of accounts in the book of Revelation provide evidence that these wars are going to produce what could very well be severe nuclear destruction. The descriptions of the destruction caused could only result from incredibly large explosions occurring all over the world. These explosions would produce scorching temperatures that could melt rock and metal. They will also rearrange the contour of the earth as well as destroy any form of life. A world-wide nuclear war will result in massive destruction and death that should be a warning to those who continue to refuse to recognize the sovereignty of God and Jesus Christ. We will see much more detail regarding such events as we move along through this book.

Along with this destruction and death caused by war there are also going to be many severe natural disasters taking place. A series of plagues very similar to those inflicted on the Egyptians during the time of Moses will be reenacted. You may recall that when the Pharaoh of Egypt refused to free God's people, God would send a plague on the nation of Egypt. Each plague was more severe than the previous one. You can read about it in Exodus 5:1 through Exodus 12:32. We will see a very similar thing happening during the Tribulation, but on a much wider scale and with much more intensity. There are going to be wars and catastrophes occurring all over the world, the likes of which have never before been seen by mankind. At this point some of you may be wondering how a loving God would allow this kind of suffering. Well, you need to know that in spite of all the things that happen during the

Tribulation that will prove without any doubt the existence of God, many people will continue to choose evil rather than the saving message of salvation.

The only way God can get their attention is by continually turning up the heat so that they can see that without God they have no hope, that they are not able to control their own future. At the end of the day everything is under God's control. If you do not believe that see if you can find someone who has lived forever and been able to prevent their own death. Or what about disease? How many people who have AIDS can control their own future? How many people with terminal cancer are able to reverse the end result of that condition? The more we try to control things without God the more difficult life will become. The more we turn our lives over to the care of God following the path the Holy Spirit sets before us, the better it gets and the easier it gets. The harder people try to control the future, the higher the odds of their being brought down and the worse their situation will become. *"All who fear the LORD will hate evil. Therefore, I hate pride and arrogance, corruption and perverse speech"* (Proverbs 8:13, NLT); *"Pride goes before destruction, and haughtiness before a fall"* (Proverbs 16:18, NLT); *"Pride ends in humiliation, while humility brings honor"* (Proverbs 29:23, NLT).

For some people during the Tribulation the message of God will become clear. They will repent[6] and turn to God

---

6   Changing one's mind, coming to a new way of thinking; Op. Cit., Achtemeier, S. 861.

for salvation. They will call out to Christ as a result of all the suffering that is going on in the world and as a result they will be saved. Others, however, will continue to curse God for what is taking place. The book of Revelation makes it very clear that in spite of the fact that people see what God is doing, they will curse Him rather than turning to Him for help.

Revelation 16:17-21:

[17] *Then the seventh angel poured out his bowl upon the air, and a loud voice came out of the temple from the throne, saying, "It is done."* [18] *And there were flashes of lightning and sounds and peals of thunder; and there was a great earthquake, such as there had not been since man came to be upon the earth, so great an earthquake was it, and so mighty.* [19] *The great city was split into three parts, and the cities of the nation's fell. Babylon the great was remembered before God, to give her the cup of the wine of His fierce wrath.* [20]*And every island fled away and the mountains were not found.* [21] *And huge hailstones, about one hundred pounds each, came down from heaven upon men; and men blasphemed (cursed)* [7]*God because of the plague*[8] *of the hail, because its plague was extremely severe.*

We see all of this suffering going on throughout the Tribulation. It continues to get worse and worse, all the way

---

7   Certain other translations.
8   Destruction and loss of life.

up to the end of the Tribulation. As the Tribulation draws to an end there will be one final battle of enormous magnitude. That is, of course, the Battle of Armageddon. Most of us have heard the term but very few people know what it actually means or what it refers to. This battle will involve hundreds of millions of troops along with the most devastating high tech weapons of war. Sometime during that battle, Christ will appear in the darkened sky as a blazing light form, like a brilliantly shining star. He will be surrounded by His saints and angels. In case you are not quite sure what the term saint means, it refers to anyone throughout history who has placed their faith in the promises of God and Jesus Christ. All of these saints are going to be with Him when He returns to the earth during the Battle of Armageddon. Many people believe the term saint refers to those who have been awarded a special position in Christ's kingdom because of the good life they have lived. That is absolutely not true. There is nothing in Scripture to support that position. Christ does not have favorites. All believers share equally in the wealth of the King and will live like royalty in Heaven.

Christ will defeat all the armies of the earth at the Battle of Armageddon with a plan that no general in history ever had the ability or power to perform. He will then immediately establish His thousand year rule over the earth. During that period of time He will lock Satan in what Scripture refers to as the *"Bottomless Pit."* This is not Hell but a special place of incarceration especially for Satan and his demons.

Hell is a place where nonbelievers are sent when they die and, contrary to popular belief, Satan does not rule in Hell; God rules over Hell. The dominion of Satan is on the earth. Hell is simply a temporary holding place for nonbelievers until the end of the millennial kingdom when the final judgment will take place. At that time all nonbelievers throughout history will be sentenced to the Lake of Fire for eternity. During this thousand year reign of Christ on the earth (the Millennium) which occurs prior to the creation of the New Heaven and the New Earth, life is going to be almost perfect. Those people who accepted Jesus Christ as their Savior are going to be ruling with Him in positions of authority. You might find yourself governing the territory of Hawaii or Australia. The chances are very good that the thing you may have most desired in life, and never achieved, is the very thing you will be blessed with while you are ruling with Christ during the Millennial Kingdom. What form that will take is impossible to determine but you can let your imaginations run free in this regard, and no matter what you come up with, it will be far short of just how wonderful it will actually be.

During this thousand-year kingdom (Millennium) much of the pain, sickness, resentment, jealousy, debt, rejection, or competition people experience now will no longer be present. People will love one another. Those who rejected Christ throughout history will not be there. They will be in Hell where they will remain until the end of the Millennium. At that time they will be judged and sentenced for eternity.

At the end of the thousand years Christ is going to release Satan. Satan will immediately, in his deceiving way, convince millions to join his army. As that army converges from all over the world to attack Christ in Jerusalem, God will suddenly destroy that army and cast Satan into the Lake of Fire where he will spend eternity. Again I remind you that he will not rule in the Lake of Fire, but rather will be just another inhabitant there. God will rule over the Lake of Fire and we will see more about that later.

Immediately after this will be what is called in Scripture, *"The Great White Throne Judgment."* All those who have been in Hell throughout history are going to stand before the Great White Throne. They will then be sentenced to the Lake of Fire where they will spend eternity. This is not going to be a pleasant place. Revelation 21:8 tells us that this will be a lake that burns with fire and brimstone.[9] It is not a place where any sane person would want to spend eternity. There is going to be unending agony in this place. We will see much more of what Scripture says about it as the study unfolds.

But we might want to take a moment here to consider something. Why do you suppose Christ endured the most

---

9   Brimstone: Sulphur, a greenish-yellow nonmetallic substance that is highly flammable. It is used in the modern manufacturing of matches and gunpowder. Sulphur is associated in popular belief with divine punishment by fire (Gen. 19:24; Rev. 14:10). Op. Cit., Achtemeier. Easton, M.G.: *Easton's Bible Dictionary.* Oak Harbor, WA.

agonizing death imaginable by hanging on a cross for hours? He experienced agonizing pain with each breath He took. Could it be that this substitutionary death in payment for our sins was also meant to show us the kind of death He was saving us from? Scripture tells us that eternity in the Lake of Fire means never ending suffering and pain for those who end up there. I believe it is very possible that Christ is showing us that not only is He saving us from our sin, but He is also showing us at the same time the kind of death from which He is saving us.

The New Heaven and Earth will then be created and the capital city, the New Jerusalem, will descend onto the New Earth. All of Christ's saints will then move into this place that is more glorious than our limited imaginations could ever begin to picture. We will live in the presence of God and Jesus in this perfect environment (place) forever.

If you are not a believer you need to recognize the reality of the consequences of rejecting the Gospel of Jesus Christ. Without understanding this reality the unbeliever may continue to turn his back on Christ. The reality of Hell, the Lake of Fire, and the catastrophes that will occur during the last three-and-a-half years of the Tribulation can be avoided. Mankind still lives in the age of grace, which means you could have your salvation right now, today. If you have never asked Christ to be your Savior, you could have salvation right at this very moment. You do not have to go out and do good deeds to clean up your life. You do not have to run through a check list or go to a priest and confess your sins. You do not have to do penance. In fact you do not have to do anything at all to earn your salvation.

Salvation comes through God's grace. Grace means unmerited or undeserved favor. You can have it today. It is a free gift from God. If you would like an iron clad guarantee that you are going to Heaven, tell God, tell Jesus, tell the Holy Spirit that you are a sinner in need of a Savior and that you believe in your heart that Jesus is the one-and-only Savior who can wipe away all your sins so that God will no longer see them. God will grant you salvation through His grace. If you are willing right now to confess that you are a sinner and need a Savior in order to have everlasting life, you can assure your presence with God in Heaven throughout eternity. There is no other way to get there. If you still have some doubts about God, tell Him exactly what they are, and if you really want to know the truth about God, ask Him to reveal it to you. He promises that He will (Matthew 7:7).

Now the sequence of events between the beginning of the Tribulation and the Great White Throne Judgment can be very confusing. So let me provide a general outline of what happens during this period of time in the sequence in which it occurs:

- The beginning of the seven-year Tribulation will occur when a world government is formed and Israel will sign a seven year treaty that will supposedly finally bring peace to the Middle East.

- If you are familiar with politics and conspiracy,[10] it may not surprise you that this government will not succeed for very long. There will soon be arguing within the ranks and before long wars will be breaking out all over the world bringing death and famine to much of the world's population. At about the same time God will initiate natural disasters throughout the world that will bring additional death, starvation, and epidemics.

- There will be a movement begun before the start of the Tribulation to bring all people together in a common religion so that there will be no more wars in this world over religion. You will be introduced to a man who will lead that attempt to bring the world together in one religion, eventually leading to a one world government, and he will be known as The False Prophet. He will also be a very important person in the Antichrist's rise to world power.

- With all this going on and it being obvious that the world is no longer able to function harmoniously with individual nations bickering all the time over various issues, world leaders will decide that the world could

---

10   A combination of persons for a secret, unlawful, or evil purpose.

best be governed if it was divided into ten regional nations, each governed by a king or ruler.

- From this new ten nation grouping of world government the Antichrist will come out of nowhere and rapidly rise in power to the place where he will overthrow three of these kings and kingdoms, and because of the enormous popular support he has among the people, he will be appointed world ruler and will soon also declare that he is the Messiah the Jews were expecting, and demand that all the people of the world worship him.

- We will do some traveling back and forth through many of the Old Testament books of prophecy because much of the detail of the story of Revelation is found in these prophetic books.

- You will also find that as we look at this book and many of the prophetic books we will encounter a considerable amount of symbolism, which speaks of something by identifying it with something else that might give more meaning to the text. For example, ten toes refer to ten kings. The Antichrist is described as rising out of the sea, having ten horns and seven heads. As difficult as some of these passages are to interpret accurately, it is my intention to attempt to the best of my ability to make it all understandable to the average reader, even if a person is not that familiar with the Bible.

- There is going to be unprecedented[11] horror during the Tribulation especially in the last three-and-one half years. Christians and Jews throughout the world will be severely persecuted and murdered. But God will be right there for the believer, bringing you through.

- You will observe Antichrist as he prepares for victory in a battle (Armageddon) where he expects to overthrow Christ and His people and crown Satan as the one and only God.

- There are a number of Bible scholars whom I admire very much and have used much of their commentary as resources for this book. It is their scholarly opinion that the event known as the Rapture of the Church is going to occur before the Tribulation begins. They make some good arguments for holding this position, but as I mentioned earlier I think otherwise.

- At the end of the Tribulation the earth will have been torn to shreds and be incapable of supporting life. Whoever is left alive among both believers and unbelievers, the believers being identified as sheep, and the unbelievers identified as goats, will be assembled at the Valley of Jehoshaphat where the "Sheep and Goat Judgment" will take place. All unbelievers who rejected Christ right up until the end will be condemned to Hell awaiting the "Great

---

11   The likes of which has never been seen before.

White Throne Judgment," which will take place after the thousand years, the Millennium, a time in which Christ will return to earth and rule from Jerusalem.

- Those sentenced to Hell will remain there for a thousand years and then they will be sent to the Lake of Fire which is even worse. There will also be a remnant of believing Jews who come to faith in Christ before the end of the Tribulation, and they will enter the Millennium alive in their earthly bodies to repopulate Israel and live in the land that God originally promised them. Those born in the Millennium will have the same kind of bodies as their parents, just like those we have today. All believers, from Adam until the end of the Tribulation (with the exception of the Jewish remnant and the believing Gentiles who live through the Tribulation), will have new resurrected bodies that are perfect in every way and will last forever. These bodies will be just like Jesus' resurrected body with many of the same capabilities. If those who enter the Millennium in earthly bodies die, they will not be raised and given resurrected bodies until the end of the Millennium.

- After the separation of the sheep (believers) and the goats (unbelievers) and Jesus' recreating this world after the destruction of the Tribulation, the thousand year millennium will begin with Jesus being the ruler over all the earth. Life will be nearly perfect in every

way because Jesus will deal swiftly and harshly with
those who commit sin.
- During this time Satan will be incarcerated (locked)
  in the Pit, which is very much like a prison.

Revelation 20:1-3 (NKJV):

[1] *Then I saw an angel coming down from heaven, having the key
to the bottomless pit and a great chain in his hand.* [2] *He laid hold
of the dragon, that serpent of old, who is the Devil and Satan,
and bound him for a thousand years;* [3] *and he cast him into the
bottomless pit, and shut him up, and set a seal on him, so that he
should deceive the nations no more till the thousand years were
finished. But after these things he must be released for a little while.*

- At the end of the Millennium, Heaven will descend
  to the earth, and all things will be perfect for those
  who have believed, and I might add beyond our
  ability to conceive.

So with this brief introduction in mind let us begin to take
a look at the wonderful book of Revelation.

BACKGROUND INFORMATION FOR THE STUDY OF THE BOOK OF REVELATION

IT IS ALMOST impossible to undertake a study of End Time prophecy and the book of Revelation without a working knowledge of the history of Israel. So that is where we will begin. The nation and people of Israel have an incredible history. I spent a good deal of time researching this subject and then one evening I opened up the *Holman Illustrated Bible Dictionary*, and there it was, everything I had been looking for. I was so impressed with the way this subject was covered that I decided to quote their description word for word. So here it is, and I trust it will provide you a solid foundation on which to build your understanding.

THE LAND OF ISRAEL[1]

The following introductory material on *"The Land of Israel"* has been taken from the *Holman Illustrated Bible Dictionary*, Chad Brand, Charles Draper, Archie England, eds., (Nashville: Holman Bible Publishers, 2003), s.v. and is used by permission.

"The most common name in the Old Testament for the land where the history of Israel takes place is Canaan. It occupies about 9,500 square miles, an area about the size of the state of Vermont, the upstate of South Carolina, or the country of Belgium. Canaan, or Palestine, reaches from the Mediterranean Sea on the west, to the Great Arabian Desert on the east, to the Lebanon and Anti-Lebanon Mountains on the north, and the Sinai Desert on the south. It is about 150 miles from north to south and 75 miles from east to west. The very location of Israel profoundly affected what was to happen to her over the centuries, for she sat uncomfortably in the middle of the "Fertile Crescent" (including Egypt, Palestine, Mesopotamia, Anatolia, and Armenia, or to use modern names: Egypt, Lebanon, Syria, Turkey, Jordan, Iraq, and Iran). This area was the very matrix of humankind, a veritable cradle for civilization.

---

1   *Holman Bible Dictionary* © 2003 Holman Bible Publishers, Nashville, TN

"Due to its strategic location, it served as a land bridge between Asia and Africa, a meeting place, and a contested battlefield for many ancient powers, including Egypt, Assyria, Babylonia, Medo-Persia, Greece, and Rome. To this day it remains one of the most geopolitically sensitive and important areas of the world.

"It is an arid[2] and exotic [unusual][3] land of great variety [with many natural resources]. Mountains in the north are in stark contrast [a lot different] to the Arabah[4] and the lowest point on the earth, the **Dead Sea**, some 1,300 feet below sea level.[5]

"**The Pre-exilic Period** *The Patriarchal Period* Biblical interest in Canaan begins with the call of Abram (Gen. 12). His journey to Canaan occurred about 2092 B.C. He left his home of Ur of the Chaldeans in Mesopotamia earlier with his family but lingered in Haran where his father Terah died. With Sarai, his wife, and Lot, his nephew, he came at last to Canaan. Abram was not a nomadic shepherd tending sheep and goats but rather a merchant prince who traded with

---

2   Dry; footnote added.

3   Brackets added.

4   Arabah (burnt up). Place-name meaning "dry, infertile area" and common Hebrew noun meaning desert with hot climate and little rainfall. Chad Brand, Charles Draper, Archie England, ed., *Holman Illustrated Bible Dictionary*, (Nashville: Holman Bible Publishers, 2003), s. v. "," WORD*search* CROSS e-book. http://www.biblestudytools.com/dictionary/arabah/

5   Op. Cit., *Holman Illustrated Bible Dictionary*.

monarchs and commanded a security force of 318 men to guard his family and his assets. The names of people and places and events described have a ring of authenticity, and we may be confident that the Abraham cycle is a reliable historical record. Abraham received a promise from God that the land of Canaan would be given to his descendants forever, but the only land he ever owned in the land of promise was a burial plot for Sarah and himself. Initiating a pattern, the younger of Abram's son, Isaac, was the child of the promise. Isaac had twin sons, Jacob and Esau. Continuing the pattern, the younger of the twins, Jacob, became the child of the promise. His 12 sons became the namesakes for the 12 tribes of Israel, but the child of the promise, Judah, was not the hero of his generation, rather Joseph became the savior of his family.

"There is no reason to doubt that Joseph really existed. His story (Gen. 37–50) accurately reflects the history of Egypt in the 19th century B.C. Joseph's story falls into three parts: Joseph and his brothers in Canaan, Joseph alone in Egypt, and Joseph in Egypt with his father Jacob (by this time renamed Israel), his brothers, and their families.

"One of the younger sons but favored by his father, Joseph was resented deeply by his brothers who sold him into slavery and told his father he was dead. In Egypt he repeatedly overcame great obstacles until he rose to the right hand of Pharaoh.[6] Famine sent his brothers to Egypt for food where

---

6   A ruler of ancient Egypt.

they came before Joseph who, after testing them, brought his father's family to live in safety in Egypt about 1875 b.c. The Joseph stories exhibit an overwhelmingly Egyptian context that fits well what is known of this period. Joseph's story provides the explanation for why Jacob's family and the tribes of Israel found themselves in Egypt for the next 430 years.

"**The Egyptian Period.** Several hundred years of relative silence separate the end of the story of Joseph (Gen. 37–50) from the beginning of the story told in the Book of Egypt. Joseph's story indicates that **Israel** probably entered Egypt in the middle of the illustrious[7] Twelfth Dynasty[8] (ca. 1875-1850 b.c.).

"Moses appeared early in the new kingdom era, born about 1526 b.c. His parents Amram and Jochebed sought to save his life from Pharaoh's decree, that all male Hebrew infants be killed, by setting him adrift on the Nile in a basket. His basket came to rest at the place where a daughter of Pharaoh bathed. She took the child in and raised him as the grandson of Pharaoh. Educated in the palace of Egypt, Moses received one of the finest educations in the world. Learning a spectrum of languages and a wide variety of subject matter that prepared him well to lead and govern the Israelites after they left Egypt. Moses' foster mother likely was a powerful

---

7   Well-known; celebrated.

8   A family of rulers who rule over a country for a long period of time; *also*: the period of time when a particular dynasty is in power.

woman named **Hatshepsut,**[9] who effectively controlled Egypt while Thutmose III was still a minor after his accession to the throne. **Amenhotep II**[10] (1450-1425 B.C.) was probably the pharaoh of the **exodus,**[11] which most likely occurred in 1447 or 1446 B.C.

"The Exodus from Egypt—ca. 1447b.c. The exodus from Egypt was to Israel what the Odyssey[12] was to the Greeks and what the Pilgrim Fathers are to Americans. *"So I said, I will bring you up out of the affliction*[13]*of Egypt to the land of the Canaanite and the Hittite and the Amorite and the Perizzite and the Hivite and the Jebusite, to a land flowing with milk and honey."*[14](Exodus 3:17)

"Israel arrived at **Mount Sinai** around 1447 B.C. Though various locations have been suggested, the best option for the location of Mount Sinai is the traditional site Jebel Musa in the southern end of the Sinai Peninsula. At Sinai Israel entered into covenant with Yahweh, received the Ten Commandments, and began her first experience in self-governance.

---

9   Emphasis added.
10   Emphasis added.
11   Emphasis added.
12   Odyssey:A long journey full of adventures; a series of experiences that give knowledge or understanding to someone.
13   Affliction: Suffering
14   Bible verse added.

"*The Wilderness Period—ca. 1447-1407b.c.* About a year later they started for the land of promise but were deterred[15] from entry, first by disobedience and then by God, and did not arrive in Canaan for another 40 years. God protected and preserved Israel, but the generation that refused to enter the land at God's command died out except for the two faithful spies, Joshua and Caleb.

'*Conquest of Canaan—ca. 1407-1400b.c.* One of the most dramatic stories ever told about the origin of a nation unfolded as Israel moved into the land of promise. A journey that could be made in eleven days stretched out for a total of 40 years. Near the end of this period Moses died and was buried by the Lord Himself and Joshua, an Ephraimite, assumed leadership of the nation. He is introduced as Moses' successor and as the conqueror of Canaan (Deut. 1:38; 3:21, 28; Josh. 1). Outside the book bearing his name, he is mentioned only in Exod. 17:8-16; Judg. 1:1, 2:6-9; 1 Kings 16:34; 1 Chron. 7:27; and Neh. 8:17.

"Joshua did a remarkable job of organizing and executing the plan for the conquest of the land. Miraculously Israel crossed Jordan on dry ground during flood season. Israel renewed the covenant at Gilgal where all those males were circumcised who had not been in the wilderness. The conquests were impressive, beginning with the miraculous collapse of the walls of Jericho, yet some of the existing people

---

15   Deterred: Prevented. Footnote added.

in the land were not completely driven out and remained a source of difficulty for Israel throughout her existence.

"Joshua apportioned the land to the 12 tribes according to the instructions God gave Moses, and the occupation of Canaan began. Things went well during the lifetime of those who served with Joshua, but then a dark period of serious spiritual decline began.

'Period of the Judges—ca. 1360-1084b.c. The downward spiral lasted about 280 years. The judges, *shophetim,* were more like leaders or rulers. The period was characterized by a recurring cycle of decline, oppression,[16] repentance, and deliverance.[17] The reforms never lasted, and oppression came again repeatedly. The reports of the work of the various judges are not strictly chronological and overlapped frequently, explaining how the elapsed time of 280 years is so much shorter than the aggregate[18] total of 410 years for the 15 judges mentioned. Progressive spiritual decline is seen in progressively declining character of the successive judges, until they and their people are much more like the surrounding peoples than they are like a people belonging to the one true and living God.

---

16 Oppression: Persecution. Footnote added.
17 Deliverance: Rescue from danger. In Scripture God gives deliverance (Psalms 18:50; 32:7; 44:4) often through a human agent. In the OT deliverance most often refers to victory in battle (Judg. 15:18; 2 Kings 5:1; 13:17; 1 Chron. 11:14; 2 Chron. 12:7).
18 Aggregate: Entire sum; footnote added.

"Toward the end of this period, hope emerged in the heroic saga of Naomi, Ruth, and Boaz, who demonstrate that faithful Israelites remained loyal to their covenant Lord. From this family would come the great King David.

"The last of the judges was the greatest: Samuel, a Benjaminite whose mother dedicated him to the service of the Lord. Raised by the priest Eli, Samuel became priest and judge when God excised[19] the family of Eli for its unfaithfulness. Samuel administered[20] the nation wisely and fairly, and stability prevailed[21] during the time of his stewardship. However, the people longed to be like the other nations and asked for a king.

"*The United Monarchy—ca. 1051-931b.c.* Samuel was provoked, but God commanded him to give the people what they asked for, a king of their desire, Saul, son of Kish, a wealthy Benjaminite. A tall, handsome, and humble man, Saul did not seek power and accepted it reluctantly. But, once in command, Saul demonstrated poor judgment and an ultimately fatal lack of spiritual discernment.[22]

"Saul made a good beginning by defeating the Philistines with the intervention of young David who killed the Philistine

---

19   Excised: Eliminated; footnote added.
20   Administered: Led; footnote added.
21   Prevailed: Lasted; footnote added.
22   Discernment: Judgment; footnote added.

champion Goliath foreshadowing[23] things to come. Almost immediately Saul became suspicious and resentful of David and kept him close by giving David his daughter Michal in marriage and by making David a commander of troops who reported to Saul (1 Sam. 18). Saul was determined to pass the throne to his son Jonathan and neglected the kingdom to pursue David for years, his reign lasting about 40 years.

"David was the youngest son of Jesse of Bethlehem. He served his father as a shepherd. Samuel anointed David years before his accession to the throne, and David consistently honored the king and repeatedly passed up opportunities to kill Saul. Rather than attack Saul, David ran from him for years. As Saul's kingdom disintegrated,[24] David grew stronger and gained a significant following.

'Ultimately Saul and Jonathan were slain[25] in battle, and David reigned over his tribe of Judah for seven years in Hebron, while the remaining tribes were led by Saul's son, Ish-Bosheth. After Ish-Bosheth's brutal assassination, David acceded[26] to the throne of all Israel for an additional 33 years, establishing his capital in Jerusalem. He defeated Israel's enemies and established peace for his people. David was Israel's greatest king, described by God as *"a man after*

---

23 Foreshadow: Indicating; footnote added.
24 Disintegrated: Fell apart; footnote added.
25 Slain: Killed; footnote added.
26 Acceded: Inherited; footnote added.

My heart"[27](Acts 13:22; 1 Sam. 13:14), but failed morally and spent years in personal and family turmoil as a result. David not only had an affair with the wife of one of his most loyal subordinates, but when threatened with exposure, he engineered Uriah's death. His household never knew peace again, ultimately costing the lives of some of his children. David developed the plans for the temple and gathered the resources, but because of his own sins God did not allow him to complete the project.

"At the end of David's life, the accession[28] of his son Solomon to the throne was a bloody interfamily struggle. Solomon made a marvelous beginning, building and dedicating a magnificent temple. Genuinely humble, God prospered him beyond his fondest hopes. Solomon was revered for his wisdom and maintained a kingdom expanded to five times the size of the land God promised to Abraham, extending south to the Sinai and north to the Euphrates River. Solomon became one of the most significant monarchs of his era. By the end of his 40-year reign, his kingdom was strong, but his commitment to the Lord had waned, and his latter[29] years were troubled by internal problems. Soon after his death, the united monarchy ended.

---

27 Italics added.
28 Accession: Taking over; footnote added.
29 Latter: Later; footnote added.

"The Divided Monarchy—ca. 931-586b.c. The united kingdom of the 12 tribes suddenly divided in 931/930 B.C. The 10 tribes in the north would henceforth be known as Israel or Ephraim (its most influential tribe). The two southern tribes, Judah and Benjamin, remained loyal to the house of David and was known as Judah. Even before the united kingdom was founded, the unity of Israel was fragile. Petty rivalries and jealousies were common during the period of the judges. The division between Judah and Israel was apparent even during Samuel's lifetime, but David achieved a high degree of national unity. The heavy taxes of Solomon and the forced periods of labor imposed on the people under Solomon and Rehoboam brought the matter to a head.

'Sedition[30] boiled toward the surface late in the reign of Solomon. Jeroboam, son of Nebat, was a successful supervisor of civilian labor in Ephraim for Solomon (1 Kings 11:27-28). The Prophet Ahijah from Shiloh met Jeroboam one day and tore his (Ahijah's) garment into 12 pieces, handed Jeroboam 10 of them, and announced that Jeroboam would become ruler over Israel (1 Kings 11:31). The rumor of this prophecy spread quickly and Jeroboam fled to Egypt where he found refuge with Pharaoh Shishak, a political opportunist. Peace was preserved until the death of Solomon, but then trouble

---

30   Sedition: Desire for rebellion; footnote added.

arose quickly and Rehoboam was not wise enough to salvage the tenuous[31] situation.

"Rather than easing the onerous[32] governmental burdens on the people, Rehoboam threatened to increase them, and 10 tribes rebelled, leaving the Southern Kingdom of Rehoboam containing only the tribes of Judah and Benjamin. Jeroboam, son of Nebat, became the first king of the Northern Kingdom and immediately led the people into idolatry.[33] In order to make up for the loss of religious ties to Jerusalem, Jeroboam had two golden calves fashioned for the two sites of Dan and Bethel. Because of his apostasy[34] Jeroboam's family forfeited the kingship. His name became a refrain[35] and a stereotype[36] for the evil in the reigns of the rulers of the Northern Kingdom.

"Rehoboam was attacked by Jeroboam's ally, Pharaoh Shishak (Shosenq I, ca. 945-924 B.C.), who looted the temple and then moved further into the territory of Israel, Gilead, and Edom. An inscription left by Shishak at Karnak claimed

---

31 Tenuous: Fragile; footnote added.

32 Onerous: Heavy; footnote added.

33 Idolatry: Worship of false gods; footnote added.

34 Apostasy: Act of rebelling against, forsaking, abandoning, or falling away from what one has believed. Chad Brand, Charles Draper, Archie England, ed., *Holman Illustrated Bible Dictionary*, (Nashville: Holman Bible Publishers, 2003), s.v. "," WORD*search* CROSS e-book; footnote added.

35 Refrain: Slogan; catchphrase; buzzword; footnote added.

36 Stereotype: Label; footnote added.

the defeat of 150 cities in the region. Oddly Shishak did not consolidate his gains of territory but returned to Egypt where he soon died. Rehoboam secured his kingdom and turned over a stable nation to his son Abijah, who reigned only two years. He failed in an attempt to reunite the tribes. Abijah's son Asa reigned 41 years in Judah. He partially, but not entirely, reversed the religious deterioration of Judah.

The north also was divided once into two factions, which further confuses the issue. During the divided kingdom era each nation had 19 kings. The kings of the north came from nine dynasties (families) while all the kings of Judah were descended from David. The 19 kings of the north ruled from 930-722 B.C.; the average length of each reign was relatively brief. The kings of the south served from 930 to 586 B.C., demonstrating the greater stability and continuity of life in Judah. All the kings of the north are evaluated in Kings and Chronicles as bad, while the kings of Judah were partly bad and partly good kings. Ironically, the worst of the kings was from Judah: Manasseh, who sacrificed one of his own children as a pagan sacrifice.

"During the Israelite monarchies, great nations came across the biblical stage as their affairs intersected those of Judah and Israel. Because the focus of the biblical record is on God's people, only vignettes[37] and brief glimpses are provided of the larger history of the era. The details provided

---

37   Vignettes: Sketches; fragments; small part; brief stories; footnote added.

in the Bible are confirmed repeatedly by the archives[38] and artifacts[39] of various kinds left by other ancient kingdoms.

"The relationship between Israel and Judah fluctuated[40] from hostile[41] to civil[42] to fraternal[43] over the life of the Northern Kingdom. Sometimes they were allied.[44] Overall both kingdoms enjoyed periods of peace and prosperity. An ominous[45] development was the emergence of Syria as a major power about the time of the division of the Israelite kingdom (ca. 930 B.C.). By about 850 B.C. **Damascus** was the capital of the most powerful state in the region. Assyria was in a time of domestic turmoil,[46] which allowed more autonomy[47] for other nations. After about a century of weakness,

---

38   Archives: Records; files; libraries; footnote added.

39   Artifacts: Remains; ruins; historical objects; footnote added.

40   Fluctuated: Changed; wavered; footnote added.

41   Hostile: Unfriendly; of or relating to an enemy;www.merriam-webs ter.com/dictionary; footnote added.

42   Civil: Polite but not friendly: only as polite as a person needs to be in order to not be rude; footnote added. Op. cit., *Merriam.*

43   Fraternal: Friendly; brotherly; Footnote added.

44   Allied: Joined in a relationship in which people, groups, countries etc., agree to work together; Op. Cit., *Merriam;* footnote added.

45   Ominous: Dangerous; footnote added.

46   Turmoil: National (countrywide) state of confusion or disorder; footnote added.

47   Autonomy: The power or right of a country, group, etc., to govern itself; Op. Cit., Merriam; footnote added.

however, an Assyrian resurgence[48] (ca. 745 B.C.) changed the geopolitical balance and foreshadowed future trouble for the Israelite kingdoms.

"Syria became isolated and surrounded by territory under Assyrian control. With Syria thus preoccupied[49] with problems of her own, Judah prospered most notably under the long reign of the good king Hezekiah. However, the end of Israel was just around the corner.[50]

"The last century of the Northern Kingdom (eighth century B.C.) was marked by the ministry of four great prophets: Amos, Hosea, Micah, and Isaiah, as well as Jonah. With perfect clarity they saw the demise[51] of Israel and eventually Judah. Yet both nations believed themselves to be invincible[52] because of their relationship with Yahweh.[53] Most

---

48 Resurgence: A growth or increase that occurs after a period without growth or increase; Op. Cit., *Merriam;* footnote added.

49 Preoccupied: Concerned; footnote added.

50 Emphasis added.

51 Demise: downfall; footnote added.

52 Invincible: Unbeatable; indestructible; Footnote added.

53 Yahweh: The most common designation for God; footnote added; T. Desmond Alexander and David W. Baker, ed., *Dictionary of the Old Testament Pentateuch: A Compendium of Contemporary Biblical Scholarship,* (Downers Grove, Illinois: InterVarsity Press, 2003), WORD*search* CROSS e-book, Under: "GOD, NAMES OF."

of the people ignored the prophets and clung to delusions[54] of grandeur[55] and safety.

"Tragically the Assyrians swept Israel away after the fall of Samaria in 722 B.C. Twice, perhaps, Assyria came against Judah (701 and 688 B.C.) but was unable to conquer her because of divine[56] intervention. Judah continued for another 135 years, often as a vassal[57] state of Assyria. Jerusalem ultimately fell in 587-586 B.C. to the Babylonians under Nebuchadnezzar, who displaced[58] Assyria as the dominant[59] world power late in the seventh century B.C. (ca. 612-609).

"**The Babylonian Exile** The Babylonians deported most of the people of Judah. The **Neo-Babylonian**[60] ascendancy[61]

---

54 Delusions: A belief that is not true: a false idea; footnote added; Op. Cit., *Merriam-Webster*.

55 Grandeur: Greatness; footnote added.

56 Divine: Godly; footnote added.

57 Vassal: A person in the past who received protection and land from a lord in return for loyalty and service; Op. Cit., *Merriam-Wester*; footnote added.

58 Displaced: Replaced; footnote added.

59 Dominant: More important, powerful, or successful than most or all others; Op. Cit., *Merriam-Wester*; footnote added.

60 The effects of the Babylonian conquest of Carchemish and Hamath were impressive indeed and Babylon regained the position of dominant world power under King Nebuchadnezzar. Walter C. Kaiser Jr., *A History of Israel*, (Nashville, Tennessee: Broadman & Holman, 1998), WORD*search* CROSS e-book, 390, 391.

61 Ascendancy: Rise to power; footnote added.

was short lived. Babylon fell to her former ally, the Medo-Persian Empire in 539 B.C.

"The Postexilic Period Shortly after the fall of Babylon, Cyrus the Great, the Persian king, allowed conquered peoples to relocate to their native lands (Ezra 1:2-4). The Jews began returning to Judah about 537 B.C. Under the leadership of Zerubbabel, Ezra, and Nehemiah, Jerusalem was resettled and a second temple was built. A measure of autonomy existed throughout this period. The OT[62] era ended about 400 B.C. with the ministry of the Prophet Malachi.

"The Intertestamental Period The period of Persian domination[63] ended with the conquests of Alexander the Great, beginning in 332 B.C. Palestine changed hands several times between the Seleucid and Ptolemaic successors of Alexander. Greek domination of Palestine continued until the Jews succeeded in establishing an independent kingdom in a war that began in 167 B.C. under the leadership of an aged priest Mattathias and his sons, who became known as the Maccabees. In 63 B.C. Roman control of Palestine was established by the Roman General Pompey. The region was subdivided for purposes of governance by the Romans who sanctioned[64] local rulers but also maintained control through the presence of the Roman military.

---

62   OT: Old Testament; footnote added.

63   Domination: World rule; footnote added.

64   Sanctioned: Allowed; permitted; footnote added.

"**The New Testament Period and Beyond** Roman control of Palestine continued beyond the NT[65] era, culminating[66] in the first Jewish War with Rome, ca. A.D. 66-72, in which the temple and Jerusalem were decimated[67] (A.D. 70). Finally, after another war in the second century A.D. (ca. 135), the Jews were scattered throughout the Roman Empire. Palestine remained in Roman hands until about A.D. 400."[68]

—Walter C. Kaiser, Jr. and Charles W. Draper

---

65 NT: New Testament; footnote added.

66 Culminating: Ending; footnote added.

67 Decimated: Destroyed; footnote added.

68 Chad Brand, Charles Draper, Archie England, ed., *Holman Illustrated Bible Dictionary*, (Nashville: Holman Bible Publishers, 2003), s.v. "," WORD*search* CROSS e-book," I", Israel, Land of.

DOCTRINE OF PREDESTINATION

I WOULD LIKE for us to take a close look at this doctrine, and let us begin with Revelation 13:8. My purpose in doing this is to establish a sound basis for my questioning of the **Doctrine of Predestination**[1] as it is most frequently presented. That is why I will spend a considerable amount of time on this subject in an attempt to provide adequate evidence that this has long been a misinterpreted doctrine. It is my hope

---

1   The sovereign determination and foreknowledge of God. Some theologians connect divine predestination with the central events of salvation history, especially the death of Jesus as foreordained by God. In Calvinist theology the doctrine of predestination more specifically holds that God has from all eternity chosen specific people to bring into eternal communion with himself. Some Calvinists add that God has also predestined (or ordained) the rest of humankind for damnation. *Pocket Dictionary of Theological Terms*.

to provide you with this understanding which I believe is needed as we proceed with our study.

Reading Revelation 13:8 one might assume that God decided just who would be saved and who would not be saved way back even before the earth was created. *"All who dwell on the earth will worship him, everyone whose name has not been written from the foundation of the world in the book of life of the Lamb who has been slain."* Those who hold fast to the doctrine of *predestination* often cite this verse to substantiate their belief. We also see another verse in the book of Revelation that might support that theory as well: *"The beast that you saw was, and is not, and is about to come up out of the abyss and go to destruction. And those who dwell on the earth, whose name has not been written in the book of life from the foundation of the world, will wonder when they see the beast, that he was and is not and will come"* (Revelation 17:8).

Based on these verses I would assume that everyone would like to see his or her name written in the *"Book of Life,"* for at the last judgment, according to Revelation 20:15, *"whosoever was not found written in the book of life was cast into the lake of fire."*

So how does one's name get written into the Book of Life? Those who believe in predestination would say that God, for whatever reason, preselected some people to be saved and then simply leaves the rest of the names out, leaving them to their own devices. But let me suggest an alternative consideration: *"Then Moses returned to the LORD, and said, 'Alas, this people has committed a great sin, and they have made a god of gold for themselves.* ³² *But now, if You will, forgive their sin—and if not, please blot me out from Your book which You have written"* (Exodus 32:31-32). *"May they be blotted out of the book of life and may they not be recorded with the righteous"* (Psalm 69:28). *"You have rebuked the nations, You have destroyed the wicked; You have blotted out their name forever and ever"* (Psalm 9:5).

Jesus further clarifies this when in Revelation 3 He says: *"He who overcomes will thus be clothed in white garments; and I will not erase his name from the book of life, and I will confess his name before My Father and before His angels"* (Revelation 3:5). Perhaps, in the beginning, God wrote in His Book the name of every person born, as a kind of birth record in His Book of Life. Throughout his/her lifetime each person is given ample evidence as to the existence and grace of God. They are invited to make Him Lord of their lives (Romans 1:20-23; 6:23; 10:9-10). Those that do receive Jesus as their Savior and make Him their Lord, thereby assure that their names remain in and are not erased out of *the Book of Life.* But the names of those who consistently reject God are blotted out, erased, from the Book of Life. When the books are opened at the Great White Throne judgment, there will only be a blank space where their name should have been. *"And I saw the dead, the great and the small, standing before the throne, and books were opened; and another book was opened, which is the book of life; and the dead were judged from the things which were written in the books, according to their deeds.* ¹³ *And the sea gave* *up the dead which were in it, and death and Hades gave up the dead which were in them; and they were judged, every one of them according to their deeds" (*Revelation 20:12-13).

I found some support for this theory in the *Lehman Straus Commentary*:

> "The 'book' referred to could be the register of all who ever lived, giving the right to eternal life to those whose names had not been blotted out. This register of genealogy is possibly referred to by Moses when he prayed to Jehovah, 'Oh, this people have sinned a great sin, and have made them gods of gold. Yet now, if Thou wilt forgive their sin—; and if not, blot me, I pray Thee, out of Thy book which Thou hast written' (Exodus 32:31-32). Now it seems that all Israelites were registered in the book, *else how could some be blotted out,* for God said toMoses,'Whosoever hath sinned against Me, him will I blot out of My book'" (verse 33).[2]

> "The Psalmist wrote, 'Let them be blotted out of the book of the living, and not be written with the righteous' (Psalm 69:28). This verse seems to teach that the unrighteous had their names in the book and at a given time their names were erased so that only the names of the righteous remained. A word from Nehemiah seems to confirm this view: 'And my God put into mine heart to gather together the

---

2   *Lehman Strauss Commentary – The Prophecies of Daniel,* p.355.

nobles, and the rulers, and the people, that they might be reckoned by genealogy. And I found a register of the genealogy of them which came up at the first, and found written therein' (Nehemiah 7:5). Another significant verse which sheds light on this discussion comes to us toward the close of the Biblical record: 'He that overcometh, the same shall be clothed in white raiment; and I will not blot out his name out of the book of life, but I will confess his name before My Father, and before His angels' (Revelation 3:5). Now since the overcomers are the believers (1 John 5:5), then it follows that they cannot be blotted out of the register. We conclude that it looks as though all names are there at some time, thereby giving all an opportunity to receive eternal life until the name is blotted out.[3]

"At which point is one's name blotted out? We cannot speak with dogmatic assurance about all of the details, but I would guess that the name of the unbeliever might remain until death, or the Rapture of the Church, or the second coming of Christ to earth at the end of the seventieth week. Those in Daniel 12:1 who are delivered are the redeemed of the tribulation."[4]

During the coming reign of Antichrist, those believers living at that time will demonstrate *their overcoming faith* by

---

3   Ibid.

4   Ibid.

not worshiping him, even at the cost of their lives (Revelation 13:15). In any age, the overcomers are those who are not afraid to confess Christ as their Lord and Savior (Luke 12:8). They will end up in Heaven. The *"fearful,"* however, which have not come to faith in Christ, will end up in the Lake of Fire (Revelation 21:8).

You see we all sin and not one single person who has sinned is going to make it into Heaven by their own efforts. That of course means that if God had not sent Jesus, who has never sinned, and who willingly offered Himself as the perfect sacrifice to pay for our sins, we would all go to Hell. A sinless sacrifice was necessary for God to forgive sin. Those who are willing to believe in what Jesus taught will be saved and go to Heaven when they die. It is in that way we can be *"born again"* into a new life where God will see us as sinless because of our faith in His Son, Jesus Christ, who became that perfect sacrifice. When God looks at a believer He no longer sees his or her sin because in its place He sees His Son who is without sin and who became our substitute, our Savior. He took the flogging and tortuous death to pay the penalty for our sin. God sent Him to save us from our sin because He loves us so much.

You may wonder why God would require such a sacrifice. I would advise that you not try too hard to figure that out because it is one of those things that only God knows for sure. But I can give you a thought that I know to be true. Sin is such a serious violation against God's perfect nature that He cannot allow sin in His presence. It was so serious a violation that it meant the shedding of blood was the only way for God to forgive sin. That blood sacrifice had to be made by a human being who was sinless. Since there was no one on earth that could do this, God Himself took the form of a human and came down to earth as the Christ Child. He would grow to be the Man that could provide what God required.

But we must participate in this miracle by reaching out and accepting this free gift from God by believing. Those who do not are going to stand before God with each sin they ever committed visible to Him, and thereby be sentenced to an eternal (never ending) Hell of 24/7 torment. All one has to do to obtain this salvation is to trust in God by believing Him and accepting Christ's substitutionary death as payment for their sins. If they choose, and the choice is offered to all people, to accept Christ, they are saved and their name remains in the *Book of Life*. If they refuse to accept God's free gift, their names will be erased from the *Book of Life* upon their death. Those who reject God over and over and over again seal their own fate, and in effect choose to be punished instead. They harden their own hearts, God does not do it, and in so doing they can no longer come to faith in Jesus. You can ignore or deny Jesus enough times so that you will build a wall between you and Christ. A wall so high you cannot see the other side. You yourself could make Jesus unreachable by continually pushing Him away, and if you do that, you will be among those who are sentenced to Hell and eventually the

Lake of Fire for eternity.Because He wanted everyone to be saved, God created within them a calling to come to Him: "*For everyone who calls on the name of the LORD will be saved*" (Romans 10:13, NLT).

All people have a built in awareness of God. The Jews were called by God as a select people that would know Him, obey Him, and then teach the Gentiles about Him. But that conscience that we all have can also serve as a calling from God. That would mean of course that all people are called, and if that is the case why would God predestine (predetermine) only certain people to be saved?

Please read these following verses carefully:

Romans 1:1-7:

[1] *Paul, a bond-servant of Christ Jesus, called as an apostle, set apart for the gospel of God,*[2] *which He promised beforehand through His prophets in the holy Scriptures,* [3] *concerning His Son, who was born of a descendant of David according to the flesh,* [4] *who was declared the Son of God with power by the resurrection from the dead, according to the Spirit of holiness, Jesus Christ our Lord,* [5] *through whom we have received grace and apostleship to bring about the obedience of faith among all the Gentiles for His name's sake,* [6] *among whom you also are the called of Jesus Christ;* [7] *to all who are beloved of God in Rome, called as saints: Grace to you and peace from God our Father and the Lord Jesus Christ.*

All Gentiles are called to the obedience of faith in Jesus Christ (verses 5-6). It would follow then that they are all predestined to bear Christ's image.[5]

Romans 8:28-30:

[28] *And we know that God causes all things to work together for good to those who love God, to those who are called according to His purpose.* [29] *For those whom He foreknew, He also predestined to become conformed to the image of His Son, so that He [Jesus][6] would be the firstborn among many brethren;* [30] *and these whom He predestined, He also called; and these whom He called, He also justified; and these whom He justified, He also glorified.*

All people are given the ability to be aware of God (Romans 1:19-20). If they seek after knowledge that will make them understand God, God will reveal Himself to them. He will give them what they need to know to help them choose Jesus as their Savior. It is their free choice to accept or reject the gift. You may accept or reject that position; that is your free choice, but it is the best way I know of taking the Bible as a whole text to explain this subject of predestination.

Now how is God going to bring this obedience through faith to all the Gentiles? By His grace. When anyone comes to God confessing he/she is a sinner in need of a Savior and claims Jesus to be that Savior, God by His grace gives them

---

5   Op. Cit., Richards, Larry; *Bible Reader's Companion*, P.744.

6   Brackets mine.

salvation and the ability to be obedient by His grace through the presence of the Holy Spirit of God who comes to live within them.

We get another hint that some people will be blotted out of the Book of Life in Exodus 32.

Exodus 32:30-35 (NLT):

[30] *The next day Moses said to the people, "You have committed a terrible sin, but I will go back up to the LORD on the mountain. Perhaps I will be able to obtain forgiveness for your sin." [31] So Moses returned to the LORD and said, "Oh, what a terrible sin these people have committed. They have made gods of gold for themselves.[32] But now, if you will only forgive their sin—but if not, erase my name from the record you have written!" [33] But the LORD replied to Moses, "No, I will erase the name of everyone who has sinned against me. [34] Now go, lead the people to the place I told you about. Look! My angel will lead the way before you. And when I come to call the people to account, I will certainly hold them responsible for their sins." [35] Then the LORD sent a great plague upon the people because they had worshiped the calf Aaron had made.*

However, those that are blotted out will certainly not be believers because the Bible tells us once we are saved, we are saved forever: *"Therefore there is now no condemnation for those who are in Christ Jesus"* (Romans 8:1). Once you are saved you can never lose that salvation!

Daniel also spoke of names written in the "book."

Daniel 12:1:

[1] *"Now at that time Michael, the great prince who stands guard over the sons of your people, will arise. And there will be a time of distress such as never occurred since there was a nation until that time; and at that time your people, everyone who is found written in the book, will be rescued."*

And what about free choice? God wants people to make the choice to follow Him. If they are predestined for salvation, does that not remove the responsibility for the decision from the individual? God sent Jesus for the purpose of providing salvation for the whole human race, not for just a few. *"For the Son of Man came to seek and to save **the lost**"* (Luke 19:10 ESV). This verse does not say *"some of the lost,"* or *"those who were predestined to be saved."* It says *"**the lost.**"* That means **all of the lost**, and that is why God desired everyone to be saved: *"The Lord does not delay His promise, as some understand delay, but is patient with you, **not wanting any to perish but all to come to repentance**."* (2 Peter 3:9 HCSB).

If God predestined certain people to be saved, the Bible would have to say that Jesus came to save those that He had predestined, or elected for salvation. After all, we know that everything we read in the Bible is true and there is no falsehood in Christ. That would also mean that He would never intend to mislead us. I also find the following from one of the reference books I have used to be helpful:

"The word translated *'elect'* is generally found in the plural and refers either to the members of God's people as a whole or to those in a particular local church (Romans 8:33; Colossians 3:12; 1 Thessalonians 1:4; 2 Timothy 2:10; Titus 1:1; 1 Peter 1:1–2; 2 Peter 1:10; Revelation 17:14; cf. Romans 16:13 and 2 John 1:13, which have the singular form). The use of the plural may partly be explained by the fact that most of the NT [New Testament][7] letters are addressed to groups of people rather than to individuals. More probably, however, the point is that God's election is concerned with the creation of a collective people rather than the calling of isolated individuals.[8]

"The word *'election'* emphasizes that becoming one of God's people is due to God's initiative,[9] prior to all human response, made before time began (Ephesians 1:4; cf. John 15:16, 19).It is God who has called men and women to be his people, and those who respond are elect."[10]

I would suggest then that the elect are both Jews and Gentiles. The relationship between God's call and human response is explained in Matthew 22:14: "For many are called, but few are chosen." Although God calls many through the

---

7   Brackets mine.

8   Op. Cit., *Easy-to-Read Commentary Series*.

9   Initiative: The act of starting something; In this situation God starts the process of salvation within a person.

10   Op. Cit., *Easy-to-Read Commentary Series*.

Gospel, only some of those respond to the call and become His elect people. The text sheds no light on the mystery of why only some choose to become God's people. When men and women refuse the Gospel, it is **because they have become hardened** as a result of sin and their trust in their own works. Scripture does not go beyond that point in explaining, and neither should Christians.[11]

Do you think God would go through the intricate and time consuming task (1,600 years in the writing) of preparing a perfect *Manual for Living* (Bible), from the time of Moses, to a hundred years after the birth of Christ if He had already determined who would go to Heaven and who would go to Hell? I think not. And what about Satan? Why would he work so hard to keep and bring people over into his camp if he knew that God had already determined who would be saved and who would not?

---

11   Ibid.

GOD'S COVENANTS

THIS IS SUCH a rich topic of study; we will take some time here to examine the covenants (promises) between God and man. It is the fulfillment of these covenants that God made to His prophets that we see being fulfilled in the Last Days. A covenant (*berith* in Old Testament Hebrew, *diatheke* in New Testament Greek) is a promise or an agreement between God and man. A covenant may be conditional or unconditional. There are eight important covenants in the Bible:[1]

1. **The covenant with all repenting sinners** to save them through Christ. This covenant is unconditional (See Titus 1:1–2; Hebrews 13:20).
2. **The covenant with Adam**
   Genesis 1:28; 2:15–16; 3:15–19.

---

1   H. L. Willmington, *The Complete Book of Bible Lists*, Wheaton, IL: Tyndale House Publishers, 1987), WORD*search* CROSS e-book, 92.

a. Before the Fall—that he could remain in Eden as long as he obeyed. This was conditional.[2]

b. After the Fall—that God would someday send a Savior. This was unconditional.[3]

3. **The covenant with Noah.**
    Genesis 8:21–22

a. That the earth would not be destroyed by water again.

b. That the seasons would continue until the end. This was unconditional.

4. **The covenant with Abraham.**
    Genesis 12:2–3, 7; 13:14–17; 15:5, 18; 17:8

a. That God would make Abraham the founder of a great nation.

b. That God would someday give Palestine forever to Abraham's seed. This was unconditional.

5. **The covenant with Moses and Israel.**
    Exodus 19:3–8; Leviticus 26; Deuteronomy 28.

a. That Israel could have the land at that time to enjoy if they obeyed.

b. That Israel would forfeit all God's blessings if they disobeyed. This was conditional.

6. **The covenant with David.**
    2 Chronicles 13:5; 2 Samuel 7:12–16; 23:5.

---

2   Conditional: God will make it happen if the people obey Him.

3   Unconditional: God will make it happen no matter what the people do

a. That from David would come an everlasting throne.
b. That from David would come an everlasting kingdom.
c. That from David would come an everlasting king. This was unconditional.

7. **The covenant with the Church.**
   Matthew 16:18; 26:28; Luke 22:20; Hebrews 13:20–21.
   a. That Christ would build his Church with his own blood.
   b. That all the fury of Hell would not destroy it.
   c. That he would perfect all the members of his Church. This was unconditional.

8. **The new covenant with Israel.**
   Jeremiah 31:31–34; Isaiah 42:6; 43:1–6; Deuteronomy 1:1–9; Hebrews 8:7–12
   a. That God would eventually bring Israel back to himself.
   b. That he would forgive their iniquity and forget their sin.
   c. That he would use them to reach and teach Gentiles.
   d. That he would establish them in Palestine forever. This was unconditional.

THE RAPTURE OF
THE CHURCH

THERE ARE FOUR main passages we need to study to even have a glimmer of hope as to *when the Rapture of the Church will occur, and when Jesus will return.* There are a great many conclusions that various theologians and commentators have arrived at, and some of them simply baffle me. Then there are others who make their explanation so complicated that I would be surprised if they really understood it themselves. So here is my best effort to provide as much solid information as is available in the Scriptures, and even then I cannot be certain that my conclusions are the most accurate. This is a very, very difficult book to interpret, and all of us are only human. We also need to understand that God does not want us to know everything and we must accept that fact, having faith that what we cannot understand or know is still going to be *more wonderful than we could ever imagine.* The evidence about to be presented results in a conclusion that few have reached. I believe we may have come upon some different conclusions that you may find fascinating. These conclusions are different from other expositors, but are completely in accord with Scripture.

Let us begin with the first passage in:

1) 1 Thessalonians 4:13-17 (RSV):

[13] *But we would not have you ignorant, brethren, concerning those who are asleep* [dead],*that you may not grieve as others do who have no hope.* [14] *For since we believe that Jesus died and rose again, even so, through Jesus,* **God will bring with him those who have fallen asleep** [died].[1]

The death and resurrection of Jesus are proven historical events. Because Christians know these events took place, they can be equally certain that the souls of believers who have died will be with Christ when He comes for His living saints to *meet Him in the air* at the *Rapture.* The bodies of the dead saints[2] will have been raised to join with their souls, no matter what the condition of that body. Even if it has turned to dust, those bodies as well as those of the living saints at the time will receive their new, perfect bodies that will remain alive forever. Please do not ask me how God is going to give

---

1   Brackets mine.

2   People who have died since the day Jesus rose from the grave.

skeletons from the grave or dust mixed with dirt new bodies or skeletons from bodies in the sea. If you are experiencing some confusion regarding how a fifteen hundred year old body that may be nothing more than part of a sandstorm can be reunited with its soul which is in Heaven and be recognizable as it was when it was alive on earth, you are not alone. But let me just suggest this as a possible answer: "*Then the LORD God formed man of dust from the ground, and breathed into his nostrils the breath of life; and man became a living being*" (Genesis 2:7). If God can create a life that way, He is certainly capable of rebuilding that same life in basically the same way. Nobody knows the answer, but that is what God says He is going to do, so that is how the process will work. The prophecy of the Rapture[3] is as sure to be fulfilled as the prophecies of Christ's death and resurrection were fulfilled.[4]

Continuing with 1 Thessalonians 4:15-17:

[15] *For this we declare to you by the word of the Lord, that we who are alive, who are left until the coming of the Lord, shall not*

---

3   Rapture: The event that will take all living believers and those who have died since the time of Christ to Heaven and in the process provide them with new living bodies that will last forever.

4   John Walvoord and Roy Zuck, ed., *The Bible Knowledge Commentary: An Exposition of the Scriptures by Dallas Seminary Faculty*, (Colorado Springs, CO: Cook Communications, 1985), WORD*search* CROSS e-book, 704.

precede those who have fallen asleep. [16] *For the Lord himself will descend from heaven with a cry of command, with the archangel's call, and with the sound of the trumpet of God. And the dead in Christ will rise first;* [17] *then we who are alive, who are left, shall be caught up together with them in the clouds to meet the Lord in the air; and so we shall always be with the Lord.*

This is not the Second Coming. The raptured Church, those dead or alive, which will also include Jewish Christians who have accepted Christ as Savior by this time in the Revelation, will be raised and lifted up to meet the Lord in the air, and escorted by Him into Heaven.

We can definitely identify this as the Rapture of the Church, just as we can identify 1 Corinthians 15:52 as the Rapture of the Church. So if the trumpet in verse 52 is the last trumpet, then the trumpet here in 1 Thessalonians 4:16 must also be the last trumpet. *"In a moment, in the twinkling of an eye, at the last trumpet; for the trumpet will sound, and the dead will be raised imperishable, and we will be changed"* (1 Corinthians 15:52).

Now there are a number of stages involved with the Rapture. It begins with Jesus descending from Heaven into the planetary heavens, where the sun, moon, and stars are located. You might be more familiar with the terms, *"outer space"* or *"upper atmosphere."* As Jesus descends, a *great shout will* be heard, kind of like a military leader issuing a command to charge. This will be the command for the Rapture and the resurrection of Christians to begin. Then the voice of the archangel, Michael, will be heard. Jesus gives the command and it is Michael's job to set it in motion. Then there will be the sound of a trumpet, which in Jewish culture was a call to battle, worship, or some other major event. Bodies of dead Christians from the Church Age[5] will be lifted first from their graves and then they will be joined immediately by all Christians who are alive at that time. They will all meet Christ in the planetary heavens, and be escorted into Heaven itself.[6] So Heaven will now have added the resurrected eternal bodies of all saints[7]since Christ's First Coming (circa A.D. 30). *Old Testament believers* will not be resurrected until after the Tribulation, as will the Tribulation saints that die between the time of the Rapture and the end of the Tribulation.

The Bible does not tell us what form our souls will have in Heaven before the resurrection. In 1 Thessalonians 4:14, Paul uses the term *"sleep"* to describe death. The analogy he is making here is that the Bible looks at death as a temporary stoppage of physical activity until the person awakes at the time of the Rapture. But also, just like in sleep, mental activity remains active, and that is basically the state of the soul in

---

5   From the ascension of Christ to the Rapture.

6   Op cit., Fruchtenbaum, p. 146.

7   The name given to all Christians, Romans 1:7; 8:27; 12:13; 15:25,31; 16:2.William Wilberforce Rand, ed., "SAINT," in *A Dictionary of the Holy Bible*, (New York: American Tract Society, 1859), WORD*search* CROSS e-book, Under: "SAINT".

Heaven.[8] However, you should not get the idea that Heaven is a place where there are only clouds and spirits floating around in a gaseous, vaporous condition like Casper the Friendly Ghost. Do not forget that God is a Spirit and there can be no one or nothing more real than He is. So it is my recommendation that you realize that if you die before the Rapture, and are a believer, whatever time you might have in Heaven will be a very real experience in a very real place, and you will be having the time of your life. Contrast that to those souls in Hell,who will be experiencing the most miserable conditions imaginable with no hope for those conditions to ever come to an end throughout all eternity.

"To meet the Lord" (1 Thessalonians 4:17*)*. The Greek expression for the verb is *eis apantesin;* this refers to the custom of sending an official delegation out of the city to meet a visiting dignitary (Matthew 25:6; Acts 28:15-16). They would go out to accompany the dignitary and return with him to the city. The implication is that the risen and raptured Christians will leave earth and go to meet Jesus in the air and He will then escort them to Heaven. There they will receive their new resurrected bodies and a short time later return with Him to earth to establish God's Kingdom on the earth.[9]

---

8   Op. Cit., Fruchtenbaum.

9   Ibid.

2) The Second Passage is:

1 Corinthians 15:50-58:

[50] *Now I say this, brethren, that flesh and blood*[10] *cannot inherit the kingdom of God; nor does the perishable*[11] *inherit the imperishable.*[51] *Behold, I tell you a mystery;*[12] *we will not all sleep, but we will all be changed, 52 in a moment, in the twinkling of an eye, at the last trumpet; for the trumpet will sound, and the dead will be raised imperishable, and we will be changed 53 For this perishable must put on the imperishable, and this mortal must put on immortality. 54 But when this perishable will have put on the imperishable, and this mortal will have put on immortality, then will come about the saying that is written, "DEATH IS SWALLOWED UP in victory.* [55] *"O DEATH, WHERE IS*

---

10   Physical bodies; Richard E. Oster, Jr., Ph.D., *The College Press NIV Commentary – 1 Corinthians*, ed. Jack Cottrell, Ph.D. and Tony Ash, Ph.D. (Joplin, Missouri: College Press Publishing Co., 1995), WORD*search* CROSS e-book, 389.

11   Perishable: Term some translations (KJV, REB, NRSV) use to describe the present, mortal body (1 Corinthians 15:42, 50,53-54), which is subject to death and decay. Chad Brand, Charles Draper, Archie England, ed., *Holman Illustrated Bible Dictionary*, (Nashville: Holman Bible Publishers, 2003), s.v. ".," WORD*search* CROSS e-book.

12   Mystery: In Daniel a mystery (Aramaic *raz*) was a revealed secret, something that could not be understood apart from divine revelation or explanation (Dan. 2:17-47; 4:9) Brand, Charles Draper, Archie England, ed., *Holman Illustrated Bible Dictionary*, (Nashville: Holman Bible Publishers, 2003), s.v. ".," WORD*search* CROSS e-book.

YOUR VICTORY? O DEATH, WHERE IS YOUR STING?"
56 The sting of death is sin, and the power of sin is the law; 57 but thanks be to God, who gives us the victory through our Lord Jesus Christ. 58 Therefore, my beloved brethren, be steadfast, immovable, always abounding in the work of the Lord, knowing that your toil is not in vain in the Lord.

This is the Rapture, the same event we saw in 1 Thessalonians 4:16 and it occurs at the last trumpet. The seventh trumpet will blow and immediately the dead in Christ (those who have accepted Christ as Savior) shall rise from their graves. Now it only makes sense that if the Rapture occurs at the last trumpet, it would have to occur after the seventh trumpet and before the first Bowl Judgment, because the seventh trumpet contains the seven bowl judgments. Therefore the Rapture would have to occur just before the bowl judgments near the end of the Tribulation. Should the last trumpet be the same as the seventh trumpet? Hold that thought.

Keep in mind that, based on what we have and will be studying about the Rapture, there will have to be some length of time between the Rapture and the Second Coming of Christ, because we see Tribulation saints under the altar in Revelation 6:9, so the Rapture could not come at the end of the Tribulation, which eliminates the possibility of a post-tribulation Rapture.[13] There is another passage that I think

---

13 Post-Tribulation:Meaning the Rapture would not occur until the end of the Tribulation or after it is over.

confirms that the Rapture will not occur until near the end of the Tribulation: *"For then there will be a great tribulation, such as has not occurred since the beginning of the world until now, nor ever will. ²²Unless those days had been cut short, no life would have been saved; but for the sake of the elect those days will be cut short"* (Matthew 24:21-22).

Jesus is telling His disciples about the Tribulation in the End Times. He is basically saying that if the Tribulation lasted any longer than the seven years, no one would survive including the people that came to salvation after the Rapture and the end of the Battle of Armageddon, which ends the seven year Tribulation. Verse 22 tells us that saved people (the elect) are going to be alive during most of the Tribulation, which again confirms to me that the Rapture will not occur until sometime after the blowing of the seventh trumpet (introducing God's wrath).

Now to be fair to the Pre-Tribulation Rapture folks, they say that the last trumpet means the last trumpet blown at the end of the festival of the Feast of Trumpets. I have found this claim lacking in substance and here is one very good reason why. Numbers 29:1–6 describes the fall season of festivals commencing with the Day of the Blowing [of Trumpets], later called *Rosh Ha-Shanah*—The New Year. This instrument was the *ram's horn* (šôpar) rather than the silver trumpets blown over the burnt and fellowship offerings at other festivals (Numbers 10:1–10). The Feast of Trumpets used a ram's horn, not a trumpet.I can find no evidence that the Feast of Trumpets is connected to 1 Corinthians 15:52. This seems like a real stretch by the pre-tribulation folks to justify their position as to when the Rapture will occur. It seems rather obvious that the evidence points to a Pre-wrath or Post-Tribulation Rapture, and as we have seen the post-tribulation Rapture is not possible, leaving us with the pre-wrath viewpoint.[14]

If that is correct then this trumpet would also be the seventh trumpet and the last trumpet. We will look at the seventh trumpet passage next. First Corinthians 15:50 says that flesh and blood is perishable (lasts only for a short while), and the Kingdom of God is imperishable (lasts forever). We see here that a change of body is necessary for those who are raptured before they can enter Heaven. Flesh and blood cannot enter the Kingdom of God nor corruption inherit incorruption. Because of sin, the human race has become vulnerable to corruption[15] which leads to death because bodies that contain sin cannot last forever. Therefore the physical human body has to be changed to a new, perfect, heavenly body that can enter Heaven and last forever. So during the resurrection process Jesus changes our earthly, sinful bodies into perfect, heavenly, sinless bodies that are fit for Heaven. Nothing sinful can be allowed in God's kingdom, and the

---

14   R. Dennis Cole, *New American Commentary – Volume 3b: Numbers*, (Nashville, TN: Broadman & Holman, 2000), e-book, 476.

15   Corruption: Dishonesty; immorality.

only way for sin to be removed from an earthly body is by believing that Jesus Christ made Himself a perfect sacrifice for our sin. Without that confession of faith a person will never see Heaven, and the only other place a sin-filled person can go is Hell. You see, those who deny Christ will also be given some type of physical form that will be imperishable, but it will remain corruptible (sinful) and therefore will need to be made of some highly fire resistant material to endure the intense heat of their final prison in the Lake of Fire.

Sin and death entered the world because Adam and Eve opened the door to both when they allowed Satan to convince them to doubt God. We all have inherited that same sin nature. A body vulnerable to sin, death, and corruption must be changed and be made perfect before it can enter the sinless environment of God in Heaven.[16]

Verses 51-53 of 1 Corinthians 15 tell us that an unknown number of people will not sleep (die) before the Rapture occurs. And all this is going to happen when the *"last trumpet"* sounds. Now theologians have held a number of views (perhaps I should just say, *"argued"*) about the meaning of 1 Corinthians 15:52 since it was written; and they will probably continue to do so until it all begins to take place. I find most of the views to have little if any Scriptural backing and therefore I am not going to waste your time by evaluating the different positions. I will comment, however, that I am

---

16   Op. Cit., Fruchtenbaum, p.147.

often disappointed in the majority of commentaries I read when doing research. They are either simply wrong or explain things in a way that few people could understand.

3) Now let us take a look at the third passage:

<u>Revelation 11:15-19:</u>

[15] *Then the seventh angel sounded* [seventh trumpet];[17] *and there were loud voices in heaven, saying, "The kingdom of the world has become the kingdom of our Lord and of His Christ; and He will reign forever and ever."* [16] *And the twenty-four elders, who sit on their thrones before God, fell on their faces and worshiped God,* [17] *saying, "We give You thanks, O Lord God, the Almighty, who are and who were, because You have taken Your great power and have begun to reign.* [18] *"And the nations were enraged, and Your wrath came, and the time came for the dead to be judged, and the time to reward Your bond-servants the prophets and the saints and those who fear Your name, the small and the great, and to destroy those who destroy the earth."* [19] *And the temple of God which is in heaven was opened; and the ark of His covenant appeared in His temple, and there were flashes of lightning and sounds and peals of thunder and an earthquake and a great hailstorm.*

---

17   Brackets mine.

**This is the Coronation ceremony where Christ
is crowned king over all the earth.**

Jesus is not yet descending. However, Jesus begins to reign
at the sound of the trumpet. Christ has taken over as the
King of the world. The sounding of the seventh trumpet was
to bring *the third woe* (verse 14), but instead of a description
of calamity, an announcement is made of the advent[18] of
the kingdom of God. The nature of the third woe is given
in detail later. This is the announcement that the time had
come for Christ to take the throne as King and Ruler over
the entire earth even though *"The Kingdom"* would not be
established on earth until the bowl judgments have ended.
So Christ assumes the throne but He is still in Heaven. This
passage looks to the future,for it speaks of Christ beginning
to rule. It then describes the events that occurred after Jesus
began to reign over the earth from Heaven until His return
and the establishment of His kingdom headquarters in Israel
[Jerusalem (Revelation 11:15-18)].

The scene is located in Heaven. For it is there that John
hears the Trumpet sound,and sees the *"Temple of God"* opened,
and hears the *"voices"* and *"thunderings"* that accompany
the devastation of the earth by the *"earthquake"* and *"hail."*
This announcement comes before the great events that are
to follow, which will be the most remarkable and important

---

18   Advent: Second Coming of Christ at the end of the Tribulation. The
first Advent was Jesus' birth.

that have ever happened on this earth.[19] The wording of the announcement reminds us of Psalm 2. The kingdom of our Lord and the Kingdom of His Christ have been established on earth.

Psalm 2:1-12:

[1] *Why are the nations in an uproar and the peoples devising a vain [useless]*[20] *thing?* [2] *The kings of the earth take their stand and the rulers take counsel together against the LORD and against His Anointed, saying,* [3]*" Let us tear their fetters apart And cast away their cords from us!"* [4] *He who sits in the heavens laughs, the Lord scoffs at them.*[5]*Then He will speak to them in His anger and terrify them in His fury, saying,* [6]*" But as for Me, I have installed My King Upon Zion, My holy mountain.* [7]*" I will surely tell of the decree of the LORD: He said to Me, 'You are My Son, today I have begotten You.* [8] *'Ask of Me, and I will surely give the nations as Your inheritance, and the very ends of the earth as Your possession.* [9] *'You shall break them with a rod of iron, You shall shatter them like earthenware.'* [10] *Now therefore, O kings, show discernment; Take warning, O judges of the earth.* [11] *Worship the LORD with reverence and rejoice with trembling.* [12] *Do homage to the Son, that He not become angry, and you perish in the way,*

19   Larkin, Clarence. *The Book of Revelation: A Study of the Last Prophetic Book of Holy Scripture*, (Philadelphia: Rev. Clarence Larkin Estate, 1919), WORD*search* CROSS e-book, 105-107.

20   Brackets mine.

for His wrath may soon be kindled. How blessed are all who take refuge in Him!

> "The consummation [complete in every detail] *of God's plan itself occurs with the sounding of the seventh trumpet in Revelation 11:15-19.* Accordingly, the *'twenty-four elders'* (symbolizing the Church)[21] address the deity as *'Lord God Almighty, the One who is and who was.'* John's more complete form of this title has been *'the one who is, and who was, and who is to come.'* At this point in the vision, the Lord has already 'come' again."[22]

If you look at Revelation 11:15 and Psalm 2:2, 6, 10, 12, it seems relatively certain that God has installed Jesus as king over the earth while He is still in Heaven before His Second Coming. This cannot be the Rapture because we see the twenty-four elders representing the Church already in Heaven. They must have been raptured sometime earlier. We see here that people down on the earth are still receiving warnings about their fate if they do not accept Christ. So

---

21   The Church at the beginning of the Tribulation will include both Jewish Christians and non-Jewish Christians. The combined Church is here represented by the 12 tribes of Israel and the 12 prophets. More on the 24 elders will be discussed in Chapter 4,

22   Christopher A. Davis, Ph.D., *The College Press NIV Commentary – Revelation*, ed. Jack Cottrell, Ph.D. and Tony Ash, Ph.D. (Joplin, Missouri: College Press Publishing Co., 2000), WORD*search* CROSS e-book, 243-244.

there must be some time left before the end of the Tribulation and Christ's actual return to earth. All of this makes Satan's servants on the earth hopping mad and they formulate a plan to knock Jesus off His throne (Revelation 11:18). However, little do they know that the wrath of God (the seven bowl judgments) is about to fall on them, and to top it all off they will be annihilated in the end at the Battle of Armageddon.

As the forces of Antichrist are preparing to get rid of Jesus and His army when Jesus returns, God unleashes the seven bowls of wrath on the people of the earth (unbelievers). Then Jesus will return to Mount Zion in Jerusalem and destroy all the armies of Antichrist that wanted to defeat Him and take control of the world and never again have to worry about Jesus interfering with their grand plans. Then after the forces of Antichrist and Satan are defeated, and the Tribulation ends, Jesus will begin to reign over all the earth. The sheep and goats will be judged (Sheep and Goat Judgment), with believers entering the Millennium, some in their *earthly bodies* and others in their *resurrected bodies*. There will be more on this later.

So Christ will return and the nations will be enraged and try to kill Him and His army at Armageddon but they will be soundly defeated before they even fire a shot. Then in Revelation 11:19 it speaks of the temple in Heaven.

> "John saw God's temple in heaven. Most likely this was not a physical temple sitting in the clouds, for the

point is made later that there would be no temple in the New Jerusalem because 'the Lord God Almighty and the Lamb are its temple' (21:22 nlt). John had already seen God's throne and the altar in heaven (4:2; 6:9; 8:3). What John was seeing is the place where God dwells and the Ark of the Covenant, which had always symbolized God's presence and faithfulness among his people. God's promises would be fulfilled and his purposes completed."[23]

4) The fourth Passage:

Matthew 24:29-31:

[29] *"But immediately after the tribulation of those days THE SUN WILL BE DARKENED, AND THE MOON WILL NOT GIVE ITS LIGHT, AND THE STARS WILL FALL from the sky, and the powers of the heavens will be shaken.* [30] *"And then the sign of the Son of Man will appear in the sky, and then all the tribes of the earth will mourn, and they will see the SON OF MAN COMING ON THE CLOUDS OF THE SKY with power and great glory.* [31] *"And He will send forth His angels with A GREAT TRUMPET and they will gather His elect from the four winds, from one end of the sky to the other.*

"Matthew 24:27 indicates that the return of Jesus to the earth will be sudden, like a stroke of lightning. The event

23   Bruce B. Barton et al., *Life Application Bible Commentary – Revelation*, (Wheaton, IL: Tyndale, 2000), WORD*search* CROSS e-book, 132.

that immediately precedes His return is the gathering of the Gentile nations at Armageddon."[24] It is pretty clear in verse 29 that the scene takes place after the Tribulation ends, which strongly suggests this scene takes place at the beginning of the seventy-five day interval from the end of the Tribulation until the Millennium begins.

Now who are God's elect that are being referred to in Matthew 24:31? God's elect are all those throughout history who have come to believe in Jesus as their Lord and Savior. But here we have a specific group of God's elect and they are all the believers who do not die in the Tribulation and will be entering the millennial kingdom in their earthly bodies. Those that do not die are the followers of Jesus who will be gathered from all around the world and assembled before Christ for the *"Sheep and Goat Judgment."* Now you may be wondering what *"election"* (the elect) means. Well the source I found that seemed to have the best definition said this:

> *"Election:* God chooses on the basis of His sovereign will for his creation granting salvation by His grace through faith. In the Old Testament, God elects a people (Israel), its king (David), and the city of Jerusalem. The chosen [elect] are under obligation to live by God's will and to be His servants (e.g., Deut.

---

24 Warren W. Wiersbe, *The Bible Exposition Commentary – New Testament, Volume 1*, (Colorado Springs, CO: Victor, 2001), WORD*search* CROSS e-book, 89.

7:6-11; 1 Chron. 16:9-13; Jer. 33:19-26; Amos 3:2).
In the New Testament, election is focused on Jesus
Christ as the elect one. Through faith and discipleship,
his followers are called *'elect'* (e.g., Mark 13:20-27;
Matthew 22:14; Titus 1:1; 1 Peter 1:2; 2:9-10)."[25]

Some will argue that the *"elect"* in Matthew 24:31 are
the Jewish remnant[26] who are saved. I disagree and suggest
that the elect are all the believers who are left alive on the
earth at the end of the Tribulation, and they are now all
considered Christians, including the Jewish remnant who
have accepted Jesus Christ as their Lord and Savior. They are
brought together to be part of the *"Sheep and Goat Judgment."*
The *"elect,"* the *"sheep"* that are all saved will be allowed into
the Millennial Kingdom, and they will still remain in their
earthly bodies. Two other passages describing The Sheep and
Goat Judgment are: *"His winnowing fork is in His hand, and
He will thoroughly clear His threshing floor; andHe will gather
His wheat into the barn, but He will burn up the chaff with
unquenchable fire"* (Matthew 3:12).

---

25 *Harper's Bible Dictionary.*

26 Remnant: Something left over, especially the righteous people of God
after divine judgment. Op. Cit., *Holman Dictionary.*

Matthew 13:24-30:

[24] *Jesus presented another parable to them, saying, "The kingdom of heaven may be compared to a man who sowed good seed in his field.* [2] *"But while his men were sleeping, his enemy came and sowed tares among the wheat, and went away.*[26]*" But when the wheat sprouted and bore grain, then the tares became evident also.* [27]*" The slaves of the landowner came and said to him, 'Sir, did you not sow good seed in your field? How then does it have tares?'* [28]*" And he said to them, 'An enemy has done this!' The slaves said to him, 'Do you want us, then, to go and gather them up?'* [29]*" But he said, 'No; for while you are gathering up the tares, you may uproot the wheat with them.* [30]*'Allow both to grow together until the harvest; and in the time of the harvest I will say to the reapers, "First gather up the tares and bind them in bundles to burn them up; but gather the wheat into my barn."*

Here is another source that arrives at the same conclusion:

> "The people who make up God's *elect* are from all the nations. They are literally *"from the four winds"* (cf. Isaiah 43:6; Daniel 7:2; Zechariah 2:6; Revelation 7:1) and *"from one end of the sky to another."* The gathering of the elect here is similar to John's words about the gathering of the wheat into the barn (Matthew 3:12). It is a bit different from Jesus' parable about the tares or wicked people being gathered out of his Kingdom (Matthew 13:40-41; cf. 25:46). The description of one being taken and another being left is similar

(Matthew 24:40-41). Whatever the imagery, *the point of these passages is the separation of the righteous from the unrighteous at Christ's return."*[27]

If you do not agree that the elect are all believers including the Jews, you need to study the following verses and then decide for yourselves who you think the elect are. *"Therefore I endure everything for the sake of the **elect**, that they also may obtain the salvation that is in Christ Jesus with eternal glory"* (Matthew 24:24 ESV).

"For this reason I endure all things for the sake of those who are chosen, so that they also may obtain the salvation which is in Christ Jesus and with it eternal glory" (2 Timothy 2:10).

1 Peter 1:1-2 (ESV):

*Peter, an apostle of Jesus Christ, To those who are **elect** exiles of the dispersion in Pontus, Galatia, Cappadocia, Asia, and Bithynia, [2]according to the foreknowledge of God the Father, in the sanctification of the Spirit, for obedience to Jesus Christ and for sprinkling with his blood: May grace and peace be multiplied to you.*

---

27 Philip W. Comfort, *Cornerstone Biblical Commentary – Volume 11: Matthew and Mark*, (Carol Stream, IL: Tyndale House, 2005), WORD*search* CROSS e-book, 315.

Romans 8:31-35 (ESV):

*[31] What then shall we say to these things? If God is for us, who can be against us? [32] He who did not spare his own Son but gave him up for us all, how will he not also with him graciously give us all things? [33] Who shall bring any charge against God's **elect?** It is God who justifies. [34] Who is to condemn? Christ Jesus is the one who died—more than that, who was raised—who is at the right hand of God, who indeed is interceding for us. [35] Who shall separate us from the love of Christ? Shall tribulation, or distress, or persecution, or famine, or nakedness, or danger, or sword?*

Now remembering our focus passage here is Matthew 24:29-31, I would now like to include Luke 21:25-33:

[25] "There will be signs in sun and moon and stars, and on the earth dismay among nations, in perplexity at the roaring of the sea and the waves, [26] men fainting from fear and the expectation of the things which are coming upon the world; for the powers of the heavens will be shaken. [27] "Then they will see THE SON OF MAN COMING IN A CLOUD with power and great glory. [28] "But when these things begin to take place, straighten up and lift up your heads, because your redemption[28] is drawing near." [29] Then He told them a parable: "Behold the fig tree and all the trees;[30] as soon as they put forth leaves, you see it and know for yourselves

---

28 Redemption: A term associated in current English usage with a transaction involving the release of an item (or person) in exchange for some type of payment. *Harper's Bible Dictionary.*

that summer is now near.[31] *"So you also, when you see these things happening, recognize that the kingdom of God is near.*[32] *"Truly I say to you, this generation will not pass away until all things take place.*[33] *"Heaven and earth will pass away, but My words will not pass away.*

Matthew 24:29-31:

[29] *"But immediately after the tribulation of those days THE SUN WILL BE DARKENED, AND THE MOON WILL NOT GIVE ITS LIGHT, AND THE STARS WILL FALL from the sky, and the powers of the heavens will be shaken.* [30] *"And then the sign of the Son of Man will appear in the sky, and then all the tribes of the earth will mourn, and they will see the SON OF MAN COMING ON THE CLOUDS OF THE SKY with power and great glory.* [31] *"And He will send forth His angels with A GREAT TRUMPET and they will gather His elect from the four winds, from one end of the sky to the other.*

This also describes Christ's Second Coming. Those who have accepted Him as Lord and Savior, and are still alive at the end of the Tribulation are about to be granted citizenship in God's Millennial Kingdom. At the end of the thousand years they will all go to Heaven.

Revelation 16:13-16 (NLT):

And I saw three evil spirits that looked like frogs leap from the mouths of the dragon, the beast, and the false prophet. [14] *They are demonic spirits who work miracles and go out to all the rulers of the world to gather them for battle against the Lord on that great judgment day of God the Almighty.* [15] *"Look, I will come as unexpectedly as a thief! Blessed are all who are watching for me, who keep their clothing ready so they will not have to walk around naked and ashamed."* [16] *And the demonic spirits gathered all the rulers and their armies to a place with the Hebrew name Armageddon.*

Revelation 19:11-15 (NLT):

Then I saw heaven opened, and a white horse was standing there. Its rider was named Faithful and True, for he judges fairly and wages a righteous war. [12] *His eyes were like flames of fire, and on his head were many crowns. A name was written on him that no one understood except himself.* [13] *He wore a robe dipped in blood, and his title was* **the Word of God.** [14] *The armies of heaven, dressed in the finest of pure white linen, followed him on white horses.* [15] *From his mouth came a sharp sword to strike down the nations. He will rule them with an iron rod. He will release the fierce wrath of God, the Almighty, like juice flowing from a winepress.*

> "The cosmic changes mentioned in Matthew 24:29 precede the return of Jesus Christ to the earth.[29]
>
> "We are not told what 'the sign of the Son of man in heaven' is, but the people on earth at that time will recognize it. When Jesus comes for the Church, He

---

29   Op Cit., Comfort.

will come in the air and His people will be caught up to meet Him in the air (1 Thessalonians 4:17).[30]

"This event will have special meaning for Israel. Jesus will return at that hour when Israel is about to be defeated by the Gentile armies. He will rescue His people, and they will see Him and recognize that He is their Messiah (Zech. 12:9–14). There will be a national repentance, national cleansing, and national restoration under the gracious leadership of their Messiah."[31]

"Historic *pre-millennialism* sees the period [Tribulation][32] as a future time of intense trouble on earth prior to Christ's return, but holds the church will go through the tribulation. The church must endure the tribulation, but not God's wrath."[33]

Take note of what Jesus said to the church in Philadelphia in <u>Revelation 3:10-11</u>:

'Because you have kept the word of My perseverance, I also will keep you from the hour of testing, that hour which is about to come upon the whole world, to test those who dwell on the earth.

---

30   Ibid.

31   Ibid.

32   Brackets mine.

33   Trent C. Butler, ed., "TRIBULATION," in *Holman Bible Dictionary*, (Nashville, TN: Holman Bible Publishers, 1991), WORD*search* CROSS e-book, Under: "TRIBULATION."

[11] *'I am coming quickly; hold fast what you have, so that no one will take your crown.*

Some maintain that Matthew 24:31 is the trumpet that triggers the Rapture, but it is not. This prophecy taught by Jesus will take place at the end of the Tribulation or the beginning of the seventy-five day interval between the Tribulation and the start of the Millennial Kingdom.

In summary Matthew 24:31 describes the Second Coming of Christ as well as the gathering of all the faithful from every corner of the earth to The Sheep and Goat Judgment where they will be blessed by God and allowed to enter the Millennial kingdom in their earthly bodies. So what conclusion can we draw from these four verses? First, we can conclude that there is no final, perfect answer to explain the *"last trumpet."* There are trumpets being blown all over the place for a wide variety of occurrences. However, I believe we can determine in what sequence the events of the Rapture will occur.

I cannot quite understand how anyone could come to the conclusion that the Rapture will occur before the Tribulation (Pre-Tribulation Rapture) or in the middle of the Tribulation. Those who believe the Rapture will occur at the end or after the Tribulation are on more solid ground, but I must come to the conclusion that the Rapture will occur at the sound of the seventh trumpet just before the bowl judgments of God's wrath are released (**Pre-Wrath Rapture**). Go back and look at the evidence and prayerfully make your own decision. If you do not agree with me, that is your choice.

- 1 Thessalonians 4:13-17 describes the Rapture.
- 1 Corinthians 15:50-58 describes the Rapture.
- Revelation 11:15-19 describes the coronation of Jesus in Heaven. It is neither the Rapture, nor the Second Coming.
- Matthew 24:29-31 describes the Second Coming of Jesus and the gathering of all remaining believers who are still alive at the end of the Tribulation.

Whenever these events occur and how they occur may surprise us all when they actually happen. One thing, however, is for certain. The glory, splendor, and wonder of the Rapture and Christ's Second Coming will knock your socks off. I hope I will see all of you there.

THE DEAD

ADDITIONAL INFORMATION THAT will be helpful to us as we progress in this study is a clarification of terms used in reference to the dead, both believers and unbelievers. Believers, of course, are those who have placed their faith in Christ's substitutionary death and resurrection in payment for their sins. Unbelievers are those who have rejected God and Christ and must stand before God covered with every sin they have committed and thereby pay the penalty for sin which is eternity in the Lake of Fire, which will be discussed in more detail later in the study. Hopefully this will allow for a better understanding of the End Time prophecies and events that we will encounter in both the Old and New Testaments.

- Let us look first at the term, *"Sheol,"* which is a Hebrew word found only in the Old Testament. This was the place that both the *righteous and unrighteous* expected to go when they died. It was a place of soul consciousness, which means that the body is in the

grave, but the soul is alive and functioning in some kind of physical form. There are several different divisions within Sheol. The *righteous side of Sheol* was referred to as *Abraham's Bosom (Paradise)* and was relocated to Heaven at the time of Jesus' resurrection. Since that time the reference Hades alone is used to describe what most of us commonly refer to as *Hell.*[1]
HADES = HELL

Revelation 6:8 tells us that death comes on a horse, and Hades (a symbol of death) comes close behind. Matthew 16:18 tells us the Church will be built upon a rock and the gates of Hades (Hell) will not be victorious against it. Here the place of the dead (complete with gates and bars) is a symbol for death. Christians will die, but death (the gates of Hades) will not be able to hold them, just as they were unable to hold Christ in the grave. He (Jesus) who burst out of Hades (overcoming death) will bring His people out as well. This is also the meaning of Acts 2:27 (quoting Psalm 16:10):[2] *"For You will not abandon my soul to Sheol; Nor will You allow Your Holy One to undergo decay."* Let us also read this from a contemporary translation: *"For you will not leave my soul*

---

1   Ibid.
2   Trent C. Butler, ed., "TRIBULATION," in *Holman Bible Dictionary*, (Nashville, TN: Holman Bible Publishers, 1991), WORD*search* CROSS e-book, under: "TRIBULATION".

among the dead or allow your holy one to rot in the grave" (NLT). Christ has conquered both death and Hades. He appears in Revelation 1:18 as the one holding the keys which open or close (control) both.[3]

IN THE OLD TESTAMENT

Before Jesus' resurrection, this chart shows the structure of:

<u>Sheol/Hades</u>
(Located in the center of the earth)

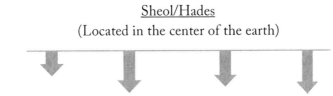

Paradise

Abraham's Bosom	**Hades (Proper)**	**The Abyss**	**Tartarus**
(Righteous Dead)	(The Unrighteous Dead) Also known as **The Pit** Also known as **Hell** Also known as **Apollyon**	(Fallen Angels Only)	(Fallen Angels from the time of flood only)

Anyone who died in Old Testament times went to either **Paradise (Abraham's Bosom) or Hades** (proper). **Heaven, Abraham's Bosom, Paradise**; all three are the same. Abraham's Bosom (Paradise) was relocated to Heaven when Jesus was resurrected (rose from the dead). Now the righteous

---

3   Ibid.

dead go immediately to Heaven when they die. Hades remains right where it is (2 Corinthians 5:6-8) and that's still where unbelievers end up. There was a large chasm between Abraham's Bosom and Hades. People could see and hear one another, but they could not get to one another.

IN THE NEW TESTAMENT

After Jesus' resurrection, this chart shows the
structure of Hades only
(Those in Paradise or Abraham's Bosom
were taken to Heaven)

HADES

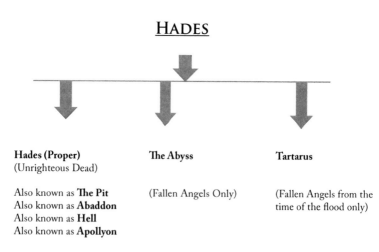

Hades (Proper)
(Unrighteous Dead)

Also known as **The Pit**
Also known as **Abaddon**
Also known as **Hell**
Also known as **Apollyon**

The Abyss

(Fallen Angels Only)

Tartarus

(Fallen Angels from the
time of the flood only)

DURING THE 1000 YEAR REIGN (MILLENNIUM) OF CHRIST ON EARTH

IN HADES

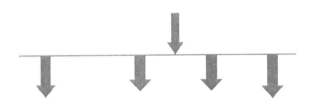

Hades (Proper) (Unrighteous Dead)	**The Abyss**	**Tartarus**	**Lake of Fire**
Also known as **The Pit** Also known as **Abaddon, Gehenna, and Appolyon** Also known as **Hell**	Fallen Angels	Fallen Angels from the time of the flood only	Antichrist and False Prophet

ON EARTH

Jesus reigning from Jerusalem
Glorified believers ruling with Jesus

IN HEAVEN

**Resurrected saints will have access
between Heaven and earth
Also home of the righteous that die
during the Millennium
Where God Dwells
Holy Angels**

THEN COMES ETERNITY

HEAVEN/THE NEW JERUSALEM

God

Jesus

The Holy Spirit

All Resurrected Believers of All Time

Holy Angels

Heaven, The New Jerusalem, will descend to the New Earth

The Lake of Fire/Gehenna

All People Who Did Not Accept Christ as Their Savior
Satan
Fallen Angels
False Prophet
Antichrist
Hades no longer exists–All inhabitants
transferred to the Lake of Fire[4]

---

4   Op. Cit., Larkin, p. 75.

SHEEP AND GOAT JUDGMENT

SOMETHING ELSE WE should have a working knowledge of before we begin chapter one is the Sheep and Goat Judgment at the end of the Tribulation.

Matthew 25:31-33:

31 "But when the Son of Man comes in His glory, and all the angels with Him, then He will sit on His glorious throne. 32 "All the nations [Gentiles][1] will be before Him; and He will separate them from one another, as the shepherd separates the sheep from the goats; 33 and He will put the sheep on His right, and the goats on His left."

> Christians are not saved by doing good works.
> Christians do good works because they are saved.

---

1   Brackets mine.

The Son of Man in verse 31 is Jesus. He will come and set up His throne in the Valley of Jehoshaphat, just outside Jerusalem. *"All the nations"* (πάντα τὰ ἔθνη) in verse 32, may most accurately be translated *"Gentiles"* (non-Jews).[23] Both sources indicated here in the footnotes suggest this will include all Gentiles who survive the Tribulation and are alive at the Second Coming of Christ, both believers and nonbelievers. Christ will then separate them according to who believed in Him and by the way in which they treated the Jews during the course of the Tribulation. The sheep, those who supported the Jews, will be on His right and the goats, which persecuted the Jews, will be on His left. Only true believers will risk protecting the Jews during the Tribulation. One-third of all the Jews in the world will come to faith in Christ before the end of the Tribulation. They will repopulate the Promised Land of Israel just as God promised thousands of years before.

The right is the preferred side in ancient texts. In the few scenes of judgment where it occurs, the right side is for the righteous and the left for the wicked. Sheep were also considered more valuable than goats, and characteristics like this may have influenced how these terms would be

2   Vincent, Marvin Richardson: *Word Studies in the New Testament.* Bellingham, WA: 2002, S. 1:135.

3   Schwandt, John; Collins, C. John: *The* ESV *English-Greek Reverse Interlinear New Testament.* Inc., 2006; 2006, S. Matthew 25:32

understood. For instance, sheep were associated with good while goats were associated with trouble (Matthew 25:34-40).[4]

The sheep will be judged in the manner described in Matthew 25:34 and will enter the Millennial Kingdom still in earthly bodies but ready to enjoy the perfect rule and government under Jesus Christ. They will also be the ones who repopulate the earth in the same manner people have been populating the earth for thousands of years. This will be a time of near perfection in government and personal relationships, and mankind will finally experience peace on earth, good will toward men.

These Gentile sheep will be those who helped the Jews during their time of need as they were forced to flee into the wilderness without even the opportunity to pack a lunch. The sheep will provide food, clothing, and shelter for them, at a time when it could mean their death to do so. They will show kindness to the Jews by visiting them in prison, and providing them medical care when they need it.

As evidence of the new lives people demonstrated in Matthew 25, after being saved and receiving the Holy Spirit of God within them, Jesus cites their deeds of kindness done to His *"brothers" (Jews,* verse 40) which He considers the same as doing it to Him. These are acts only believers would do for

---

4   Keener, Craig S.; InterVarsity Press: *The IVP Bible Background Commentary: New Testament.* Downers Grove, Ill.: InterVarsity Press, 1993, S. Mt 25:32. Op. Cit., Keener.

other believers in this time of great tribulation. Nonbelievers will not even give the time of day to believers. And even if they extend the same courtesies to one another, nonbelievers are not considered Christ's brothers and will not therefore receive salvation.

Someone might be saying, *"Is this guy trying to teach a doctrine of salvation by works?"* Absolutely not! There is only one way to salvation and eternal life and that is through God's grace by faith in Jesus' work on the cross, dying for our sins in our place. The idea that helping one's neighbor will earn one salvation and eternity in Heaven is definitely not what is meant here, although that is what God wants us to do for one another. No one at any time in the history of the world was ever saved by good works. The Old Testament saints were saved by faith (Hebrews 11); the New Testament saints were and are saved by faith in Jesus Christ (Ephesians 2:8–10). People today are saved the same way. However, it is because of salvation that believers desire to do well. They want to do good because the Holy Spirit is now living within them. He makes people want to do the right thing. He also makes people feel guilty if they are thinking about doing the wrong thing, and He makes them regret what they have done if they actually commit the act. *"So then, while we have opportunity, let us do good to all people, and especially to those who are of the household of faith"* (Galatians 6:10). *"And do not neglect doing good and sharing, for with such sacrifices God is pleased"* (Hebrews 13:16).

But doing good is not the way people are saved.

What we have here is what James referred to in James 2:14-26, where he said that what we do with our lives demonstrates our faith. These Gentile sheep are *demonstrating their faith* in Christ by what they do for the Jews. These sheep will be sent into the Messianic (Millennial) Kingdom to inhabit the Gentile nations there, and they will enter the Kingdom in their earthly bodies without experiencing death or resurrection.

Now we come to the Jew haters, the Anti-Semites. These are the people who were loyal to Satan and Antichrist in their attempt to annihilate the Jews. These miserable Satan worshippers will have done everything possible to rid the earth of the Jews. They killed them, they tortured them, raped the Jewish women, stole from them, humiliated them, drove them from their land, and blasphemed their God. **They will be killed and sent to Hell.** End of story.

Matthew 25:41, 45-46:

[41] *Then He will also say to those on His left, 'Depart from Me, accursed ones, into the fire which has been prepared for the devil and his angels;...* [45] *"Then He will answer them, 'Truly I say to you, to the extent that you did not do it to one of the least of these, you did not do it to Me.'* [46] *"These will go away into eternal punishment, but the righteous into eternal life."*

We see a prophecy by Joel in the Old Testament predicting this very same event.

Joel 3:1-2:

"For behold, in those days and at that time, when I restore the fortunes of Judah and Jerusalem, ² I will gather all the nations and bring them down to the Valley of Jehoshaphat. And I will enter into judgment with them there, on behalf of my people and my heritage Israel, because they have scattered them among the nations and have divided up my land."

In the future the Lord will restore the fortunes of Judah and Jerusalem, in fulfillment of Moses' promise.[5]

Deuteronomy 30:1-10 (NLT):

[1] *"In the future, when you experience all these blessings and curses I have listed for you, and when you are living among the nations to which the LORD your God has exiled you, take to heart all these instructions. ² If at that time you and your children return to the LORD your God, and if you obey with all your heart and all your soul all the commands I have given you today, ³ then the LORD your God will restore your fortunes. He will have mercy on you and gather you back from all the nations where he has scattered you. ⁴ Even though you are banished to the ends of the earth, the LORD your God will gather you from there and bring you back again. ⁵ The LORD your God will return you to the land that*

---

5   John Walvoord and Roy Zuck, ed., *The Bible Knowledge Commentary: An Exposition of the Scriptures by Dallas Seminary Faculty*, (Colorado Springs, CO: Cook Communications, 1985), WORD*search* CROSS e-book, 1421.

belonged to your ancestors, and you will possess that land again. Then he will make you even more prosperous and numerous than your ancestors! [6] *"The LORD your God will change your heart and the hearts of all your descendants, so that you will love him with all your heart and soul and so you may live!* [7] *The LORD your God will inflict all these curses on your enemies and on those who hate and persecute you.* [8] *Then you will again obey the LORD and keep all his commands that I am giving you today.* [9] *"The LORD your God will then make you successful in everything you do. He will give you many children and numerous livestock, and he will cause your fields to produce abundant harvests, for the LORD will again delight in being good to you as he was to your ancestors.* [10] *The LORD your God will delight in you if you obey his voice and keep the commands and decrees written in this Book of Instruction, and if you turn to the LORD your God with all your heart and soul.*

All people who died up to the time of this judgment of sheep and goats by Jesus, who did not believe in Jesus as Savior *would already be in Hell.* Those who have died believing in Jesus would be in Heaven. Therefore, this judgment will involve only those who are left alive at the end of the seven-year Tribulation, and will include both believers and unbelievers. The believers (sheep) will be placed on God's right, the unbelievers (goats) to His left. *"Then the King will say to those on His right, 'Come, you who are blessed of My Father, inherit the kingdom prepared for you from the foundation of the world'"* (Matthew 25:34). These sheep will then be allowed to enter the Millennial Kingdom of God, the first destination on their way to Heaven. The unbelievers will not be so fortunate for they have chosen to be sent to Hell. *"Then He will also say to those on His left, 'Depart from Me, accursed ones, into the eternal fire which has been prepared for the devil and his angels'"* (Matthew 25:41).

There will also be some other folks in the Millennial Kingdom with these sheep. There will also be the glorified saints who by this time will have received their new resurrected bodies (Revelation 20:4-6). These saints are believers who died throughout history up to the end of the Tribulation.

The goats will be sent to Hell and remain there until the Great White Throne Judgment at the end of the Millennium, when they will be sentenced to The Lake of Fire for eternity. This is the same judgment scene that we see in Revelation 20:11-15, which takes place at the end of the Millennium (the thousand years), when all who have been confined in Hell throughout history, since the time of their death, will come out of Hell and stand before the Great White Throne of God, be declared guilty, and sentenced to the Lake of Fire for all eternity.

Christ as King invites the sheep to come and inherit the millennial kingdom where they will live under the earthly rule and reign of Christ for 1,000 years. At the end of the 1,000 years, the Great White Throne Judgment will take place in space somewhere *("the earth and the heaven having fled away,"* Revelation 20:11). That judgment will include all people throughout history who died and went to Hell.

Whether it could also include those who were born and saved and then died during the Millennial Kingdom is hard to say because the Bible does not give us any specific information in that regard.

Now as we conclude this section, we do not want to play down the impact of the salvation of one-third of all the Jewish people on the earth. Just as Gentile believing Christians are being saved and resurrected, at the same time one-third of the Jews will be saved and enter the Millennial Kingdom in their earthly bodies as well.

REGATHERING OF ISRAEL

Now JUST A quick look at God's promise to Israel that when Christ returns at the end of the age to establish His kingdom on earth, all Jews will be returned to the land they were originally promised and rule with Him during the thousand year Millennium. The prophets in the Old Testament foretold of a miracle that would bring the Jews back into their land.[1]

Moses anticipated the judgmental scattering of Israel into all parts of the earth because of national sin; he also foresaw the End Time gathering of all the remaining outcasts of Israel. In Deuteronomy he prophesied that national repentance would be followed by a national re-gathering:[2]

---

1   J. Vernon McGee, *Thru The Bible with J. Vernon McGee*, (Nashville, TN: Thomas Nelson, 1983), WORD*search* CROSS e-book, under: "Chapter 24".

2   John Phillips, *The John Phillips Commentary Series – Exploring the Gospel of Matthew: An Expository Commentary*, (Grand Rapids, MI: Kregel Publications, 2005), WORD*search* CROSS e-book, 453-454.

Deuteronomy 30:3-5:

[1] *"So it shall be when all of these things have come upon you, the blessing and the curse which I have set before you, and you call them to mind in all nations where the LORD your God has banished you,* [2] *and you return to the LORD your God and obey Him with all your heart and soul according to all that I command you today, you and your sons,* [3] *then the LORD your God will restore you from captivity, and have compassion on you, and will gather you again from all the peoples where the LORD your God has scattered you.* [4] *"If your outcasts are at the ends of the earth, from there the LORD your God will gather you, and from there He will bring you back.*

[5] *"The LORD your God will bring you into the land which your fathers possessed, and you shall possess it; and He will prosper you and multiply you more than your fathers.*

The rebirth of the state of Israel in our day and the re-gathering of the Jewish people to their ancestral homeland do not completely fulfill the prophecy of Moses. Although many Jews have returned to Israel, many more remain scattered around the world, and Israel is still rejecting Christ. Israel is not yet the olive branch being grafted back into its former special relationship with God (Romans 11:17-24). It is the fig tree barren of all that could minister to Christ, but putting forth its end-time leaves (Matthew 24:32). "Israel is being regathered today not in anticipation of the coming of Christ to reign, but in anticipation of the coming of the antichrist to ruin."[3]

Jews that come to accept Christ as their Savior will be gathered from all around the world along with all the Gentile believers for the Sheep and Goat Judgment. All believers will be allowed to enter into the Millennial Kingdom in their earthly bodies. One-third of the Jews will be saved, but two-thirds will go to destruction (Hell).

---

3   Ibid.

HISTORY OF GOD'S TEMPLE

IN ORDER TO understand the purpose for God's Temple, we must begin by familiarizing ourselves with the Tabernacle. Because the physical properties of the Tabernacle reflected God's desired relationship with His people, we can see that symbolism taking shape. To really understand the background of the Tabernacle, one must examine what the symbols meant to ancient Israelites.

The Tabernacle was a very elaborate[1] tent. It was built during the wilderness period, when the people of God were traveling from Egypt to the Promised Land and were all living in tents. Thus it is understandable that the Tabernacle, which came to represent God's residence on earth, would be constructed in the form of a tent. The book of Exodus

---

1   Elaborate: made or done with great care or with much detail: having many parts that are carefully arranged or planned; http://www.merriam-webster.com

tells us that God gave detailed instructions for the building of His Tabernacle. God told Moses in detail how to build the Tabernacle according to the pattern shown him on the mountain beginning in Exodus 25. After the instructions were given and before they were carried out, Israel turned away from God and worshiped the golden calf (Exodus 32). Moses, though, interceded[2] for his people and God forgave them. The last part of the book of Exodus narrates how Israel carried out God's construction plans to the letter (Exodus 35-38). When the building was finished, God filled it with His cloud of glory, symbolizing His holy presence among His people (Exodus 40:34-38).

The Tabernacle was modest by ancient temple standards. The cherubim atop the Ark of the Covenant symbolize a throne; thus God is seated on His throne above the Cherubim.[3] Other ancient Near Eastern temples (e.g., Minoan, Assyrian, and Hittite) had tables of offering, but in Israel's Tabernacle the priests rather than a deity consumed the bread (Leviticus 24:9). Sacrificial altars regularly appear in ancient temples, along with standard types of sacrifices: thank offerings, sin offerings, and atonement offerings. But most ancient peoples also had offerings to persuade deities to send rain or other

---

2   Intercede: to try to help settle an argument or disagreement between two or more people or groups: to speak to someone in order to defend or help another person.

3   1 Samuel 4:4; 2 Sam. 6:2; 2 Kings 19:15; Psalm. 80:1; 99:1; Isaiah 37:16; cf. Numbers 7:89; Ezekiel 9:3.

favors; Yahweh promised His people that they would be blessed if they simply kept His covenant.[4]

Temples with sacrificial altars, which God's Tabernacle had, needed incense altars to cover the stench of burning flesh. Lampstands were also necessary in such temples so priests could see in the sanctuary which did not have any openings to allow in the light of day. Many ancient Near Eastern temples provided the deity with a throne, footstool, lamp, table, chest and bed. The Tabernacle had no chest or bed, which would suggest that God does not have bodily needs and does not sleep. Of course God is not contained by a human body and has no need for human comforts.[5] God tells His people: *"But I* [God] *do not need the bulls from your barns or the goats from your pens. For all the animals of the forest are mine, and I own the cattle on a thousand hills"* (Psalm 50:9-10 NLT).

People also understood that an earthly Temple merely reflects the glory of God's heavenly home. The earthly pattern had to correspond with the heavenly to help people understand what Heaven will be like. Just as pagan temples often pointed to the heavens as the home of their deities (e.g., the blue, star-studded ceilings of Egyptian temples), Israel could worship God in His Tabernacle yet acknowledge that He fills Heaven and earth (1 Kings 8:27; Isaiah 66:1-2). God's Temple did not confine God; it merely provided a

---

4   Op. Cit., *Easy-to-Read Commentary Series.*

5   Ibid.

place for the worshiper to approach the deity with appropriate reverence. The Tabernacle came to symbolize God's presence among His people (Exodus 33:9-11). During the wilderness wanderings, the Tabernacle signified God's presence as a divine warrior. Numbers 2 presents a picture of the Israelite camp as it was on the march from Egypt to the Promised Land.The Tabernacle is a tent pitched in the midst of the tribes. In other words, God's tent occupies the place of the *warrior-king*in a battle camp. So when the Tabernacle was taken down, the ark, which was normally housed in the holy of holies, led the march, which began with the acclamation *"Rise up, O Lord! May your enemies be scattered; may your foes flee before you"* (Numbers 10:35). And when the ark comes to rest at a new campsite, the cry is *"Return, O Lord, to the countless thousands of Israel"* (Numbers 10:36).[6]

One who longed for God might desire to be in His "Tabernacle," that is, dwelling in His presence like the priests and Levites[7] who served in the Temple.[8] God promised that

---

6   Ibid.

7   Levites: All the descendants of Levi (Ex. 6:25; Lev. 25:32; Josh. 21:3, 41); also the distinctive title of that portion of the tribe that was set apart for the service of the sanctuary and subordinate to the priests (Num. 8:6; Ezra 2:70; John 1:19). Merrill Unger, *The New Unger's Bible Dictionary*, (Chicago: Moody Press, 1957), s.v. "," WORD*search* CROSS e-book.

8   Ps. 15:1; 27:5; 61:4; Levites wrote many of the Psalms: 1 Chron. 16:4-6, 41-42; 25:1-7; 2 Chron. 29:30.

His Tabernacle would be with His people forever, for His covenant (promise) was that He would dwell with them and be their God.[9]

The Gospel of John begins by announcing that the very Word of God took on human form. In the words of John 1:14, *"The Word became flesh and made his dwelling among us. We have seen his glory, the glory of the one and only Son, who came from the Father, full of grace and truth"* (NIV). In Greek, *"made His dwelling"* (skenoo) is a verbal form of the word for Tabernacle.[10]

In this way the author of the Gospel intends us to see Jesus as the fulfillment of the Tabernacle. God is indeed present among men and women, and can reveal Himself anywhere. *"But now you have been united with Christ Jesus. Once you were far away from God, but now you have been brought near to him through the blood of Christ. Now all of us can come to the Father through the same Holy Spirit because of what Christ has done for us. So now you Gentiles are no longer strangers and foreigners. You are citizens along with all of God's holy people. You are members of God's family. Together, we are his house, built on the foundation of the apostles and the prophets. And the cornerstone is Christ Jesus himself. We are carefully joined together in him, becoming a holy temple for the Lord. Through him you Gentiles are also being made*

---

9   Ezekiel 37:27; cf. Ezekiel 43:7, 9; Exodus 29:45-46.

10   Op. Cit., *Easy-to-Read Commentary Series.*

part of this dwelling where God lives by his Spirit" (Ephesians 2:13, 18-22, NLT).

Revelation 21:1-4:

[1] *"Then I saw a new heaven and a new earth; for the first heaven and the first earth passed away, and there is no longer any sea.* [2] *And I saw the holy city, new Jerusalem, coming down out of heaven from God, made ready as a bride adorned for her husband.* [3] *And I heard a loud voice from the throne, saying, "Behold, the tabernacle of God is among men, and He will dwell among them, and they shall be His people, and God Himself will be among them,* [4] *and He will wipe away every tear from their eyes; and there will no longer be any death; there will no longer be any mourning, or crying, or pain; the first things have passed away."*

As noted above, the Tabernacle of Exodus probably pointed to a heavenly Tabernacle. Jewish people in the first century A.D. often paralleled the heavenly and the earthly (e.g., the heavenly Sanhedrin); naturally the rabbis and various End Time writers pictured a Temple in Heaven.[11]

Hebrews 8:1-3, 6-7 (NLT):

[1] *Here is the main point: We have a High Priest who sat down in the place of honor beside the throne of the majestic God in heaven.*

---

11   Leland Ryken, James C. Wilhoit, Tremper Longman, ed., *Dictionary of Biblical Imagery*, (Downer's Grove, IL: InterVarsity Press, 1998), WORD*search* CROSS e-book, 837-839.

² There he ministers in the heavenly Tabernacle, the true place of worship that was built by the Lord and not by human hands. ³ And since every high priest is required to offer gifts and sacrifices, our High Priest must make an offering, too. ⁶ But now Jesus, our High Priest, has been given a ministry that is far superior to the old priesthood, for he is the one who mediates for us a far better covenant with God, based on better promises.⁷ If the first covenant had been faultless, there would have been no need for a second covenant to replace it.

Now that we have access to the heavenly house of God in Christ, we need no longer resort to the earthly one. Contemporaries like Philo allegorized[12] the Tabernacle: linen represented the earth, dark red the air, the seven-branched lampstand the seven planets, and so forth. The writer of Hebrews observes that the holiest place in the Tabernacle was off limits to anyone but the high priest once a year (Hebrews 9:6-7), and that this condition was carried on right up until Jesus' resurrection, until God revealed Himself fully to His people (Hebrews 9:8-10; cf. Revelation 11:2). But Jesus, as

---

12   A method of interpretation ("allegorizing"), especially biblical interpretation, that seeks to find a deeper moral, theological, spiritual meaning behind the words and literal imagery of the text. Walter A. Elwell and Philip W. Comfort, "ALLEGORY," in *Tyndale Bible Dictionary*, (Wheaton, IL: Tyndale House Publishers, 2001), WORD*search* CROSS e-book, 29.

the High Priest after the order of Melchizedek[13] (Hebrews 5:5-6), has accomplished all that was necessary to bring believers into God's presence.

Hebrews 9:1-28 (NLT):

1 That first covenant between God and Israel had regulations for worship and a place of worship here on earth. ⁸ By these regulations the Holy Spirit revealed that the entrance to the Most Holy Place was not freely open as long as the Tabernacle and the system it represented were still in use. ⁹ This is an illustration[14] pointing to the present time. For the gifts and sacrifices that the priests offer are not able to cleanse the consciences of the people who bring them. 10 For that old system deals only with food and drink and various cleansing ceremonies—physical regulations that were in effect only until a better system could be established. 11 So Christ has now become the High Priest over all the good things that

---

13   Hebrews 7:1 *(a)* Scholars disagree on the position occupied by this priest. Some are quite sure that he was an Old Testament incarnation of Christ Jesus Himself. Others believe that he was a strange, unusual character who was a type of the Savior. The evidence is not too clear, and the reader may use either conclusion that he feels the Scriptures justify. Walter L. Wilson, *A Dictionary of Bible Types*, (Grand Rapids, MI: Wm. B. Eerdmans, 1957; repr., Peabody, MA: Hendrickson, 1999), WORD*search* CROSS e-book, under: "MELCHIZEDEK".

14   Illustrate, Illustrated, Illustration: To give examples in order to make (something) easier to understand; to explain or decorate a story, book, etc., with pictures.

*have come. He has entered that greater, more perfect Tabernacle
in heaven, which was not made by human hands and is not part
of this created world. 12 With his own blood—not the blood of
goats and calves—he entered the Most Holy Place once for all time
and secured our redemption forever. 13 Under the old system, the
blood of goats and bulls and the ashes of a young cow could cleanse
people's bodies from ceremonial impurity. ¹⁴ Just think how much
more the blood of Christ will purify our consciences from sinful
deeds so that we can worship the living God. For by the power
of the eternal Spirit, Christ offered himself to God as a perfect
sacrifice for our sins. ¹⁵ That is why he is the one who mediates a
new covenant between God and people, so that all who are called
can receive the eternal inheritance God has promised them. For
Christ died to set them free from the penalty of the sins they had
committed under that first covenant.*

Now all believers have direct access to God's presence
(Hebrews 4:16), the reality toward which the Tabernacle in
Israel's midst always pointed.[15] When they approach His
throne room in Heaven they always find the welcome mat
telling them to come right in: "*Therefore let us draw near
with confidence to the throne of grace, so that we may receive
mercy and find grace to help in time of need*" (Hebrews 4:16).
Revelation's images of God's heavenly throne room remind
us of the Tabernacle during the wilderness wandering of
the Jews. Revelation declares that the Tabernacle that long

---

15   Op. Cit., Ryken, et. al.

represented God's dwelling among His people will be among His people forever.

Revelation 21:3-4:

[3] *And I heard a loud voice from the throne, saying, "Behold, the tabernacle of God is among men, and He will dwell among them, and they shall be His people, and God Himself will be among them,* [4]*and He will wipe away every tear from their eyes; and there will no longer be any death; there will no longer be any mourning, or crying, or pain; the first things have passed away."*

Despite Ezekiel's vision of an eschatological[16] temple (Ezekiel 40—46), Revelation is interested only in what that Temple ultimately symbolized: God dwelling with His people (Ezekiel 43:7-12; cf. Ezekiel 11:16; 36:27; 37:14, 27-28; 39:29). In keeping with John's teaching (John 14:23; 15:1-6), God and the Lamb will be their people's Temple, and they will need no other (Revelation 21:22; cf. Revelation 3:12).[17] What John was actually seeing here was the place where God dwells and the Ark of His covenant as symbolic

---

16 Refers to the biblical doctrine of last things. The doctrine of last things normally focuses on a discussion of the return of Christ at the end of the age, the coming judgments, various expressions of the kingdom of heaven and the kingdom of God, the nature of the glorified body, and the prospects for eternal destiny. Chad Brand, Charles Draper, Archie England, ed., *Holman Illustrated Bible Dictionary*, (Nashville: Holman Bible Publishers, 2003), s.v. ","*WORDsearch* CROSS e-book.

17 Op. Cit., Ryken, et.al.

of God's presence and faithfulness among His people. That John saw the Ark also assured the readers of John's Gospel of God's presence and protection in their coming trials. John is promising through this symbolism that God's promises would be fulfilled and His purposes accomplished. In this vision of God's open Temple, John saw heavenly worship before God Himself. There would be no sin that would ever again separate God and His people.[18]

The Temple (Tabernacle) which Moses made followed the pattern in Heaven. "*And the sanctuary*[19] (Temple) *of God in Heaven was opened*" (Revelation 11:19) means that God is dealing now with Israel. "*Was opened*" promises worship and access to God. All of this points to the nation Israel. The focus of attention is on the ark of God, the symbol of God's presence with His people. God's glory rested on the ark, and God's Law was within the ark, beautifully illustrating that

---

18   Barton B. Bruce et al., *Life Application New Testament Commentary*, (Wheaton, IL: Tyndale House, 2001), WORD*search* CROSS e-book, 1239.

19   Sanctuary: "Sanctuary" refers to the place where God appeared and/ or dwelt, as indicated by the presence of the ark. God's Word was kept there and issued forth from it. There God's people gathered for sacrifice, for hearing the covenant word, for worship and prayer, and for the celebration of the major feasts. Walter A. Elwell and Philip W. Comfort, "SANCTUARY," in *Tyndale Bible Dictionary*, (Wheaton, IL: Tyndale House Publishers, 2001), WORD*search* CROSS e-book, 1165.

the two must never be separated. He is the holy God and must deal righteously with sin. But He is also the faithful God who keeps His promises to His people. This vision of the ark would greatly encourage God's suffering people to whom John sent this book. "God will fulfill His promises!" John was saying to them. *"He will reveal His glory! Trust Him!"*[20]

The Ark of the Covenant disappeared when **Nebuchadnezzar**[21] destroyed the Temple and took **Judah** captive into Babylon 600 years before Christ. At that time *"all the vessels of the house of God, great and small, and the treasures of the house of the Lord"* were also taken to Babylon (2 Chronicles 36:18), as were the brass and other metals that adorned[22] the Temple (2 Kings 25:13-20). No mention, however, was made of the ark, the most important and perhaps most costly item in the Temple (the ark was overlaid with pure gold, and the mercy seat and cherubim were of pure gold). It also was certainly the most significant item to the writers of the accounts in 2 Kings, 2 Chronicles, and Jeremiah (chapter 52, as well as the book of Lamentations). There wasn't anything said about the ark when

---

20 Op. Cit., Barton.

21 Nebuchadnezzar: Babylonian king (605-562 B.C.) who captured and destroyed Jerusalem in 586 b. c.; Walter A. Elwelland Philip W. Comfort, "SANCTUARY," in *Tyndale Bible Dictionary*, (Wheaton, IL: Tyndale House Publishers, 2001), WORD*search* CROSS e-book, 1165.

22 Adorn: To make (someone or something) more attractive by adding something beautiful.

Cyrus commissioned the rebuilding of the Temple and sent back all its vessels as well (Ezra 1:1-11).[23]

It seems impossible that God would have allowed the ark to be destroyed. When it was captured earlier by the Philistines, in the days of Samuel, Saul, and David, God saw that it was kept for almost a hundred years until David finally returned it to the Tabernacle in Jerusalem.[24, 25] Men through the centuries have been almost as intrigued with the search for the Ark of the Covenant as they have with the search for Noah's ark. The ark was not in Zerubbabel's Temple [rebuilt Temple, 515 B.C. (Ezra 5:1–6:22)], nor the Temple of Herod, nor in the Tribulation Temple. Neither is there any mention of it even in the Millennial Temple described in Ezekiel 40—48. People have rumored it is somewhere in a cave in Ethiopia, or in the Arabian Desert, or somewhere else.[26] But there is no mystery as to where it is. God showed John, when He revealed to him the Apocalypse,[27] that it was

---

23 Henry M. Morris, *The Revelation Record*, (Wheaton, IL: Tyndale House Publishers, 1983), WORD*search* CROSS e-book, 211-205.

24 1 Samuel 4:4, 11, 22; 1 Chronicles 15:28; 16:1.

25 Op. Cit., Morris.

26 Ibid.

27 The word apocalypse (unveiling) is derived from Revelation 1:1, where it refers to the ascended Jesus' revelation to John of the consummation (to bring to completion, conclude) of the age. Walter A. Elwell, ed., *"Apocalyptic,"* refers to the end of history as we know it and the beginning of God's 1,000 year kingdom on the earth.

safely stored in the *Heavenly Temple*. No doubt the two tables of the Ten Commandments are there as well. If God could transport Enoch and Elijah to Heaven, and if the resurrected Christ could ascend to Heaven, He would be more than able to remove the ark from Jerusalem before Nebuchadnezzar's armies sacked the Temple, and then have it safely moved to the true Tabernacle in the *New Jerusalem* under construction in Heaven.[28]

And there it will remain, until after the *Millennium*, when the New Jerusalem (which itself is the true Tabernacle—Revelation 21:3) will descend from God out of Heaven to the earth. The city is itself a Tabernacle, and since *"the Lord God the Almighty and the Lamb are its Temple"* (Revelation 21:22), there will be no Temple within the city. But the ark of God's covenant will be there, with its mercy seat possibly constituting His very throne, or at least representing the throne whereon He will meet with His people forevermore.

The hill on which the Temple stood was called **Mount Moriah**(2 Chronicles 3:1). *"The highest of mountains…lifted above the hills,"* does not have any reference to the elevation of *Mount Moriah* (also referred to as **Mount Zion**). Rather it suggests that Jerusalem will be the home of the King of the World and *"all the nations will stream into it."* God will at this time restore the nation of Israel to glory and bless all the nations of the world, which are all people in all nations of the

---

28   Op. Cit., Morris.

world who have accepted Christ as their Savior. The rest will go to Hell.

The prophet Isaiah looked ahead to the time (the Millennium) when God's righteous kingdom would be established and the Temple would become the center for the worldwide worship of the Lord. Everyone will want to visit Jerusalem to worship God and Christ in the Temple. In Isaiah's day, the Jews were worshipping the false gods of the Gentiles; but the day would come when the Gentiles would give up their phony religions and worship the true God of Israel. During the Millennium the Jewish Temple will be rebuilt, and the Word of God will go forth from Jerusalem to govern the nations of the world.[29]

"The mountain of the house of the Lord" refers to the mount where the Temple was built (and where the Millennial Temple will be built, Ezekiel 40-43). Often in the Scriptures mountains refer to governmental authorities (Daniel 2:35; Amos 4:1). Here God's rule from the Temple will be unquestioned. Jesus will be considered the highest authority on earth. The idea that Christ will rule the world from the Temple Mount in Jerusalem is repeated often in Isaiah's prophecies.[30] Isaiah clearly wanted his readers to be aware that God would protect His covenant nation, Israel, despite

---

29 Wiersbe, Warren W.: *Be Comforted.* Wheaton, Ill.: Victor Books, 1996, c1992 (An Old Testament Study), S. Is 2:1.

30 Isaiah 11:9; 25:6-7; 27:13; 30:29; 56:7; 57:13; 65:11, 25; 66:20.

their disobedience and even though they would go into captivity.[31] These words provided hope for the Jewish people while they were still in captivity in Babylon. They knew that their captivity would eventually end and they would be free.

---

31 Walvoord, John F.; Zuck, Roy B.; Dallas Theological Seminary: *The Bible Knowledge Commentary: An Exposition of the Scriptures.* Wheaton, IL: Victor Books, 1983-c1985, S. 1:1037.

The Millenium

When Jesus Christ has returned and defeated the enemies, He will set up a kingdom here on earth and rule it for one thousand years. This is called the Millennium. It will be a wonderful time of peace. Satan will be locked up so that he cannot prowl about as a lion, seeking whom he may destroy (1 Peter 5:8). There will be no war and no poverty. Worship of the Lord and living according to God's Word will prevail (Isaiah 2:2-4; Micah 4:1-4).

The attraction that will draw people to Jerusalem at that time will be the Lord's ways…paths… Law, and Word which were described in Isaiah 2:3, and which will be made known from that place. **Zion** is referred to dozens of times by Isaiah as a synonym for **Jerusalem**. During the Millennium, which will be the thousand year rule of Jesus on this earth headquartered in Jerusalem, people everywhere will realize that God's spoken Word is essential to their lives. As we are told in Isaiah 2:3, they will want to know it (He will teach us) and to live according to it (walk in it).[1]

In Matthew 24 Jesus gave a brief overview of the entire Tribulation period prior to His return. Then He then spoke of the abomination that causes desolation. This abomination was spoken of by Daniel when he referred to the disruption of the Jewish worship which will have been reinstituted in the **Tribulation Temple** (Daniel 12:11), and the establishment of the worship of the world dictator, the Antichrist, in the Temple. He will make the Temple abominable[2] (and therefore desolate) by setting up in the Temple an image of himself to be worshiped (Revelation 13:14-15). Such an event will be clearly recognizable by everyone.[3]

Matthew 24:15 (NLT):

[15] *"The day is coming when you will see what Daniel the prophet spoke about—the sacrilegious object that causes desecration standing in the Holy Place."*

---

1   Ibid.

2   Abominable: abhorrent, detestable, hateful, horrid, odious. *Merriam-Webster's Collegiate Thesaurus.*

3   Op. Cit, Walvoord/Zuck, S. 2:77.

2 Thessalonians 2:4 (NLT):

⁴ He will exalt himself and defy everything that people call god and every object of worship. He will even sit in the temple of God, claiming that he himself is God.

Revelation 13:14-15 (NLT):

And with all the miracles he [False Prophet]⁴ *was allowed to perform on behalf of the first beast, he deceived all the people who belong to this world. He ordered the people to make a great statue of the first beast* [Antichrist], *who was fatally wounded and then came back to life. He was then permitted to give life to this statue so that it could speak. Then the statue of the beast commanded that anyone refusing to worship it must die.*

Then after everything on the earth has been destroyed at the end of the Tribulation, there will be a new Temple built for the Millennial Kingdom of Christ. The Millennial Temple is discussed in Ezekiel 40–48 as well as in Zechariah: *"Tell him, 'This is what the Lord says: Here is the man called the **Branch**. He will branch out from where he is and build the Temple of the Lord. Yes, he will build the Temple of the Lord. Then he will receive royal honor and will rule as king from his throne. He will also serve as priest from his throne, and there will be perfect harmony between his two roles'"* (Zechariah 6:12-13 NLT).

---

4   Brackets added.

This is a picture of the Messiah in the dual role of Priest and King when He returns to earth to rule during the Millennium. *Branch* suggests a person of humility and lowliness. He will be a native to His land and not a foreigner. The Messiah will be both Priest and King (Zechariah 6:13; Hebrews 5:10; Psalm 110:4) uniting in one person both the priestly and kingly authorities. These two functions will be blended in the Person of the Messiah[5]and God will rule not only in our hearts, but over the entire world.[6]

"The Branch" (Zechariah 6:12) was a reference to the Messiah. It is a name given to identify Jesus Himself. He came to earth some two-thousand years ago as the Branch, "a root out of dry ground"(Isaiah 53:2). He was called the **root from Jesse** and by the time Christ was born the royal line of David was living in poverty and obscurity, "the root out of a dry ground." You might liken the comparison to a beautiful rose growing in a sea of weeds.

So the Millennium is ruled by and focused on Jesus, our Messiah, our King, and our Priest. Everyone in the world will be living in a glorious time and they will willingly come to worship Him and bow at His feet.

---

5   Pfeiffer, Charles F.: *The Wycliffe Bible Commentary: Old Testament.* Chicago: Moody Press, 1962, S. Zec 6:12.

6   Richards, Larry: *The Bible Reader's Companion.* Wheaton, Ill.: Victor Books, 1991, S. 578.

MILLENNIAL TEMPLE

WHEN ISRAEL ENTERS the Millennium there will be a Temple here on earth. But then a Millennial Temple will be built. Ezekiel chapters 40–42 contain a description of this Temple. Those chapters detail the vision[1] that Ezekiel is shown of the Temple that will be in Jerusalem during the millennial Kingdom.[2]

The Messiah will build *"the Temple of the Lord,"* the Millennial Temple: *"For this is what the Lord says: In just a little while I will again shake the heavens and the earth, the oceans and the dry land. [7] I will shake all the nations, and the treasures*

---

1   A supernatural presentation of certain scenery or circumstances to the mind of a person either while awake or asleep, Isaiah 6:1-13l Ezekiel 1:1-28; Daniel 8:1-27; Acts 26:13. William Wilberforce Rand, ed., "VISION," in *A Dictionary of the Holy Bible*, (New York: American Tract Society, 1859), WORD*search* CROSS e-book, Under: "VISION".

2   Op. Cit., McGee, "CHAPTERS 40—48".

of all the nations will be brought to this Temple. I will fill this place with glory, says the Lord of Heaven's Armies. ⁸ The silver is mine, and the gold is mine, says the Lord. ⁹ The future glory of this Temple will be greater than its past glory, says the Lord. And in this place I will bring peace. I, the Lord, have spoken!" (Haggai 2:6-9 NLT).

Ezekiel 40:38-43 (NLT):

³⁸ A door led from the entry room of one of the inner gateways into a side room, where the meat for sacrifices was washed. ³⁹ On each side of this entry room were two tables, where the sacrificial animals were slaughtered for the burnt offerings, sin offerings, and guilt offerings. ⁴⁰ Outside the entry room, on each side of the stairs going up to the north entrance, were two more tables. ⁴¹ So there were eight tables in all—four inside and four outside—where the sacrifices were cut up and prepared. ⁴² There were also four tables of finished stone for preparation of the burnt offerings, each 31-1/2 inches square and 21 inches high. On these tables were placed the butchering knives and other implements for slaughtering the sacrificial animals. ⁴³ There were hooks, each 3 inches long, fastened to the foyer walls. The sacrificial meat was laid on the tables.

Ezekiel 42:15-20 (NLT):

¹⁵ When the man had finished measuring the inside of the Temple area, he led me out through the east gateway to measure the entire perimeter. ¹⁶ He measured the east side with his measuring rod, and it was 875 feet long. [17] *Then he measured the north side, and it was also 875 feet.* [18] *The south side was also 875 feet,* [19] *and the west side was also 875 feet.* [20] *So the area was 875 feet on each side with a wall all around it to separate what was holy from what was common.*

"Beginning in Ezekiel 40, Ezekiel was led on a tour of the future **Millennial Temple** which he recorded in remarkable detail. This tour was given by someone, probably an angel, whose appearance was like bronze."[3]

Ezekiel 47:1-2 (NLT):

[1] *In my vision, the man brought me back to the entrance of the Temple. There I saw a stream flowing east from beneath the door of the Temple and passing to the right of the altar on its south side.* [2] *The man brought me outside the wall through the north gateway and led me around to the eastern entrance. There I could see the water flowing out through the south side of the east gateway.*

This is just one of the reasons we know this is the Millennial Temple. None of the other temples have rivers flowing from them. One feature in the Millennium will be a life-giving river flowing from the Temple. Many think this refers only symbolically to the blessings that flow from God's presence. But nothing in the passage suggests that Ezekiel had anything in mind other than a literal river. The inclusion of details such as the fishermen (Ezekiel 47:10) and the

---

3   Ibid.

salty swamps and marshes (Ezekiel 47:11) lend a touch of realism to the passage. These details become meaningless if the passage is only symbolic. In the Millennium this river will be another visible reminder of God's presence and blessing.[4]

As this new river enters the Dead Sea, the water there will become fresh. The Dead Sea, now some six times saltier than the ocean, will become completely salt-free—truly a miracle of God! This now lifeless body of water will then support life so that wherever the river flows everything will live. Fishermen will line the shores of the river and catch many different kinds of fish there.[5] Another way God will provide for Israel is by the trees on the riverbanks that will bear fruit year-round. The fruit will provide food and their leaves will provide healing. How healing will come from the leaves is not clear, but sickness will be virtually eliminated. God will use these trees to meet people's physical needs.[6]

The city will be laid out as a square 7,875 feet on each side and will cover approximately 2.2 square miles (48:16). Jerusalem will be surrounded by a band of land 4371½ feet wide, which will serve as pastureland for flocks and herds belonging to people living in the city (Ezekiel 48:17). On

---

4   Op. Cit., Walvoord, *S. 1:1313*.

5   Walvoord, John F.; Zuck, Roy B.; Dallas Theological Seminary: *The Bible Knowledge Commentary: An Exposition of the Scriptures*. Wheaton, IL: Victor Books, 1983-c1985, S. 1:1313.

6   Op. Cit., Walvoord, S. 1:1315.

either side of the city limits will be two pieces of land 3.3 miles long (verse 18) and 1.65 miles wide (verse 15). This farmland will be cultivated to supply food for the workers of the city.[7]

When the Millennial Temple is established and God is enthroned in it, daily services will begin.[8] The sacrifices offered during the Millennium will be memorial in character. They will *look back* to the work of Christ on the Cross as the sacrifices of the Old Testament *anticipated* His sacrifice.

Levitical sacrifices[9] were connected with Israel's worship of God. After Christ established His Church and allowed the Temple to be destroyed and the Jews were scattered throughout the world, the **Levitical sacrificial system,** which looked forward to Christ, was replaced by the Lord's Supper, which looked back to His death and forward to His Second Coming (1 Corinthians 11:24, 26).[10] After Christ's Second Coming, the Lord's Supper will no longer be necessary because Christ will have returned. Jesus will be alive among us and we will be continually aware of His presence. Therefore, His physical presence will serve as a reminder of what He has done for us.

---

7   Ibid.

8   Op. Cit., Walvoord, S. 1:1309.

9   The main source for a description of the correct performance of sacrificial ritual is the opening section of Leviticus (Lv 1—7). *Tyndale Bible Dictionary.*

10 Op. Cit., Walvoord, Zuck.

In Old Testament times Israelites were also saved by grace through faith that the Messiah would come one day and be a living sacrifice for their sins. Obeying all of the Law according to the Old Testament system would never save anyone except Christ. Even after the founding of the Church by Christ, Jewish believers did not stop taking part in Temple worship (Acts 2:46; 3:1; 5:42) including offering sacrifices (Acts 21:26). They viewed the sacrifices as memorials of Christ's death.[11] That will be the reason for the sacrifices of the saved Jews in the Millennial Kingdom. Ezekiel 45:18-25, along with Isaiah 56:7; 66:20-23; Jeremiah 33:18; Zechariah 14:16-21; and Malachi 3:3-4 all refer to a sacrificial system in the Millennium.[12]

The Jews hardly ever obeyed the instructions for behavior that God established for them. When the Millennium begins all the Jews that are saved will remain in their earthly bodies which are still capable of sin. There will also be Gentiles who are saved and go into the Millennium in their earthly bodies that are capable of sin. So there will be a whole lot of people that are in earthly bodies who are still capable of sinning. Both the Jews and Gentiles have now been brought together as a combined Church but having just been recently saved at the end of the Tribulation they have not had the opportunity to openly worship Jesus and it seems that having some visible

11   Op Cit., Walvoord, Zuck.
12   Ibid. S. 1:1305.

forms of death, a broken body, and blood being spilled will provide a more meaningful experience in understanding just what Jesus went through for the salvation of everyone. The millennial sacrifices will differ from the Levitical sacrifices though there are some similarities.

> "...*only three of the six annual feasts under the Levitical system (cf. Lev. 23:4-44) will be followed*: two feasts celebrating national cleansing (Passover and Unleavened Bread combined as one feast) which will point back to Christ's death, and the Feast of Tabernacles that will symbolize Israel's new position in God's millennial kingdom."[13]

Zechariah 14:16-19:

"Then it will come about that any who are left of all the nations that went against Jerusalem will go up from year to year to worship the King, the LORD of hosts, and to celebrate the Feast of Booths. [17] *And it will be that whichever of the families of the earth does not go up to Jerusalem to worship the King, the LORD of hosts, there will be no rain on them.* [18] *If the family of Egypt does not go up or enter, then no rain will fall on them; it will be the plague with which the LORD smites the nations who do not go up to celebrate the Feast of Booths.* [19] *This will be the punishment of Egypt, and the punishment of all the nations who do not go up to celebrate the Feast of Booths.*

---

13   Op. Cit., Walvoord, BKC, P. 1311

That Gentiles will go to Jerusalem (cf. Isa. 2:2; 14:1; 66:23; Zech. 8:23) to worship does not mean they will become Jewish themselves. Millennial religious worship will not be a restored Judaism but *a newly formed worldwide community of believers that includes both Jews and Gentiles* which will be headquartered in Jerusalem, and will incorporate some features identical with or similar to certain aspects of Old Testament worship. Everyone will be expected to go to Jerusalem because that is where their object of worship, Jesus Christ, the King, will be located. "Jesus will be ruling on the throne of David (2 Sam. 7:13, 16; Luke 1:32) in Jerusalem (Isa. 24:23)."[14]

Worshiping annually in Jerusalem will be necessary for the people to enjoy fertility of crops. Those nations that neglect or refuse such opportunities for worship will forfeit their water supply. For most nations this simply means they will have no rain. But Egypt, whose irrigation depends not on rain (at least not directly) but rather on the flooding of the Nile, will still experience the plague of drought[15] as punishment from the LORD, as will all the nations that do not go up to celebrate the Feast of Tabernacles.[16] More information on sacrifices during the Millennium can be found in Ezekiel 40:38-43.

At this point we must answer a major question: Since all the sacrifices of the Old Testament were fulfilled in Christ,

---

14   Ibid.

15   Drought: No rain for long periods of time.

16   Op. cit. Walvoord

why are they restored again during the Millennium? I feel that the sacrifices offered during the Millennium are going to look back to the coming of Christ and His death upon the Cross in the same way that in our day the Lord's Supper looks back to them. The sacrifices will be restored here on earth to reveal to the people of Israel how they were redeemed.[17] Someone will ask why the literal offering of sacrifices will be necessary. Our salvation from sin and Hell unto Heaven was a pretty big deal, one that only God could undertake. Also, how can these prophecies be understood literally when the New Testament declares that the sacrificial system has been abolished by Christ's death? Ezekiel seems to be telling us that the sacrificial system used by the Jews before the time of Jesus will be reinstituted (Ezekiel chapters. 40-48). How can that be when the New Testament in general and the Book of Hebrews in particular is clear in declaring that Christ has by one sacrifice forever done away with the need for animal sacrifices (Hebrews 10:1-9)?[18] I am one that struggles with this reality for that reason but I can also understand the reasoning that follows. Further, it is in the Bible and therefore it is true and God has a good reason for it even if He has not made it

---

17 Ibid.
18 Norman L. Geisler and Thomas A. Howe, *The Big Book of Bible Difficulties: Clear and Concise Answers from Genesis to Revelation*, (MI: Baker Books, Grand Rapids), WORD*search* CROSS e-book, 288-290.

entirely clear to us. There are two basic interpretations of this passage of Scripture. Some take it spiritually and others view it literally.

First, some maintain that these sacrifices are not to be understood literally, but only as symbols of what was fulfilled in Christ's all-sufficient sacrifice on the Cross (Hebrews 1:1-2). They give the following reasons for their symbolic view.

1. "The New Testament teaches that Christ fulfilled and abolished the Old Testament sacrificial system and priesthood (Hebrews 8:8-10).
2. "The Book of Revelation describes the Heavenly City of the future with no temple or sacrifices, only Christ the Lamb (21:22-27).
3. "Ezekiel portrays the Gentiles as excluded from Israel's temple, which is contrary to the New Testament teaching that Jew and Gentile are one in Christ (Galatians 3:28; Ephesians 2:12-22).
4. "The New Testament speaks of the church as a spiritual Israel in which Old Testament predictions are fulfilled (Galatians 6:16; Hebrews 8:8-10)."[19]

Those who object to this symbolic viewpoint argue that the sacrifices predicted by Ezekiel could be pointing back to the Cross, just as the Old Testament ones pointed forward

---

19   Ibid.

to it. The literal interpretation looks to an actual Temple and sacrificial system, just as Ezekiel predicted it to be fulfilled during the Millennium (Rev. 20). They point out the following:

1. "Ezekiel presents a highly detailed description and historical scenes that are not compatible with a spiritual viewpoint.

2. "The Bible distinguishes between Israel and the Church (1 Corinthians 10:32; Romans 9:3-4). Promises directed to Abraham and his descendants, such as the Promised Land (Genesis 12:1-3), are certainly not fulfilled in the Church but look to fulfillment in the future (Romans 11; Revelation 20).

3. "The sacrifices mentioned by Ezekiel have absolutely no effect on a person's salvation. They are memorial in nature, looking back solely to Christ's work on the Cross, much as the Lord's Supper does for believers today.

4. "The rest of Ezekiel's prophecy will be fulfilled in a literal 1,000-year reign of Christ (Revelation 20:1-7) as He rules from a literal throne in Jerusalem (Matthew 19:28) Therefore there is no reason not to believe that these sacrifices will take place as well.

5. "The Old Testament did not see how Jew and Gentile would be joined together (cf. Ephesians 3:4-6), but they were aware that the Gentiles would be blessed

(Isaiah 11:10-16). Ezekiel's presentation does not exclude this later revelation (cf. Colossians 1:26).

6. "The Book of Hebrews speaks only of abolishing animal sacrifices as in an atoning sense, not in a memorial sense."[20]

---

20   Ibid.

DANIEL'S SEVENTY WEEKS

It was part of Daniel's schedule to pray three times each day on his knees before an open window. It is a common practice for many of us to read God's Word in the morning and then pray. Perhaps Daniel followed the same routine. Let us read the first two verses of Daniel 9 to see what Daniel discovers while reading God's Word.

Daniel 9:1-2:

¹ *In the first year of Darius the son of Ahasuerus, of Median descent, who was made king over the kingdom of the Chaldeans.* ² *In the first year of his reign, I, Daniel, observed in the books the number of the years which was revealed as the word of the LORD to Jeremiah the prophet for the completion of the desolations of Jerusalem, namely, seventy years.*

Medo-Persia had defeated the Babylonian Empire in 539 B.C. to become the new world power. As Daniel is reading the Word of God from the Book of Jeremiah he is made aware that the length of their punishment in Babylon would last seventy years, which meant it was very close to being over. Now let's look at the two verses that gave Daniel this valuable information.

Jeremiah 25:11-12:[1]

[11] *'This whole land will be a desolation and a horror, and these nations will serve the king of Babylon seventy years.* [12] *'Then it will be when seventy years are completed I will punish the king of Babylon and that nation,' declares the Lord, 'for their iniquity, and the land of the Chaldeans;[2] and I will make it an everlasting desolation.*

There is further confirmation of this in 2 Chronicles 36:20-21. As to the date of the actual writing of this prophecy in Jeremiah we can look at Jeremiah 36.

---

1   Jeremiah was called as a prophet in 626 B.C. and continued at least to the destruction of Jerusalem in 586 B.C., but continued his ministry until about 562 B.C. although his last 15-20 years were spent in Egypt.

2   "CHALDEA (chal dee' uh) refers either to a geographical locality (Chaldea) or to the people who lived there (Chaldeans). Today Chaldea lies in the country of Iraq, very close to its border with Iran, and touching upon the head of the Persian Gulf." In Old Testament times different peoples occupied southeastern Mesopotamia at various times. One such group was the Chaldeans. Tony M. Martin/Trent C. Butler, ed., "CHALDEA," in *Holman Bible Dictionary*, (Nashville, TN: Holman Bible Publishers, 1991), WORD*search* CROSS e-book, under: "CHALDEA."

Jeremiah 36:1-2:

[1] ***In the fourth year*** *of Jehoiakim the son of Josiah, king of Judah, this word came to Jeremiah from the LORD, saying,* [2] *"Take a scroll and write on it all the words which I have spoken to you concerning Israel and concerning Judah, and concerning all the nations, from the day I first spoke to you, from the days of Josiah, even to this day.*

"In the fourth year of King Jehoiakim" (ca. 605 B.C.), Yahweh (the Lord God) instructed Jeremiah to write his prophecies on a scroll. First God uses Babylon to serve His purposes providing them the power to destroy Jerusalem and take captives to Babylon. Then when their punishment is ending after 70 years God punishes Babylon for the terrible things they did to Jerusalem and the people during the captivity. It was the first year of the reign of *Darius* who was appointed king over the land of the Chaldeans (Babylon). However, the king of the entire empire of Medo-Persia was *Cyrus,* who you are about to be introduced to as well. So Cyrus was the head guy and Darius was ruler over one of the many kingdoms that were under the control of Cyrus.[3]

Why was it necessary for God to punish Israel? Because Israel's disobedience to God had been going on for hundreds of years and God gave them opportunity after opportunity

---

3   Chad Brand, Charles Draper, Archie England, ed., *Holman Illustrated Bible Dictionary*, (Nashville: Holman Bible Publishers, 2003), s.v. ",", WORD*search* CROSS e-book.

to repent, be forgiven, and be obedient to the things God instructed them to do for their own good. But they loved their sin and would always return to it, just as most people have from the days of Adam and Eve to the present. What would you think of a person who was told by their boss that they could name their own salary, have all the authority they wanted in their job, a new Mercedes every six months, a private plane, yacht, and a luxury house in every garden spot of the world, if they would promise not to eat lunch in the lobby, which they heartily agree to? The next day when the boss came in just before noon, there was the employee sitting on the floor in the lobby eating lunch? You would probably say that person was really stupid. But that is exactly what the great majority of people in this world do every day.

God had not allowed any room for doubt when He told the Israelites about the good things that would happen if they obeyed Him and the bad things that would happen if they did not obey Him (Leviticus 26). Unfortunately for the Jews as a nation, just like the people today, they wasted no time disobeying God from the very beginning, not only regarding the Sabbath rest, but in many other ways, and did so repeatedly in spite of God's warnings of punishment. So many people lose out on the good things of life because they refuse to listen to God's wisdom (good sense) as to what is best for them. Therefore, instead of receiving the best things in life, they receive God's punishment because, like any good parent, He tries to make His children accountable for their actions, so that they will change their behavior in order to start receiving the good things. For the most part God does not do these things to people, but rather He allows the punishment to occur because the people have brought it upon themselves by choosing sin in place of God's promises for leading a righteous life. They cause their own problems because they love their sin. That too is stupid! But the same kind of behavior continues to go on as it has for thousands of years.

God clearly explained His instructions regarding the Sabbath Rest to the Jews through Moses at Mount Sinai, where Moses also received the Ten Commandments. Here are the instructions God gave them about the Sabbath Rest every seven years, which they pretty much ignored.

Leviticus 25:1-7 (NLT):

While Moses was on Mount Sinai,[4] *the Lord said to him,* [2] *"Give the following instructions to the people of Israel. When you have entered the land I am giving you, the land itself must observe a Sabbath rest before the Lord every seventh year.* [3] *For six years you may plant your fields and prune your vineyards and harvest your crops,* [4] *but during the seventh year the land must have a* Sabbath year of complete rest. It is the Lord's Sabbath. Do not plant your fields or prune your vineyards during that year. [5] *And don't store away the crops that grow on their own or gather*

---

4   Emphasis added.

the grapes from your unpruned vines. The land must have a year of complete rest. ⁶ But you may eat whatever the land produces on its own during its Sabbath. This applies to you, your male and female servants, your hired workers, and the temporary residents who live with you. ⁷ Your livestock and the wild animals in your land will also be allowed to eat what the land produces.

In addition **seven "sevens"** (forty nine years) brought them to the Year of Jubilee, Leviticus 25:8-12 (NLT): *"In addition, you must count off seven Sabbath years, seven sets of seven years, adding up to forty-nine years in all. ⁹ Then on the* **Day of Atonement** *in the fiftieth year, blow the ram's horn loud and long throughout the land. ¹⁰ Set this year apart as holy, a time to proclaim freedom throughout the land for all who live there. It will be a jubilee year for you, when each of you may return to the land that belonged to your ancestors and return to your own clan. ¹¹ This fiftieth year will be a jubilee for you. During that year you must not plant your fields or store away any of the crops that grow on their own, and don't gather the grapes from your unpruned vines.¹² It will be a jubilee year for you, and you must keep it holy. But you may eat whatever the land produces on its own.*

Since Israel and Judah refused to keep the Sabbath Rest for almost five-hundred years, God required from the land 70 Sabbath years (70 x 7 = **490 years**) that Israel was to be under God's punishment.And they had no one to blame but themselves because God had told them what He would do if they were disobedient. No one could say that God was not patient with the Israelites because He put up with their continued disobedience for almost 500 years before He carried out the discipline He had said would come if they did not obey His commands. You might ask yourself, "If God did this to Israel, why would He not do it to other countries?"

So God called upon *King Nebuchadnezzar* of Babylon to attack and destroy Jerusalem, robbing all the treasures from God's Temple, and then taking many of the Jews who were not killed to captivity in Babylon. Now it seems unlikely that Nebuchadnezzar met with God and allowed God to convince him that he should attack Israel. But "God works in mysterious ways His wonders to perform." Israel was rich in gold and people resources and Nebuchadnezzar probably thought he could increase his power and wealth by capturing Israel. But in reality he was doing God's will. Ezra records God's punishment on Judah.[5]

2 Chronicles 36:15-21:

The Lord, the God of their fathers, sent word to them again and again by His messengers, because He had compassion on His people

---

5   The southern kingdom which remained after the northern kingdom's defeat and scattering. After the reign of King Solomon, Israel was divided into 2 kingdoms: the northern kingdom of Israel and the southern kingdom of Judah. People of Israel were taken captive by the Assyrians and scattered throughout the known world about 100 years before the southern kingdom, Judah, was destroyed and many of the people taken to captivity in Babylon.

and on His dwelling place; [16] but they continually mocked the messengers of God, despised His words and scoffed at His prophets, until the wrath of the Lord arose against His people, until there was no remedy. [17] Therefore He brought up against them the king of the Chaldeans who slew their young men with the sword in the house of their sanctuary, and had no compassion on young man or virgin, old man or infirm; He gave them all into his hand. [18] All the articles of the house of God, great and small, and the treasures of the house of the Lord, and the treasures of the king and of his officers, he brought them all to Babylon. [19] Then they burned the house of God and broke down the wall of Jerusalem, and burned all its fortified buildings with fire and destroyed all its valuable articles. [20] Those who had escaped from the sword he carried away to Babylon; and they were servants to him and to his sons until the rule of the kingdom of Persia, [21] to fulfill the word of the Lord by the mouth of Jeremiah, until the land had enjoyed its Sabbaths.

But God offered hope to the Israelites from the very beginning of their captivity. He had already promised through the prophet Jeremiah that they would be allowed to return to their home at the end of 70 years.

Jeremiah 24:5-10 (NLT):

[5] *"This is what the LORD, the God of Israel, says: The good figs represent the exiles I sent from Judah to the land of the Babylonians. [6] I will watch over and care for them, and I will bring them back here again. I will build them up and not tear them down. I will*

plant them and not uproot them. ⁷ I will give them hearts that recognize me as the LORD They will be my people, and I will be their God, for they will return to me wholeheartedly. ⁸ "But the bad figs," the LORD said, "represent King Zedekiah of Judah, his officials, all the people left in Jerusalem, and those who live in Egypt. I will treat them like bad figs, too rotten to eat. ⁹ I will make them an object of horror and a symbol of evil to every nation on earth. They will be disgraced and mocked, taunted and cursed, wherever I scatter them. ¹⁰ And I will send war, famine, and disease until they have vanished from the land of Israel, which I gave to them and their ancestors."

With this background information we now come to Daniel. Daniel was a dedicated servant of God who was deeply committed to prayer. Daniel also was no stranger to visions and visits by angels. So being the man of God that he was, Daniel took all his questions about what was happening to Israel and what was about to happen to Israel to God in order to receive wisdom and understanding. He also asks God to help His people. I would encourage you to study this prayer because Daniel knew how to pray and this has to be one of his best; in fact it has to be one of the best in the entire Bible.

Daniel 9:3-19 [emphases added]:

³ So I gave my attention to the Lord God to seek Him by prayer and supplications, with fasting, sackcloth and ashes. ⁴ I prayed to the LORD my God and confessed and said, "Alas, O Lord, the great and awesome God, who keeps His covenant and loving-kindness for those who love Him and keep His commandments, [5] *we **have sinned**, committed iniquity, acted wickedly and rebelled, even turning aside from Your commandments and ordinances.* [6] *"Moreover, **we have not listened to** Your servants **the prophets,** who spoke in Your name to our kings, our princes, our fathers and all the people of the land.* [7] *"Righteousness belongs to You, O Lord, but to us open shame, as it is this day—to the men of Judah, the inhabitants of Jerusalem and all Israel, those who are nearby and those who are far away in all the countries to which You have driven them, because of their unfaithful deeds which they have committed against You.* [8] *"Open shame belongs to us, O Lord, to our kings, our princes and our fathers, because we have sinned against You.* [9] *"To the Lord our God belong compassion and forgiveness, for we have rebelled against Him;* [10] *nor have we obeyed the voice of the LORD our God, to walk in His teachings which He set before us through His servants the prophets.* [11] *"Indeed all Israel has transgressed Your law and turned aside, not obeying Your voice; so the curse has been poured out on us, along with the oath which is written in the law of Moses the servant of God, for we have sinned against Him.* [12] *"Thus He has confirmed His words which He had spoken against us and against our rulers who ruled us, to bring on us great calamity; for under the whole heaven there has not been done anything like what was done to Jerusalem.* [13] *"As it is written in the law of Moses, all this calamity has come on us; yet we have not sought the favor of the LORD our God by turning from our iniquity and giving attention to Your* *truth. 14" Therefore the LORD has kept the calamity [disaster; tragedy] in store and brought it on us; for the LORD our God is righteous with respect to all His deeds which He has done, but we have not obeyed His voice.* [15] *"And now, O Lord our God, who have brought Your people out of the land of Egypt with a mighty hand and have made a name for Yourself, as it is this day—we have sinned, we have been wicked.* [16] *"O Lord, in accordance with all Your righteous acts, let now Your anger and Your wrath turn away from Your city Jerusalem, Your holy mountain; for because of our sins and the iniquities of our fathers, Jerusalem and Your people have become a reproach* [source of shame or disgrace][6]*to all those around us.* [17] *"So now, our God, listen to the prayer of Your servant and to his supplications, and for Your sake, O Lord, let Your face shine on Your desolate sanctuary.*

[18] *"O my God, incline Your ear and hear! Open Your eyes and see our desolations and the city which is called by Your name; for we are not presenting our supplications before You on account of any merits of our own, but on account of Your great compassion.* [19]*"O Lord, hear! O Lord, forgive! O Lord, listen and take action! For Your own sake, O my God, do not delay, because Your city and Your people are called by Your name."*

With humility[7] Daniel approached God and the first thing he offers to the Lord is his confession. He identifies

---

6   Brackets mine.

7   Modest opinion or estimate of one's own importance. Giving all the glory to God.

himself with the sins, failure, shame, and the judgment upon the people of Israel. This might surprise people that are familiar with Daniel's obedience to the Word of God, and his dedication to serving God. Here he is speaking of the nation's sins, rebellion, transgressions of the law, and their wicked deeds as if they were attached to him. Many other well-known men of the Bible such as Abraham, Aaron, David, Moses, and others had some major failures, but Daniel had what appeared to be a spotless record. Of course he too was a sinner as we all are; yet this devoted servant of God who had demonstrated such loyalty confesses all the people's sins and the curse and shame as his own. Can you see in Daniel a type of Christ who took the sins of His people upon Himself so God would forgive them?

There is something here that we should really make a part of us. We see in this man, Daniel, someone who knows how to love and genuinely feels love for his fellow man. Because he is able to love so much he makes their sin his sin, and their failure his failure. Instead of freeing himself from any blame for what the nation did and what happened to them as a result of their rebellion, he stands right with them. Someone with this kind of an attitude pleases God and we should learn a valuable lesson from Daniel. Instead of thinking of ourselves as special people because we call ourselves Christians and are therefore innocent of any wrongdoing, we like Daniel should confess the failure in which we all share as sinners and in all humility seek the face of God, confessing our sins. This is the way to blessing. Daniel pleads for the nation, for the city of Jerusalem called by the name of the Lord.[8] He reminds God that they are His people and appeals to God, admitting His anger is understandable, but asking Him to turn away from that anger and to forgive His people without delay.[9]

> "Like Moses in his prayer of intercession[10] (Exodus 32:12-13), Daniel was concerned about God's reputation (vv. 18-19). 'For your sake, O my God, do not delay' (v. 19; cf. Jeremiah 32:20: Isaiah 63:11-14). With the collapse of both Jerusalem and the temple, the nations may have assumed that Judah's God was either powerless or a delusion. Little did the nations understand that it was God who brought Israel under Babylonian control (cf. Lamentations 2:2-5)."[11]

Daniel was not able to finish his prayer for he was suddenly aware that the angel, *Gabriel,* was there with him telling

---

8   Jerusalem was considered the city of God because that was where God had His Temple, where people went to meet with God, offer sacrifices, and worship.

9   A. C. Gaebelein, *The Prophet Daniel: A Key to the Visions and Prophecies of the Book of Daniel*, (Glasgow: Pickering & Inglis, 1911), WORD*search* CROSS e-book, 119-150.

10 A prayer to God on behalf of another.

11 Mark Mangano, *College Press NIV Commentary, the—Esther & Daniel*, ed. Terry Briley and Paul Kissling (Joplin, Missouri: College Press Publishing Company, 2001), WORD*search* CROSS e-book, 272.

him that he had come to bring him skill and understanding, an answer to his prayer. Gabriel addresses him as *"greatly beloved"* and tells Daniel that when he began his prayer with humiliation and confession, he, Gabriel, received the command to fly swiftly and bring Daniel the answer to his prayer. "What an encouragement to prayer this ought to be to God's people. The moment we pray in the Spirit and in His name our voices are heard in the highest heaven."[12] Daniel was approached by the angel, **Gabriel** (Daniel 9:21), as the Jews captivity in Babylon was coming to a close. Gabriel told Daniel that God had a plan for the balance of history that would cover a time period involving 70 weeks (7-year weeks rather than 7-day weeks, for a total of 490 years).

As soon as we utter a prayer, God in heaven hears us!

We've seen that Daniel had been reading that Israel's captivity in Babylon would last for *seventy years*. The message Gabriel brought to Daniel contains more than an answer to his prayer. It was an answer to his requests concerning the people; but it also told him about the entire future of Israel from the end of the Babylonian captivity to the time of the end, when the Antichrist shall make a treaty with the Jews, then break it and attack Israel, but then the final great and

---

12   Op. Cit., Gaebelein.

glorious deliverance of Daniel's people shall come.[13] God gave Daniel *"exceeding abundantly above"* what he asked.

In the few verses which contain the words of Gabriel, events relating to the future history of Israel are predicted. The return of the Jews from the Babylonian captivity, the rebuilding of the city in time of suffering, the coming of Christ, His death, the destruction of the Temple and the city by the Romans, the misery and wars which were to follow; all of this is found in this prophecy. The end of *The Times of the Gentiles* and the final eventful week of seven years is revealed in the last verse. Let us take a look at these verses.

Daniel 9:24-27:

*"**Seventy weeks**[14]have been decreed for your people* [Daniel's people (the Israelites)][15] *and your holy city, to finish the transgression, to make an end of sin, to make atonement for iniquity, to bring in everlasting righteousness, to seal up vision and prophecy and to anoint the most holy place.* [25] *"So you are to know and discern* [understand] *that from the issuing of a decree to restore and rebuild Jerusalem until Messiah the Prince there will be seven weeks and sixty-two weeks; it will be built again, with plaza and moat, even in times of distress.*[26] *"Then after the sixty-two weeks the Messiah will be cut off and have nothing,*

---

13 Ibid.
14 Emphasis added.
15 Brackets and parentheses mine.

and the people of the prince who is to come will destroy the city and the sanctuary. And its end will come with a flood; even to the end there will be war; desolations [miseries] are determined. [27] *"And he will make a firm covenant with the many for one week, but in the middle of the week he will put a stop to sacrifice and grain offering; and on the wing of abominations will come one who makes desolate, even until a complete destruction, one that is decreed, is poured out on the one who makes desolate."*

So Gabriel tells Daniel in 9:24 that it will be seventy weeks of years to finish the transgression, make an end of sins, cover iniquity, and to bring in righteousness.

Now it is important to note that the *seventy years* Israel spent in exile in Babylon has no direct connection to the *"seventy weeks"* revealed in Daniel. The seventy weeks refers to a different kind of exile and punishment that will begin after the Israelites are allowed to return to their homeland from Babylon. Both of these situations are being described here for background as we get into more detail regarding the seventy weeks.

Considering that the Babylonian captivity was to last seventy years, Daniel could have understood Gabriel's message describing "70 weeks" to also mean years as well. Daniel's people thought in terms of sevens as we have already discussed.

These four verses in Daniel 9:24-27 are difficult verses to understand and interpret, but very prophetic in outlining what would happen to Israel from that day all the way to Christ's crucifixion. We also have here an outline of the kingdoms that would rise during those 483 years. Finally, a general idea of the events of the **seven-year Tribulation.**

To many readers of the Book of Daniel it is not quite clear what the expression *"seventy weeks"* means when it is stated that *each week represents a period of seven years.* The original Hebrew can be translated *"seventy sevens."* So please understand that the meaning of the term "seventy weeks" is "seventy sevens."[16] Walvoord provides the following description:

> "Now this word 'sevens' meaning 'weeks' may mean 'days' and it may mean 'years.' What then is meant here, seventy times seven days or seventy times seven years? It is evident that the "sevens" mean year weeks, seven years to each week. Daniel was occupied in reading the books and in prayer with the seventy years of the Babylonian captivity. And now Gabriel is going to reveal to him something which will take place in 'seventy sevens,' which means seventy times seven years. The proof that such is the case is furnished by the fulfillment of the prophecy itself. Now seventy, seven year weeks makes 490 years."[17]

---

16 John Walvoord and Roy Zuck, ed., *The Bible Knowledge Commentary: An Exposition of the Scriptures by Dallas Seminary Faculty*, (Colorado Springs, CO: Cook Communications, 1985), WORD*search* CROSS e-book.

17 Ibid.

Daniel 9:24 speaks of the great things which are to be accomplished by the end of these seventy-year weeks or 490 years. They are as follows: "(1) To finish the transgression (breaking God's laws). (2) To make an end of sins. (3) To cover iniquity (immorality). (4) To bring in the righteousness of ages. (5) To seal the vision and prophet. (6) To anoint the Holy of Holies."[18]

1. *"To finish transgression* means to lock it up or shut it in so that it can no longer spread (cf. Zechariah 5:8).
2. *To make an end of sin* means that sin shall be guarded securely: Satan and His demons will be confined and not able to roam the world as they do now.
3. *To cover iniquity* speaks of forgiveness. The first two describe the end of sinful activity; the third advises that God removes the consequences of sinful behavior.
4. *To bring in the righteousness of ages* (everlasting righteousness), clearly speaks of a righteousness[19] that will never end.
5. *To seal up vision and prophecy* means that all the predictions God made in the Bible will have come true.
6. *To anoint the Holy of Holies* predicts the Temple that will be built in the Millennium and the presence of Jesus."[20]

---

18 Ibid.
19 Being right with God and doing what is right.
20 Mark Mangano, *College Press NIV Commentary, The – Esther & Daniel*, ed. Terry Briley and Paul Kissling (Joplin, Missouri: College Press

The first three refer to the taking away of sin; the last three refer to the bringing in of everlasting righteousness and the benefits that come along with it.[21] *"For I am the LORD! If I say it, it will happen. There will be no more delays, you rebels of Israel. I will fulfill my threat of destruction in your own lifetime. I, the Sovereign LORD, have spoken"* (Ezekiel 12:25 NLT). *"Praise the LORD who has given rest to his people Israel, just as he promised. Not one word has failed of all the wonderful promises he gave through his servant Moses"* (1 Kings 8:56 NLT).

God divided His 70-week plan for Israel and the world into three periods of human history. The 490 years are divided into three periods:

> Period #1: This period of God's plan is 7 *sevens,* which equals 49 years.
>
> Period #2: This period of God's plan is 7 *sevens* plus 62 *sevens,* which equals 483 years.
>
> Period #3: This period of God's plan is 1 *seven,* which equals seven years.

Daniel 9:25: The first period of God's plan is seven *sevens,* which equals 49 years. The starting point of this particular period was **the decree to rebuild Jerusalem,** and the end of the period is the completion of this work. The complete

---

Publishing Company, 2001), WORD*search* CROSS e-book, 274.
21   Ibid.

rebuilding of Jerusalem was to take 49 years. God was revealing that the Jews would be set free from Babylonian captivity and would return home to rebuild their nation and their capital Jerusalem. Now please do not get confused by calculating these 7-year weeks from the time Daniel prayed or from the time Cyrus gave permission for the people to return and to build the Temple.

Although other decrees were issued by various kings, this decree was issued by King Artaxerxes I, written to Nehemiah in **445** B.C. (Nehemiah 2:1-8), and was the only decree that specified the rebuilding of Jerusalem, and it was not issued until almost a hundred years *after* Cyrus issued the decree that the Jews could return to Israel.

The second period of God's plan was seven *sevens* plus sixty-two *sevens*, which equaled **483 years**. The starting point for this second period was also the decree to rebuild Jerusalem, but the end of the period stretched beyond the completion of the rebuilding of Jerusalem, and continued all the way up to the coming of the Anointed One Himself, Jesus. Gabriel said that two events would take place at that time that would be of great importance.

Daniel 9:26: This period would bring about the cutting off, or death, of the Messiah, Jesus. Note that it says that Christ would not die for Himself, and if not for Himself it must be for others. Although it would seem as though He accomplished nothing when He died, He would be providing salvation and eternal life for all those who would truly place their trust in Him.[22]

The two major events Gabriel spoke of are:

First, the Romans would destroy Jerusalem and the Temple in 70 A.D.

Second, centuries of war and horrible suffering from a variety of causes would take place on earth, and this would continue right on up until the end of human history. The destruction of Jerusalem and the Temple by Rome would not end the sufferings of the nation of Israel. The Jews would continue to suffer at the hands of the Gentiles until the return of Jesus. We then are told that the people who destroy the city of Jerusalem will be the people of the *prince (ruler)* who will come to be the world ruler during the Tribulation. This clearly points to the future Antichrist who is also made known in other places in the Book of Daniel.[23]

Daniel 8:23:

[23] *"In the latter period of their rule, When the transgressors have run their course, A king will arise, Insolent and skilled in intrigue* [trickery].[24]

---

22   *The Preacher's Outline & Sermon Bible, Daniel, Hosea,* (Chattanooga: Leadership Ministries Worldwide, 2008), WORD*search* CROSS e-book, under: "C. Daniel 9:20-27".

23   Ibid.

24   Brackets mine.

Daniel 7:8:

[8] *"While I was contemplating the horns, behold, another horn, a little one, came up among them, and three of the first horns were pulled out by the roots before it; and behold, this horn possessed eyes like the eyes of a man and a mouth uttering great boasts.*

Daniel 7:24:

[24] *'As for the ten horns, out of this kingdom ten kings will arise; and another will arise after them, and he will be different from the previous ones and will subdue three kings.'*

Daniel 9:27: The third period of God's plan was one seven, which equals seven years. Keep in mind that God's plan for the world will be completed in this period. However, these seven years will be a time of frightening suffering and misery under the rule of the **Antichrist**. *"He"* in verse 27 is most definitely the Antichrist. If we have not already, we should now be aware that there is a long period of time between the sixty-ninth and seventieth weeks, a time that will also see centuries of war and suffering. Christ warned the world of violence, natural disasters, and false messiahs.

Matthew 24:5-7:

[5] *"For many will come in My name, saying, 'I am the Christ,' and will mislead many.* [6] *"You will be hearing of wars and rumors of wars. See that you are not frightened, for those things must take place, but that is not yet the end.* [7] *"For nation will rise against*

nation, and kingdom against kingdom, and in various places there will be famines and earthquakes.

But right there to challenge the false messiahs and the lawless of this world will be the Church, the body of Christ—true believers who stand for righteousness. Although the plan that God revealed to Daniel said nothing about the Period of the Gentiles and of the Church Age, it was made known during Christ's ministry and also the ministry of the apostles (Ephesians 3:6-12 NLT).[25]

The death of Christ would bring about a new creation, a spiritual body of people that would include both Jews and Gentiles. In Christ, all prejudice and discrimination would be laid aside (Ephesians 2:11-18).[26]

How might we know that the Tribulation has begun? When Israel signs a peace treaty with a new world government for seven years, guaranteeing Israel peace and protection from all its enemies that surround them, that will be the starting gun for the seven-year Tribulation. If you are wondering how bad it will be, wait until you read chapters 6, 8, 9, and 16 of Revelation. Now we must understand that these prophecies in the Old Testament are directed only to the Jews although the rest of the world will be affected by all the tragic events of this seven year period (Tribulation).

---

25   Op. Cit., *Preachers Outline and Sermon Bible.*

26   Ibid.

"It is clear that the end of transgression, the end of sins and the covering of iniquity has a special meaning for Israel as a nation. The foundation upon which this future work of grace for God's people rests is the death of Christ. The death of Christ has made this possible for the nation, but before it becomes a reality, this period of time, 490 years, must have passed, and then the sins of His people will be finished and all the other blessings will come to them. The 483 years are already history so there are only seven years left. We should now see clearly that the blessings promised to Daniel's people and to the holy city of Jerusalem bring us to the time of the end when Jesus will return at the end of the Tribulation."[27]

Jeremiah 33:14-16 (NLT):

[14] *"The day will come, says the LORD, when I will do for Israel and Judah all the good things I have promised them.* [15] *"In those days and at that time I will raise up a righteous descendant* [*Jesus*][28] *from King David's line. He will do what is just and right throughout the land.* [16] *In that day Judah will be saved, and Jerusalem will live in safety. And this will be its name: 'The LORD Is Our Righteousness.'*

Let us take a look at a time capsule of the major events that take place within these prophecies so we have a better feel of

---

27 Ibid.
28 Brackets mine.

how actual dates correspond to the prophecies themselves. If you do not already have a pretty good understanding of "Daniel's Seventy Weeks," you are about to experience a miracle of God's ability to predict the future and therefore His ability to control everything, and I do mean everything, that goes on in our personal world as well as the world around us.

- "Isaiah began his ministry as a prophet around 740 B.C. and continued until around 686 B.C.
- "Jeremiah's call as a prophet began in 626 B.C. and ended with the destruction of Jerusalem and captivity of the people to Babylon in 586 B.C. Jeremiah, however, was not taken captive and eventually ended up in Egypt continuing his ministry until around 567 B.C. The Bible is silent regarding Jeremiah after that time.
- "Ezekiel was a priest and prophet during Israel's Babylonian exile. Ezekiel began his ministry in 593 B.C. in Babylon as one of the early captives and continued until 570 B.C.
- "Daniel was a prophet to the exiles in Babylon beginning around 606/605 B.C. and lasting until around 530 B.C.
- "Cyrus captured Babylon in 539 B.C."[29]

---

29 Philip Comfort and Walter A. Elwell, *The Complete Book of Who's Who in the Bible*, (Wheaton, IL: Tyndale House Publishers, 2004), WORD*search* CROSS e-book.

Now you can look at ten reference books regarding the Babylonian Exile and get ten different dates regarding the beginning and ending of the captivity, and they would probably all be respected authorities on the subject of the exile. So thankfully after searching for a long time I came across *"A History of Israel"* by Walter C. Kaiser Jr. In my humble opinion he provides the most realistic explanation for these two dates, and here is what he had to say:

> "The first group of captives taken to Babylon came in 605 B.C., when Daniel and his three friends, Hananiah, Mishael, and Azariah, went along with other captives from the royal family and the nobility. The **"seventy years"** (Dan. 9:2) captivity that the prophet Jeremiah had predicted in Jeremiah 25:12 and 29:10 lasted, then, from 605/6 B.C. until sometime after the famous decree of Cyrus in 538 B.C.—perhaps to 536 B.C. There is no evidence that the first return took place immediately with the issuing of Cyrus's decree in 538 B.C., as some suppose, thereby concluding that the "seventy year" reference in Jeremiah must be a "round number" which is close enough to some sixty-six years (605-539 B.C., the fall of Babylon). But it could just as well have been a full seventy years since the exact year of the first return is not known."[30]

---

30 Walter C. Kaiser Jr., *A History of Israel*, (Nashville, Tennessee: Broadman & Holman, 1998), WORD*search* CROSS e-book, 412.

Now, just for the sake of getting a clearer understanding of what is taking place, imagine it is 700 B.C. and you walk into a bookstore in Jerusalem looking for the latest bestseller, *"The Prophecy of Isaiah."* You pick up the book, pay the clerk and head home. That evening as you are reading you come across this passage:

Isaiah 44:28—45:1

"It is I who says of **Cyrus,**[31] *'He is My shepherd! And he will perform all My desire.' And he declares of Jerusalem, 'She will be built,' and of the temple, 'Your foundation will be laid.'"* [1] *Thus says the LORD to Cyrus His anointed, whom I have taken by the right hand, to subdue nations before him and to loose the loins of kings; to open doors before him so that gates will not be shut:"*

Suddenly you are gripped with fear. Here is the prophet of God who is entrusted with God's Word concerning the future, and he is in effect saying that Jerusalem is going to be destroyed and then some guy by the name of Cyrus is going to give approval for it all to be rebuilt. "Who in the world is Cyrus?" you wonder. You call the wife and kids and tell them to start packing because you are moving as soon as the house sells.

Persia had not even become a world power in 700 B.C. In fact Persia was just being formed as a small kingdom by

---

31   Emphasis added.

tribesmen in 700 B.C.[32] Cyrus (the future king of Persia) would not come along for another 150 years. Who could possibly know this other than God? And we know this prediction (prophecy) came true because history recorded it. There are over a hundred predictions in the Old Testament about the coming of the Messiah (Jesus), and all of them have come true, which is statistically impossible to happen by chance. But with God all things are possible.

Assuming that you have taken good care of yourself and had the best of health care, you now find yourself living comfortably in another country far from Jerusalem. You have almost forgotten the reason that you left there some 75 years earlier, until you pick up your newspaper and the headline grabs your attention and you begin reading what this new prophet in Jerusalem is telling the people.

Jeremiah 25:1-11:

The word that came to Jeremiah concerning all the people of Judah, in the fourth year of Jehoiakim the son of Josiah, king of Judah (that was the first year of **Nebuchadnezzar**[33] *king of Babylon),* [2] *which Jeremiah the prophet spoke to all the people of Judah and to all the inhabitants of Jerusalem, saying,* [3] *"From the thirteenth year of Josiah the son of Amon, king of Judah, even to this day, these twenty-three years the word of the LORD has come to me,*

---

32   *Holman Illustrated Bible Dictionary.*

33   Emphasis added.

and I have spoken to you again and again, but you have not listened. [4] *"And the LORD has sent to you all His servants the prophets again and again, but you have not listened nor inclined your ear to hear,* [5] *saying, 'Turn now everyone from his evil way and from the evil of your deeds, and dwell on the land which the LORD has given to you and your forefathers forever and ever;* [6] *and do not go after other gods to serve them and to worship them, and do not provoke Me to anger with the work of your hands, and I will do you no harm.'* [7] *"Yet you have not listened to Me,"* *declares the LORD, "in order that you might provoke Me to anger with the work of your hands to your own harm.* [8] *"Therefore thus says the LORD of hosts, 'Because you have not obeyed My words,* [9] *behold, I will send and take all the families of the north,' declares the LORD, 'and I will send to **Nebuchadnezzar** king of Babylon, My servant, and will bring them against this land and against its inhabitants and against all these nations round about; and I will utterly destroy them and make them a horror and a hissing, and an everlasting desolation.* [10] *'Moreover, I will take from them the voice of joy and the voice of gladness, the voice of the bridegroom and the voice of the bride, the sound of the millstones and the light of the lamp.* [11] *'This whole land will be a desolation and a horror, and these nations will serve the king of Babylon seventy years.*

So here it is again! This must be the actual collapse of Jerusalem and captivity of the people that Isaiah predicted Cyrus would free them from 75 years ago. And now Jeremiah is saying that Nebuchadnezzar would be God's servant in making this happen. You are well acquainted with the name

Nebuchadnezzar because he is the son of the Babylonian king, Nabopolassar. So now you know who will destroy Jerusalem, and sure enough that is exactly what happened in 586 B.C. as confirmed again by history.

Now fast forward a few years to Daniel, who is taken captive to Babylon 18 years before the destruction of Jerusalem, and Daniel would have been about 16 or 17 years old.[34] We see Nebuchadnezzar is beginning to make his move on Israel, although it will be another 18 years until he crushes the city and the country (Judah).

The next event on our time line is the capture of Babylon by Cyrus in 539 B.C. and the order allowing the release of the Israelites in 538 B.C., which takes us to the time of the prophecy regarding the next phase of Israel's history, the *seventy weeks.* Jeremiah's prophecy spoke of Nebuchadnezzar as being the king that God chose to take Israel captive for their 70 year punishment. Isaiah's prophecy spoke of Cyrus as the Lord's anointed (Isaiah 45:1). Israel regarded Cyrus as called and empowered by their God to free them. Under Cyrus, the Jews received permission to rebuild their Temple (Isaiah 44:28). Documents preserved in the Old Testament state that in his first year in Babylon, Cyrus issued a decree permitting the reconstruction of the house of God at Jerusalem (2 Chronicles 36:22-23; Ezra 1:1-3; 6:2-5). He also returned sacred vessels taken from the Temple by Nebuchadnezzar. Biblical

---

34 Daniel was born in 621 B.C. and taken to Babylon in 604 B.C.

descriptions of the decree say nothing about rebuilding the city, but that would be in harmony, when it was specifically commanded, with the king's policy.[35]

During excavations at Babylon, archaeologist Hormuzd Rassam (1879-82) discovered a clay barrel inscription on which Cyrus told of taking the city and of his resulting policies. Isaiah and Chronicles reflect the content of the inscription, which says that captured peoples were allowed to return home and build sanctuaries to their own gods.[36] God used Nebuchadnezzar and Cyrus to both punish and to help His people. In Ezra[37] chapter 1:1-11 we read that it was in the first year of Cyrus, King of Persia, that the Lord stirred him up, whose coming and work Isaiah had announced long before his (Cyrus) birth.[38]

Cyrus the Persian was the nephew of Cyraxares, king of Media. Media and Persia were, as a rule, very closely related. They came from the same stock; it was through

---

35 Philip Comfort and Walter A. Elwell, *The Complete Book of Who's Who in the Bible*, (Wheaton, IL: Tyndale House Publishers, 2004), WORD*search* CROSS e-book, Under: "CYRUS (THE GREAT)".

36 Ibid.

37 Ezra arrived in Jerusalem in the seventh year (Ezra 7:8) of Artaxerxes I (458 Bc.), followed by Nehemiah, who arrived in the king's twentieth year (445 B.C.; Nehemiah 2:1).

38 Isaiah began his ministry around 740 B.C.; Cyrus conquered Babylon around 537 B.C., *NASB Study Bible* notes, Isaiah 21:2; Zondervan, Grand Rapids, MI, 1995.

these kingdoms united together under the leadership of Cyraxares and Cyrus that Chaldea (Babylon) was conquered. Cyrus eventually took it by turning aside the waters of the Euphrates into another channel, and led his troops in on the river-bed under the gates of the river itself; and all of this was predicted by God. Cyrus was no mere legendary figure.[39] The announcement which Cyrus made in *Ezra 1* was important, but it only described Cyrus' approval for the building of the Temple in Jerusalem, not the city of Jerusalem.

Ezra 1:2:

"Thus says Cyrus king of Persia, 'The LORD the God of heaven, has given me all the kingdoms of the earth and He has appointed me to build Him a house in Jerusalem, which is in Judah.

So this announcement is not the starting point of the 70 year weeks. **The 70 year weeks are to begin with the word (decree, king's approval) to restore and build the city itself.** But in the Book of Ezra we also find in chapter seven what happened in the reign of **Artaxerxes,** King of Persia, known in history as *Artaxerxes Longimanus* in the seventh year of his reign. Another edict (announcement) was issued, but a careful reading will show that the command to restore and build Jerusalem was not given in the seventh year of the reign of Artaxerxes. We have to turn to the second chapter

---

39   Op. Cit., Ironside, p.261.

in Nehemiah's writings to discover the beginning of these seventy-year weeks.

According to Gabriel, the 70 *"sevens"* would begin with the issuing of the decree to restore and rebuild Jerusalem. This decree was issued by Artaxerxes Longimanus on March 5, 444 B.C. (Nehemiah 2:1-8).

Then in the twentieth year of the reign of Artaxerxes the command was given to restore and build Jerusalem. From this time then the seventy 7-year weeks begin. This 20th year of Artaxerxes was the year 445 B.C., which is proven historically. The year is not only mentioned in Nehemiah 2, but also the month; it was in Nisan.

The seventy 7-year weeks began therefore in the month of Nisan 445 B.C.

Daniel 9:25.

"So you are to know and discern [understand][40] *that from the issuing of a decree to restore and rebuild Jerusalem until Messiah the Prince there will be seven weeks and sixty-two weeks."*

So it will take 49 years to put the city of Jerusalem back into useable condition and then it will be another 434 years, for a total of 483 years, and then the Messiah will come.

What we see in Daniel 9:24-27 is truly a remarkable prediction. The exact number of years is predicted by God

---

40   Brackets mine.

through Daniel when Messiah the Prince (Jesus), who is the Hope of His people Israel, should appear. But still more remarkable is the fact that a certain event in His life on earth is predicted. It is not His birth which is to take place after the end of the 69 year weeks, but *He is to be "cut off and shall have nothing."* It is *a prediction of His death* on the cross and it happened on the exact day predicted. Exactly 483 years after the command to restore and build Jerusalem had been given; Jesus entered Jerusalem to present Himself as the Messiah, knowing that death awaited Him in a matter of days.

> *No such predictions are made with such accuracy and consistency in any other religion.*

Now if you happen to be one of those people, as I am, who have to check everyone's mathematical calculations to confirm their accuracy then what follows is just for you. You will find a breakdown of the calculations that prove beyond any doubt the perfection and accuracy of God's Word, something that could not be accomplished by anyone other than the one true God. No such predictions are made with such accuracy and consistency in any other religions or religious works.

Now every time that I have tried to calculate this formula for Daniel's seventy weeks I have ended up with more questions than when I started, until I finally ran across this explanation by Clarence Larkin. So I am going to let him explain it to you. We may have covered some of this ground earlier, but a fresh look at this miracle should be helpful to understand it fully.

> "The date of the 'commandment' is given in Nehemiah
> 2:1 as the month 'Nisan' in the twentieth year of
> Artaxerxes the king, which was the *14th day of March,*
> B.C. *445.* The day when Jesus rode in Triumphal Entry
> into Jerusalem as 'Messiah the Prince,' was Palm
> Sunday, April 2, A.D. 30 (Luke 19:37-40). But the
> time between March 14, B.C. 445, and April 2, A.D.
> 30, is more than 69 literal 'weeks.'[41] It is 445+30=475
> years. What explanation can we give for this? It is
> clear to every careful student of the Word of God that
> there is a 'Time Element' in the Scriptures. We come
> across such divisions of time as 'hours;' 'days;' 'weeks;'
> 'months;' 'years;' 'times;' 'time,' and 'the dividing of
> time.' A day stands for a year.[42]
>
> "Let us apply this scale to the 'Seventy Weeks.'
> We found that the time between the 'commandment
> to restore and build Jerusalem, and 'Messiah the
> Prince,' was to be 69 weeks, or 69x7=483 days, or if
> a 'day' stands for a year, 483 years. But we found that
> from B.C. 445 to A.D. 30 was 475 years, a difference
> of 8 years. How can we account for the difference?
> We must not forget that there are years of different
> lengths. The Lunar year has 354 days. The Calendar

---

41 Footnote mine: 69 weeks of years would be 483 years.
42 Larkin, Clarence. *Rightly Dividing the Word,* (Philadelphia: Clarence Larkin Estate, 1921), WORDsearch CROSS e-book, 257-259.

year has 360 days. The Solar year has 365 days.
The Julian, or Astronomical year, has 365-1/4 days,
and it is necessary to add one day every 4 years to
the calendar [leap years]. Now which of these years
shall we use in our calculation? We find the 'Key' in
the Word of God. In Genesis 7:11-24; 8:3,4, in the
account of the Flood, we find that the 5 months from
the 17th day of the 2nd month, until the 17th day of
the 7th month, are reckoned as 150 days, or 30 days to
a month, or 360 days to a year. So we see that we are
to use in 'Prophetical Chronology' a 'Calendar' year of
360 days.[43]

"445 B.C. to 30 A.D. = 476 years inclusively
476 x 365 = 173,740 Days
Add: Leap Years: 119 days = 173,859 Days
Add: 20 Days Inclusive (March 14 to April 2) =
173,879 Days
Calendar Year = 360 Days
173,879 divided by 360 Days = 483 Years[44]

"According to ordinary chronology, the 475 years
from B.C. 445 to A.D. 30 are "Solar" years of 365 days
each. Now counting the years from B.C. 445 to A.D. 30,
inclusively, we have 476 solar years. Multiplying these
476 years by 365 (the number of days in a Solar year),
we have 173,740 days, to which we add 119 days for

---

43 Op. cit., Larkin.
44 Ibid.

leap years, and we have 173,859 days. Add to these, 20 days inclusive from the exact number of days (483) in 69 weeks, March 14 to April 2, and we have 173,879 days. Divide 173,879 by 360 (the number of days in a 'Prophetical Year'), and we have 483 years, each day standing for a year. Could there be anything more conclusive to prove that Daniel's 69 weeks ran out on **April 2,** A.D. **30,** the day that Jesus rode in triumph into the City of Jerusalem?"[45]

"We see from this that if the 'Students of Prophecy' of Christ's day had been on the alert, and had understood Daniel's prophecy of the 'Seventy Weeks,' they would have been looking for Him, and known for certain that He was the Messiah."[46]

Luke describes the procession on that Palm Sunday when Jesus entered the city of Jerusalem and the people of Jerusalem were *"Shouting: 'BLESSED IS THE KING WHO COMES IN THE NAME OF THE LORD; Peace in heaven and glory in the highest!' Some of the Pharisees in the crowd said to Him, "Teacher, rebuke Your disciples." ⁴⁰But Jesus answered, "I tell you, if these become silent, the stones will cry out!"* (Luke 19:38-40).

Jesus' words tell us that the time had arrived for the people to be aware of who Jesus was (the Messiah). You might say history's main event was about to start. As their shouts rang

---

45 Ibid. Emphasis mine.
46 Ibid.

out, however, Jesus looked beyond them towards the Holy City of Jerusalem and said, <u>Luke 19:42-44 (NLT):</u> *"How I wish today that you of all people would understand the way to peace. But now it is too late, and peace is hidden from your eyes. [43] Before long your enemies will build ramparts against your walls and encircle you and close in on you from every side. [44] They will crush you into the ground, and your children with you. Your enemies will not leave a single stone in place, because you did not accept your opportunity for salvation."*

This is the only time in Jesus' ministry that His kingly claims were publicly announced. And no other day in His ministry satisfies the words of Daniel's vision.

> "Here then is perfect evidence that 'Messiah the Prince,' who was to be 'cut off and shall have nothing' is our Lord Jesus Christ, for He appeared in Jerusalem on exactly the day on which the 69 prophetic year weeks expired and a few days later He was put to death on the cross. No wonder the critics invent all kinds of schemes and interpretations to get rid, so to speak, of this powerful evidence of revelation."[47]

After seeing that Messiah will be cut off, we see another prophecy relating to the destruction of Jerusalem.

---

47   Ibid.

Daniel 9:26 (ESV):

²⁶ And after the sixty-two weeks, an anointed one shall be cut off and shall have nothing. And the people of the prince who is to come shall destroy the city and the sanctuary [Temple].⁴⁸ Its end shall come with a flood, and to the end there shall be war. Desolations are decreed.

> "The Hebrew phrase 'veeyn lo' translated in the authorized version, 'but not for Himself', is better translated *'and shall have nothing.'* It has been interpreted in different ways. We believe it means that He did not receive then the Messianic kingdom. He was rejected by His own and received not that which belongs to Him."⁴⁹

In this verse we see that the city which rejected the Messiah will be destroyed, including God's Temple, and that the people who will do the destroying are the people of the prince who is yet to come. This is not, by the way, a reference to the Messiah but rather to another prince that will come to rule the world during the Tribulation. But he is not the one who will destroy the city and the Temple in A.D. 70. He will be the Antichrist during the Tribulation. The people who destroy Jerusalem and the Temple will be the Romans of the first century. Many commentators suggest that the

---

48   Brackets mine.
49   Op. cit., Larkin.

relationship between people of the first century and whatever century in which the Tribulation occurs, will result from there being a revival of the Roman Empire and that revived Roman Empire will rule the world under Antichrist.

I personally find that reasoning very hard to swallow because a lot has changed since A.D. 70, and there doesn't really need to be a relationship other than knowing that Rome was brutal and evil as introduced in the first stage of the fourth beast, yet Antichrist's empire will be far worse as the fifth stage of the fourth beast. The people who will carry out the destruction here in Daniel 9:26 are therefore the Romans of the first century, and out of this Roman Empire there shall come in the future a prince. This prince or ruler of the fifth phase of the fourth empire is identical with the little horn of Daniel 7, *Antichrist*. He will be ruling the World Empire during the second half of the seven-year Tribulation as the end approaches. The people of the coming prince are the Romans of the First Century (A.D. 70) who will destroy the city and the Temple after Messiah (Jesus) has been cut off (killed) and has nothing for Himself (no earthly kingdom to rule over).

They are of the same kind of empire separated by many years. So the people who destroy the Temple and the city of Jerusalem in A.D. 70 are the Romans who slaughtered the Jews, and the world ruler in the End Times who will be just as vicious as the Romans will be, Antichrist. Both empires will be similar because of their sweeping persecution of the Jews.

Both empires will be made up of the same kind of people, only they will be separated by at least two thousand years.

For Daniel and the people of his time, this prophecy would be in their future. For those of us who have lived since the time of Christ, the first 69 weeks have already been completed, but there is one week (7 years) that still lies in our future. That period of time is of course the Tribulation.

This period of time (The Church Age) which began at the close of the 69th week has already lasted over 2000 years. During this time the Jewish people have been scattered among all the nations of the earth and the predicted miseries have been fulfilled in every generation. Yet God has preserved them physically and also as a separate race.

The one who confirms the treaty with the many for one week is **"the prince that shall come"** of Daniel 9:26. The prince that shall come, as we have seen, rises from the people who destroyed the city and the sanctuary, the Roman people in 70 A.D. The prince that shall come is the dreadful little horn, the fifth phase of the fourth empire, the world government of Antichrist. When the last seven years begin, the Jews will expect protection from Antichrist because he will be the world leader, the one in charge of government, military, and religious functions. The aim of the Jews is to control and govern Palestine, to have a Jewish state and to gain possession of the city of Jerusalem so that they may be able to have a temple and reinstate their sacrificial ceremonies.

Ezekiel 37:23-28:

[23] *"They will no longer defile themselves with their idols, or with their detestable things, or with any of their transgressions; but I will deliver them from all their dwelling places in which they have sinned, and will cleanse them. And they will be my people, and I will be their God.* [24] *"My servant David* [Jesus][50] *will be king over them, and they will all have one shepherd; and they will walk in my ordinances and keep my statutes and observe them.* [25] *"They will live on the land that I gave to Jacob [Israel] My servant, in which your fathers lived; and they will live on it, they, and their sons and their sons' sons, forever; and David My servant will be their prince forever.* [26] *"I will make a covenant of peace with them; it will be an everlasting covenant with them. And I will place them and multiply them, and will set My sanctuary in their midst forever.* [27] *"My dwelling place also will be with them; and I will be their God, and they will be my people.* [28] *"And the nations will know that I am the LORD who sanctifies Israel, when My sanctuary is in their midst forever."'*

The name of this coming King will be ***the Lord Our Righteousness.***[51] He will live up to His name as Israel's righteous God. What is righteousness? I hope you will find the following definition helpful:

---

50   Brackets mine.

51   Jesus.

"It is the action taken by God by which He pardons all the sins of those who believe in Christ, and treats them as righteous in the eye of the law, satisfying all its demands. In addition to the forgiveness of sin, justification (righteousness) declares that all the claims of the law are satisfied. The Law is not relaxed or set aside, but is declared to be fulfilled in the strictest sense; and so the person justified is declared to be entitled to all the advantages and rewards arising from perfect obedience to the law (Romans 5:1–10).[52]

"Righteousness is the reward for the person who accepts Jesus' atoning death on the cross for his/her sin. God then by His grace, declares that the person possesses a righteousness which perfectly and forever satisfies the Law. It is exactly the same as Christ's righteousness which results from His being sin free."[53]

2 Corinthians 5:21 (ESV):

"For our sake he made him [Jesus][54] *to be sin who knew no sin, so that in him we might become the righteousness of God."* [See also Jeremiah 23:1-8; Romans 4:3-8]

---

52   Easton, M.G.: *Easton's Bible Dictionary*. Oak Harbor, WA: 1996, c1897.

53   Ibid.

54   Brackets mine.

CHERUBIM AND SERAPHIM

I WOULD LIKE to begin our study of this section by identifying for you the passages that refer to angels with *"four wings"* and *"six wings."*

In Ezekiel 10:20, Ezekiel states that he knows they are **Cherubim**; and they have **four wings.** In Ezekiel 1:5-6, we see that these four living creatures have **four wings.** In Ezekiel 1:11, we see the four living creatures with **four wings.** In Isaiah 6:2, these 4 living creatures have **six wings** and praise the Lord saying, *"Holy, Holy, Holy."* In Revelation 4:8 we find the four living creatures have **six wings** and saying, *"Holy, Holy, Holy."* We also see the **Cherubim** identified in Ezekiel 10:15-17, which we will be reading in just a short time.

You should be able to see the similarities here. It is stated clearly in Ezekiel 10:20 that the four living creatures are Cherubim and they have four wings. Isaiah 6:2 states clearly that these are **Seraphim** and they have six wings and are praising the Lord saying, *"Holy, Holy, Holy."* I therefore conclude that the four living creatures with six wings are Seraphim and the four living creatures with four wings are Cherubim. Ezekiel tells us (1:22-28) that over the heads of the four living beings there was a vast area (expanse) that had the appearance of sparkling crystal. Each Cherub had two wings stretching out to the Cherubim on each side (symbolizing unity) and two wings covering its body (symbolizing humility). When the living beings moved, their wings produced a frightening noise.[1]

As Ezekiel watched the flight of the Cherubim and listened to the sound their wings were making, they suddenly stopped, lowered their wings, and stood still as a rock in complete silence (1:25). Almost immediately, Ezekiel heard the unmistakable voice of God and then saw His sapphire throne above this vast area that was above the heads of the Cherubim. Seated upon the throne was a figure that looked like a man (1:26-28). From the waist up, He looked like glowing, molten metal full of fire. From the waist down, He looked like flaming fire. Brilliant light surrounded Him and radiated from the very core of His being. His glory was like the most beautiful, dazzling rainbow imaginable.[2]

Ezekiel clearly identified the person on the throne to be God. The Lord was giving His trusted servant a glimpse of His glory. Ezekiel instinctively fell face down, humbling

1   *Preacher's Outline and Sermon Bible*–Commentary–Ezekiel.
2   Ibid.

himself before God. Being that close to the glory and holiness of God, Ezekiel immediately felt the weight of His own sin as well as the sin of the people of Israel and how far short they came of God's glory. "*For all have sinned and fall short of the glory of God*" (Romans 3:23).Ezekiel saw something that was absolutely breathtaking. Who are these incredibly beautiful and glorious living beings who are so utterly indescribable? Ezekiel does answer that question for us in Ezekiel 10:15-17: "*Then the **cherubim**[3] rose up. They are the living beings that I saw by the river Chebar. Now when the cherubim moved, the wheels would go beside them; also when the cherubim lifted up their wings to rise from the ground, the wheels would not turn from beside them. When the cherubim stood still, the wheels would stand still; and when they rose up, the wheels would rise with them, for the spirit of the living beings was in them.*" Ezekiel is simply saying that these living beings were the Cherubim, in blazing light, glory, movement, and flashing brilliance.[4]Cherubim, the plural of Cherub, are angels. They are the angels frequently referred to in the Old Testament in connection with God's divine power (for example see Psalm 80:1 and Psalm 99:1).

Solomon placed a very special design in the Holy of Holies in the Temple: "*Also in the inner sanctuary he made two cherubim of olive wood, each ten cubits high* (1 Kings 6:23).

---

3   Emphasis added.

4   *Preacher's Outline and Sermon Bible*–Commentary – Ezekiel

- The purpose of the Most Holy Placewas to house the Ark of the Covenant, which was a symbol of the very presence of God Himself (1 Kings 6:19).

- The dimensions of the Most Holy Place were thirty feet long, thirty feet wide, and thirty feet high (1 Kings 6:20). The interior covering was overlaid with pure gold.

- The two cherubim for the Most Holy Place were made of olive wood fifteen feet high, with a wing span of seven and one-half feet each, or fifteen feet from wing tip to wing tip). The wings of the two cherubim stretched from one wall of the sanctuary to the other. Standing there,the cherubim were the guardians of God's Holy Presence (Ezekiel 1:4-14, 22-28).The cherubim were also overlaid with gold (1 Kings 6:23-28).

The sanctuary symbolized the very presence of God Himself, the place where the worshiper was to meet God, feeling at one with and friendship with Him. Above all else, the one thing God wants from us is closeness and fellowship with Him. God created us primarily for friendship. He wanted friendship with a creature that had a free will, **which could choose** either to fellowship or not to fellowship with

God. Communion with God, fellowship with God, drawing close to God—this is the desire of the Lord's heart for us.

In the inner sanctuary, the Holy of Holies, the giant Cherubim were spread out over the Mercy Seat and The Ark of the Covenant as symbols guarding the holiness of God. They are in God's presence, guarding His holiness, for the purpose of expressing His power when He calls on them to do that. So in the Temple itself (Solomon's Temple) there were the *two giant Cherubim* in addition to the Ark of the Covenant with the two smaller Cherubim: *"Then the priests brought the ark of the covenant of the LORD to its place, into the inner sanctuary of the house, to the most holy place, under the wings of the cherubim"* (1 Kings 8:6). The Cherubim call attention to God's rule over all creation. Look up these verses to see what God's Holy Word says about His absolute rule over the earth and every living creature: Matthew 6:13; Acts 17:24-28; 2 Chronicles 20:6; Daniel 4:35.[5]

---

5   *Preacher's Outline and Sermon Bible*–Commentary – Ezekiel; 1:1-3:28.

REVELATION CHAPTER ONE

MESSAGES TO THE SEVEN CHURCHES

YOU HAVE PROBABLY known people who carry a rabbit's foot for good luck. Or you may have heard of religions where people go through some pretty bizarre rituals such as climbing hundreds of stairs on their knees so that they might attain some kind of blessing when they reach the top, a blessing they receive because they have pleased their god or gods. They are seeking a blessing. But they are misguided. We are about to discover a sure-fire way to get a blessing. We are going to begin with the first chapter of the book of Revelation at the first verse. The word, "revelation" means "unveiling." This book unveils, allows us to see, the glory of Jesus Christ.

Revelation 1:1-20:

The Revelation of Jesus Christ, which God gave Him to show to His bond-servants, the things which must soon take place; and He sent and communicated it by His angel to His bond-servant John, [2] *who testified to the word of God and to the testimony of Jesus Christ, even to all that he saw.* [3] Blessed is he who reads and those who hear the words of the prophecy, and heed the things which are written in it; for the time is near. [4] *John to the seven churches that are in Asia: Grace to you and peace, from Him who is and who was and who is to come, and from the seven Spirits who are before His throne,* [5] *and from Jesus Christ, the faithful witness, the firstborn of the dead, and the ruler of the kings of the earth. To Him who loves us and released us from our sins by His blood*—[6] *and He has made us to be a kingdom, priests to His God and Father—to Him be the glory and the dominion forever and ever. Amen.* [7] *Behold, He is coming with the clouds, and every eye will see Him, even those who pierced Him; and all the tribes of the earth will mourn over Him. So it is to be. Amen.* [8]*"I am the Alpha and the Omega," says the Lord God, "who is and who was and who is to come, the Almighty."* [9] *I, John, your brother and fellow partaker in the tribulation and kingdom and perseverance which are in Jesus, was on the island called Patmos because of the word of God and the testimony of Jesus.* [10] *I was in the Spirit on the Lord's day, and I heard behind me a loud voice like the sound of a trumpet,* [11] *saying, "Write in a book what you see, and send it to the seven churches: to Ephesus and to Smyrna and to Pergamum and*

to Thyatira and to Sardis and to Philadelphia and to Laodicea."
12 Then I turned to see the voice that was speaking with me. And
having turned I saw seven golden lampstands; 13 and in the middle
of the lampstands I saw one like a son of man [Jesus],[1] *clothed*
in a robe reaching to the feet, and girded across His chest with a
golden sash. 14 His head and His hair were white like white wool,
like snow; and His eyes were like a flame of fire. 15 His feet were
like burnished bronze, when it has been made to glow in a furnace,
and His voice was like the sound of many waters. 16 In His right
hand He held seven stars, and out of His mouth came a sharp two-
edged sword; and His face was like the sun shining in its strength.
17 When I saw Him, I fell at His feet like a dead man. And He
placed His right hand on me, saying, "Do not be afraid; I am
the first and the last, 18 and the living One; and I was dead, and
behold, I am alive forevermore, and I have the keys of death and of
Hades.19" Therefore write the things which you have seen, and the
things which are, and the things which will take place after these
things. 20" As for the mystery of the seven stars which you saw in
My right hand, and the seven golden lampstands: the seven stars
are the angels of the seven churches, and the seven lampstands are
the seven churches.

We will now begin a verse by verse study of this fascinating revelation from our Lord and Savior, Jesus Christ. **This is a Revelation of things yet to come and it begins at the throne of God who hands it to Jesus who gives it to an angel to give**

---

1   Brackets added.

to John; and John is to give it to all people with whom he comes in contact.

Revelation 1:1-2:

The Revelation of Jesus Christ, which God gave Him to show to His bond-servants, the things which must soon take place; and He sent and communicated it by His angel to His bond-servant John, [2] who testified to the word of God and to the testimony of Jesus Christ, even to all that he saw.

The term *"bondservant"* (δολος; *doulos*) describes someone belonging to Christ or to God. It refers to one whose service is used by Christ in extending and advancing His cause among men.[2] We are told in these first two verses that this all important message which Christ wants to deliver to His Church, His people, will be conveyed by an angel to John, who will send the message to all the churches and anyone else with whom he might come in contact. In effect, Jesus is conveying the same message through John to all of us who are believers.

Revelation 1:3:

Blessed is he who reads and those who hear the words of the prophecy, and heed the things which are written in it; for the time is near.

---

2   Strong, James: *The Exhaustive Concordance of the Bible:* Electronic ed. Ontario: Woodside Bible Fellowship. 1996 S.; G1401.

When verse three says a person is **"blessed"** if he/she reads and pays attention to this prophecy, what does it mean? Christians today use the word "bless" or "blessing" in a number of ways without really defining the term and the meaning is often vague. Someone may exclaim, "I was so blessed by..." perhaps referring to a sermon, a hymn, an event, or almost anything else that moved them in some way. Or they may sign an e-mail or letter with "Blessings" instead of "Sincerely" or "Cordially." But when the term is used in the Bible, what exactly does it mean? There are three New Testament Greek words related directly to the English word "blessing:"

Definitions of "Blessing:"

"To consecrate (a thing) by religious rite, formula, or prayer e.g., 'the bishop blessed the new church.'" "To make holy or sacred, e.g., 'And God blessed the 7th day and sanctified it.'" Genesis 2:3. "'To ask God's favor for; to commend to God's favor or protection', e.g., 'God bless mommy...daddy.'" "To wish good for; to feel grateful to." "To make happy or fortunate." "To praise, to glorify, to call holy." "'To guard or protect from evil,' e.g. 'God bless this house.'"[3] The people of God are those who enjoy His blessing (Psalm 3:8). They are described as righteous (5:12), just (Proverbs 3:33, KJV), faithful (Proverbs 28:20), and pure in heart (Psalm 24:4, 5).

---

3   Ibid.

There are a number of ways a person receives blessing from God. The first and foremost way to receive a blessing is to accept Christ as your personal Savior and know that your sins are forgiven (Romans 4:7-8). Another primary way to receive God's blessing is by delighting in His Word in the Bible, and by obeying its instructions (Joshua 1:8; Psalm 1:1-3; Deuteronomy 28:1-2; James 1:25). Another important way a Christian can receive God's blessing is by acknowledging His correction or chastening in their life and by learning and growing through it (Psalm 94:12; Hebrews 12:5-11; James 1:12) Other keys as to how to be blessed by God include being kind to the people of Israel (Genesis 12:3; Psalm 122:6), being generous (Proverbs 11:26; Malachi 3:10), fearing or reverencing God and walking in His ways (Psalm 115:13; 128:1-4). We also receive blessing from God through prayer (James 5:16; Jeremiah 29:12; 33:3), and by praising Him (Psalm 67:5-6). The phrases *"one who reads"* and *"those who hear,"* in Revelation 1:3, refer to a public reading of the book in church.[4] This is a great promise to those who are willing to listen to the prophecies and commands of this book and, where possible, put them into practice. If you do this, Jesus promises that you will be blessed.

---

4   Richards, Larry: *The Bible Reader's Companion.* Wheaton, Ill.: Victor Books, 1991, S. 907.

*God promises
blessing
to the one who reads the Book of Revelation!*

This passage (Revelation 1:3) also tells us that the time is near. Now this is an issue that has puzzled people over the years. People who read this passage, as well as certain other passages in the New Testament concerning time, have believed that such events would occur very shortly, or at least within their lifetime. However, if you were to launch a study of what this phrase actually means you would find multiple explanations regarding why Christ did not mean *"a short period of time."* In fact, the delay of Christ's return troubled early Christians as well. They thought that, according to Matthew 10:23, the Son of man should have come before the Twelve (Disciples of Christ) had finished their initial preaching mission in Judea. But Matthew tells us: *" But whenever they persecute you in one city, flee to the next; for truly I say to you, you will not finish going through the cities of Israel until the Son of Man comes."*

The persecution in Jewish Palestine would be so severe that disciples of Jesus would have no safe place to go until Jesus' return. Persecution would cause disciples to flee (compare Matthew 2:13; Acts 14:5-6; 17:14) from one city to another (Matthew 10:23; 23:34). This persecution in Israel would not fully come to an end until the Son of Man's return.[5] In the

---

5   (Kümmel 1957:61-62).

end, however, Israel would repent (Matthew 23:39), just as the prophets had spoken (for example, Deuteronomy 4:30; Jeremiah 31:33; Ezekiel 37:23; Hosea 2:14-23; 11:5-11; 14:1-7; Malachi 4:6).[6]

Also, according to Mark 9:1 and 13:30, one living at that time might get the impression that at least some of them should have lived to see Jesus' Second Coming. In Mark 9:1 (NLT) we read: *"Jesus went on to say, 'I tell you the truth, some standing here right now will not die before they see the Kingdom of God arrive in great power!'"* The next few verses give some clarity as to what Christ may have meant. Mark 9:2-8 goes on to show how three disciples did see Christ in all His glory at the Transfiguration. So Peter, James, and John did see the Kingdom of God arrive in great power when they saw Jesus in His resurrection glory at the Transfiguration.[7]

Mark 13:28-30 (NLT):

28 Now learn a lesson from the fig tree. When its branches bud and its leaves begin to sprout, you know that summer is near. 29 In the same way, when you see all these things taking place, you can know that his return is very near, right at the door. 30 I tell you the truth; this generation will not pass from the scene before all these things take place.

---

6   *The IVP New Testament Commentary Series – Matthew.*
7   Matthew. 17:1–8; Mark. 9:2–8; Luke. 9:28–36.

"The word '*generation*' *(genea* γενεα) is used in Matthew 11:16, 12:41, 23:36; Mark 8:12, and Luke 17:25, and in all of these places there can be no reasonable doubt but that the word refers to the generation of men living at the time of Jesus. But the situation in which the word is used here, speaks of the Great Tribulation period, the Antichrist, the Second Coming of Christ, and the return of Jews to their homeland, Israel. The generation of men alive when Jesus spoke these words could therefore not be alive at this future time. The people referred to here are those who will be living in the End Times not the people Jesus was speaking to in the early part of the first century. The reference here was used in the papyri manuscripts in the sense of '*race* or *ancestry.*' It described family origins and history. It was used in a will to speak of a person's descendants. The meaning here refers to '*race,*' the '*Jewish race.*'"[8]

According to Kenneth Wuest, therefore, Mark 13:30 could be translated: "*I tell you the truth, this generation of the Jewish race will not pass from the scene before all these things take place.*" "That is the generation that will be alive when the Tribulation begins."[9] It therefore seems quite obvious that the phrases "*near,*" and "*at hand*" in Revelation 1:3, and "*must soon take place,*" and "*shortly come to pass*" in Revelation 1:1, do not

---

8   Wuest, Kenneth S.: *Wuest's Word Studies from the Greek New Testament:* Grand Rapids: Eerdmans, 1997, c1984, S. Mk 13:28.

9   Ibid.

mean that these prophecies were to be fulfilled right away in John's day. They were to be fulfilled in the Tribulation.

As time passed and many Christians died, doubt arose as to whether there would be a resurrection of the dead (1 Corinthians 15:12-19). Paul explained that Christ was the *"first fruits* of the resurrection"[10] and that at His Second Coming the dead would be made alive (1 Corinthians 15:20-23). In 1 Thessalonians 3:13, Paul says that at Christ's Second Coming He will bring *"His saints"* with Him. Peter suggests several reasons for the delay but insists that "THE DAY OF THE LORD"[11] may still come at any time:[12]

2 Peter 3:3-9 (NLT):

Most importantly, I want to remind you that in the last days scoffers will come, mocking the truth and following their own desires. 4 They will say, "What happened to the promise that Jesus is coming again? From before the times of our ancestors, everything has remained the same since the world was first created." 5 They deliberately forget that God made the heavens by the word of his command, and he brought the earth out from the water and surrounded it with water. 6 Then he used the water to destroy the ancient world with a mighty flood. 7 And by the same word, the

---

10 The first one to be raised from the dead.

11 *Word Studies in the New Testament.*

12 Op. Cit., Achtemeier, S. 752. Matthew. 17:1–8; Mark. 9:2–8; Luke. 9:28–36.

present heavens and earth have been stored up for fire. They are being kept for the Day of Judgment, when ungodly people will be destroyed. 8 But you must not forget this one thing, dear friends: A day is like a thousand years to the Lord, and a thousand years is like a day. 9 The Lord isn't really being slow about his promise, as some people think. No, he is being patient for your sake. He does not want anyone to be destroyed, but wants everyone to repent.

There is one other point concerning the meaning of "near" in Mark 13:39. Consider the time of your own death. Many of these things will certainly apply the moment you die. That could make many of these things quite "near." None of us know when we are going to be called from this earth. If we do not receive Jesus Christ as Savior before our death, our eternity is sealed outside His kingdom, and that is forever. Once you are dead there is no going back. There is no purgatory and there are no second chances. There is no way for anyone to appeal their case to a higher court. Therefore, the message in this book about the importance of receiving and obeying Christ today is critical: *"And inasmuch as it is appointed for men to die once and after this comes judgment"* (Hebrews 9:27).

The clear purpose of the book of Revelation is to let us know what is to come to pass. It shows God's servants the future and all that they have to look forward to. It tells us that if we believe God and trust Christ as our Savior, we are in store for great blessings, both in eternity and in this life as well. How do we know that the promise of blessing refers to both our life here on earth and also in Heaven for eternity? Because the Bible tells us so. For example the Bible tells us we have blessings on earth: *"God blesses those who are humble, for they will inherit the whole earth"* (Matthew 5:4). Also see Matthew 5:3, 5, 8, 10; James 1:12; Revelation 14:13; 19:9; 20:6.

Now we need to be sure that we understand something, so we are going to repeat ourselves a little bit. We saw earlier that this book is addressed to the bond-servants of Christ. If you want to understand this book you must be willing to become a bond-servant of Jesus. If you want to understand this book you need to receive Christ as your Savior. If you are not ready to do that you need to at least ask Him to reveal Himself to you. Confess that you are having trouble accepting Him for who He is. He will honor your honesty and desire to know Him. He will reveal the truth to you as you study along in this book, if you open yourself to that truth. The only way you will understand this book or any other book of the Bible is to submit yourself to Christ. If you have difficulty in understanding the Bible it is because you have not opened your mind to God's truth. When I was an atheist I used to open the Bible hoping to find some answers. But I just could not understand it.

> The key to understanding the Book of Revelation:
> Receive Jesus as your personal Savior.

If you ignore the message of this book throughout your life, there is only one place that you can go when you die, and that is to Hell. People have many different theories on what might happen to them when they die. Some feel they will simply die and there will be nothing else. Others feel they will become angels in Heaven. Still others think they will come back to this life in another form. Unfortunately these ideas are only speculation on their part. None of them are founded on the truth that God reveals to us in the Bible. I often am gripped with terror when I hear anyone utter the words, *"I THINK."* The Bible tells us that everyone who has ever lived on the face of the earth since Adam will live for eternity after they die:

Revelation 20:11-15 (NLT):

11 And I saw a great white throne and the one sitting on it. The earth and sky fled from his presence, but they [unbelievers][13] *found no place to hide.12 I saw the dead, both great and small, standing before God's throne. And the books were opened, including the Book of Life. And the dead were judged according to what they had done, as recorded in the books.13 The sea gave up its dead, and death and the grave gave up their dead. And all were judged according to their deeds.14 Then death and the grave were thrown into the lake of fire. This lake of fire is the second death.15 And anyone whose name was not found recorded in the Book of Life was thrown into the lake of fire.*

---

13   Brackets mine

Matthew 25:31-46 (NLT):

31 "But when the Son of Man comes in his glory, and all the angels with him, then he will sit upon his glorious throne.32 All the nations will be gathered in his presence, and he will separate the people as a shepherd separates the sheep from the goats.33 He will place the sheep at his right hand and the goats at his left. 34 "Then the King will say to those on his right, 'Come, you who are blessed by my Father, inherit the Kingdom prepared for you from the creation of the world.35 For I was hungry, and you fed me. I was thirsty, and you gave me a drink. I was a stranger, and you invited me into your home. 36 I was naked, and you gave me clothing. I was sick, and you cared for me. I was in prison, and you visited me.' 37 "Then these righteous ones will reply, 'Lord, when did we ever see you hungry and feed you? Or thirsty and give you something to drink?38 Or a stranger and show you hospitality? Or naked and give you clothing? 39 When did we ever see you sick or in prison and visit you?' 40 "And the King will say, 'I tell you the truth, when you did it to one of the least of these my brothers and sisters, you were doing it to me!' 41 "Then the King will turn to those on the left and say, 'Away with you, you cursed ones, into the eternal fire prepared for the devil and his demons. 42 For I was hungry, and you didn't feed me. I was thirsty, and you didn't give me a drink. 43 I was a stranger, and you didn't invite me into your home. I was naked, and you didn't give me clothing. I was sick and in prison, and you didn't visit me.' 44"Then they will reply, 'Lord, when did we ever see you hungry or thirsty or a stranger or naked or sick or in prison, and not help you?' 45 "And he will answer, 'I tell you the truth, when you refused to help the least of these my brothers and sisters, you were refusing to help me.' 46 "And they will go away into eternal punishment, but the righteous will go into eternal life."

All people will live in one of two places after they die: Heaven or the Lake of Fire (the eternal Hell). Your eternity is simply in your hands, it is your choice. Now that you have read these words you can decide right now where you will go. But if you reject this truth, remember the moment after you die and find all of this is true, it will not be God's fault, it will be yours. Only a fool would choose the torment of Hell over the boundless joy of Heaven.

> There are
> Seven promises
> Of Blessings
> In the book of Revelation!

Now there are a total of seven Beatitudes, promises of blessing, in the book of Revelation. We have just read the first one in verse 3. They are as follows: 1) *"God blesses the one who reads the words of this prophecy to the church, and He blesses all who listen to its message and obey what it says, for the time is near"* (Revelation 1:3). 2) *"And I heard a voice from heaven saying, 'Write this down: Blessed are those who die in the Lord from now on.' Yes, says the Spirit, they are blessed indeed, for they will rest from their hard work; for their good deeds follow them*" (Revelation 14:13). 3) *"Look, I will come as unexpectedly as a thief! Blessed are all who are watching for me, who keep their clothing ready so they will not have to walk around naked and ashamed"* (Revelation 16:15). 4) *"And the angel said to me, 'Write this: Blessed are those who are invited to the wedding feast of the Lamb.' And he added, 'These are true words that come from God'" (Revelation 19:9). 5) "Blessed and holy are those who share in the first resurrection. For them the second death holds no power, but they will be priests of God and of Christ and will reign with him a thousand years"* (Revelation 20:6). 6) *"Look, I am coming soon! Blessed are those who obey the words of prophecy written in this book"* (Revelation 22:7). 7) *"Blessed are those who wash their robes. They will be permitted to enter through the gates of the city and eat the fruit from the tree of life"* (Revelation 22:14).

We will encounter the number **seven** many times in the book of Revelation, along with other numbers, and each has a special significance. The number seven most often carries the meaning of completeness or perfection.[14]

Revelation 1:4-5:

4 John to the seven churches that are in Asia: Grace to you and peace, from Him who is and who was and who is to come, and from the seven Spirits who are before His throne, 5 and from Jesus Christ, the faithful witness, the firstborn of the dead, and the ruler

---

14 Peloubet, F.N., Peloubet's *Bible dictionary*; Philadelphia, John E. Winston Co. (1913, 1925, 1947). P. 607.

of the kings of the earth. To Him who loves us and released us from our sins by His blood—

The seven spirits referred to in verse four refer to the Holy Spirit of God.[15] It does not suggest that there are seven spirits of God (Isaiah 11:2) but it indicates the perfection of God. We can therefore begin to see that this letter is from the Trinity, from God the Father, God the Son, and God the Holy Spirit. The letter is intended for the seven churches which were then located in Asia (modern day Turkey). However, it is also intended for all churches and all people throughout history, from the time of its writing until today. The Trinity is speaking directly to all of us.

"Faithful witness," in verse five refers to Jesus as one who always speaks the truth.

"Firstborn" means that He is excellent; He is above all others anywhere in the world.[16]

"Ruler of the kings of the earth" simply means that someday He will be ruling all the kingdoms of the earth.

Revelation 1:6:

And He has made us to be a kingdom, priests to His God and Father—to Him be the glory and the dominion forever and ever. Amen.

---

15 Robertson, A.T.: *Word Pictures in the New Testament.* Oak Harbor: 1997, S. Revelation 1:4.

16 Op., Cit., Peloubet; P. 198.

"He (Jesus) *has made us to be a kingdom."* What does that mean? Well, what is a kingdom? It is a people ruled by a king. So we are Jesus' kingdom. He is our King. His commandments are what we obey. We reverence Him as the supreme ruler in our lives. We are not isolated, but joined together into the kingdom, so we have a common life under the King. We who believe in the atoning death of Jesus Christ are all under God's rule and authority through Christ. This verse also says that He has made us priests. That means that through the blood of Christ we now have direct access to God's throne. Only certain chosen people had access to God before Jesus came.

Revelation 1:7:

Behold, He is coming with the clouds and every eye will see Him, even those who pierced Him; and all the tribes of the earth will mourn over Him. So it is to be. Amen.

That is what the book of Revelation is all about: the **Second Coming of Christ**. There are over fifteen hundred Old Testament passages that refer to the Second Coming of Jesus. One out of every twenty-five New Testament verses refers to the Second Coming of Christ.[17] So the Bible focuses much of its content on this event, when Christ will return and establish His rule on this earth. Those who pierced Christ were the Jews. They had Him crucified. All of the rest of the world, the unbelievers, will weep in sorrow and terror when

---

17   MacArthur, John Jr., *The Book of Revelation. Audio Series*, Rev.1:7.

they see Christ coming. However, the believer says, *"So it is to be, Amen."* For God's people this will be a time of rejoicing because it is the beginning of this glorious eternity that we have spoken about, and that so many of us long for. The **remnant**[18] of the nation of Israel shall see Him as He returns (Zechariah 14:4; Acts 1:11), recognize Him as their Messiah, repent, and receive Him. It will be an experience similar to that of Saul of Tarsus (the apostle Paul) when he was on his way to Damascus to persecute Christians (Acts 9).[19]

When Israel in the Old Testament asked to have a king, and God gave them Saul (not the same Saul mentioned above), the nation rejected God the Father (1 Samuel 8:5–7). In the New Testament when they asked for Barabbas, they rejected God the Son. Today, they are rejecting the pleading of God the Holy Spirit (Acts 7:51; Romans 10:21). Yet there will come a day when they shall see their King, believe, and be saved (Zechariah 12:10–11; Matthew 24:30).[20]Israel rejected their Messiah when He came to them the first time (John 1:11), but when He comes again, those Jews who are still

---

18 The Jewish remnant of Israel will be made up of one-third of the number of Jews alive during the seven-year Tribulation. This remnant will live through the Tribulation surviving the judgment of God and all the devastation that occurs to destroy those who refuse to accept Christ as their Savior and King. *Tyndale Bible Dictionary.*

19 Wiersbe, Warren W.: *The Bible Exposition Commentary.* Wheaton, Ill.: Victor Books, 1996, c1989, S. Ro 11:1

20 Ibid.

alive will recognize Him and receive Him (Revelation 1:7). In spite of what they did to His Son, God has not cast away His people (Romans 11:1–6). Israel today is suffering from a partial spiritual blindness that one day will be taken away (Romans 11:25–32). Individual Jews are being saved, but the nation as a whole is blind to the truth about Jesus Christ.[21] That will change, however, just before the end.

Before going any further we need to become aware that the book of Revelation is filled with symbolism. Symbolism means something that represents the real thing. For example, a giant that has suffered many wounds might represent the United States. You might be wondering why it was necessary to use so much symbolism. There are a couple of reasons. First, symbolism is not weakened by time. In other words, symbols can stand the test of time for hundreds or even thousands of years without relating to one particular era or culture. Symbols also impart values and arouse emotions. It is much more lifelike to speak of beasts instead of dictators. For example, several thousand years ago a pharaoh was certainly the most powerful ruler on the earth. But in today's culture people might not understand that. But people do understand the term, *"beast."* Such terms are easier to visualize and understand.[22]

---

21   Ibid

22   Ibid.

However, it was also necessary for John to disguise the message in such a way that the Roman authorities would not understand what was being said. If they had, they would have been merciless in the persecution of the churches to which these letters were directed. You will see first-hand as we read these letters that there are some very detailed descriptions of the evil that existed within the Roman Empire. The Christians could understand the meaning of the symbolism and the Romans could not.[23]

Revelation 1:8:

"I am the Alpha and the Omega," says the Lord God, "who is and who was and who is to come, the Almighty."

Here Jesus uses the first and last letters of the Greek alphabet. What He is telling us symbolically is that everything that falls between these two letters represents all knowledge. He knows everything. Jesus is stating that what He is about to say in this book is absolutely true because it is coming from the One who has all knowledge. He knows everything and He is the only One who does. His Words are completely true and accurate. Verse eight also speaks of God's eternal presence. He exists today and has always existed throughout all of time. He will also exist throughout time in the future.

---

23 Ibid.

Revelation 1:9:

I, John, your brother and fellow partaker in the tribulation and kingdom and perseverance which are in Jesus, was on the island called Patmos because of the word of God and the testimony of Jesus.

John says to the churches that he too has suffered during the time of persecution that the churches are going through. One of the reasons the book of Revelation was written was to encourage these churches that were suffering under Roman oppression. John was sent to prison for teaching the truth about Jesus Christ. In effect John is saying that he has been given this great privilege. Here he is, ninety years old, working on a chain gang on an island prison that is nothing more than a rock. It must have been very much like Alcatraz in San Francisco Bay. Suddenly Jesus reveals this vision to him. This is very important because it shows us that sometimes we gain the greatest understanding of God during times of suffering.

Revelation 1:10:

I was in the Spirit on the Lord's day, and I heard behind me a loud voice like the sound of a trumpet.

It was Sunday and John was worshipping. Suddenly he was experiencing something beyond what his human senses could comprehend. Behind him he heard the voice of Jesus and His voice had the commanding clarity of a trumpet. In Old Testament times a trumpet was often sounded before the announcement or beginning of a major event. Get the connection? John is being told that something big is coming. Jesus then speaks to John in verse 11.

Revelation 1:11:

"Write in a book what you see, and send it to the seven churches: to Ephesus and to Smyrna and to Pergamum and to Thyatira and to Sardis and to Philadelphia and to Laodicea."

John is told to write down everything that he is about to see in this vision and send it to these seven churches.

Revelation 1:12:

Then I turned to see the voice that was speaking with me. And having turned I saw seven golden lampstands;

When John turned around he saw Jesus standing among seven golden lampstands, which represent the seven churches. In the Bible, as we pointed out earlier, seven is the number of completeness and perfection. This verse tells us that this book is for all the people of God. All the churches are represented in these seven letters. Although these specific churches are no longer in existence, the letters still represent all the churches of God. The imagery of the seven golden lampstands represents the seven-branched lampstand in the Jerusalem Temple (Exodus 25:37; Zechariah. 4:2). The one people of God is represented here as seven lampstands, and walking among them is the risen Jesus Christ in all of His resurrection glory. The whole Church, therefore, is represented by each of these seven congregations.[24]

Revelation 1:13:

[13] *And in the middle of the lampstands I saw one like a son of man, clothed in a robe reaching to the feet, and girded across His chest with a golden sash.*

Each local church is the bearer of God's light in this dark world.[25] We also see that Christ is alive and at work in His Church. In fact He is right here with us now just as He was standing among the seven lampstands in this vision.

That means He is with us always; He is always standing right at our side. Christ is described as *"One like the Son of Man."* This tells us that Jesus is forever a man as well as God. Jesus was not a man before His incarnation, before His birth in Bethlehem. Before that He was God. God took the form of a man in the person of Jesus Christ. Jesus took upon Himself human flesh. But He did not take on that human flesh with the intention of discarding it someday when He returned to Heaven. Jesus will keep His humanity as well as His deity throughout eternity. Christ in some way will maintain His

---

24 Carson, D. A.: *New Bible Commentary:* 21st Century Edition. 4th ed. Leicester, England; Downers Grove, Ill., USA: Inter-Varsity Press, 1994, S. Re 1:9.

25 Wiersbe, Warren W.: *The Bible Exposition Commentary.* Wheaton, Ill.: Victor Books, 1996, c1989, S. Re 1:9.

form as a man as well as being God. Just think, there is someone like you and me in Heaven sitting at the right hand of God. But at the same time He is far different than you and me. He was made to be like His brothers and sisters, and throughout eternity He will be the **Son of Man.**[26]

We also see in this verse that Christ is wearing a robe with a golden sash, which is the dress and splendor of a king as well as a judge. This robe also reminds us of a robe that might be worn by a priest, which would remind us of the role of Christ as high priest in charge of the Church. The golden girdle He is wearing is the same type that priests wore in the Old Testament. We see this in Exodus 28, 29, 39, and Leviticus 16.[27]

Revelation 1:14:

His head and His hair were white like white wool, like snow; and His eyes were like a flame of fire.

The whiteness of His hair corresponded to that of the Ancient of Days (Daniel 7:9), a reference to God the Father. God the Son has the same purity and eternity as God the Father.[28] Having white hair was the same way God was

---

26 *Barnes' Notes on the New Testament;* Revelation 1:13.

27 Ibid.

28 Walvoord, John F.; Zuck, Roy B.; Dallas Theological Seminary: *The Bible Knowledge Commentary: An Exposition of the Scriptures.* Wheaton, IL: Victor Books, 1983-c1985, S. 2:930.

described in the Old Testament. Jesus is shown here as being purer than virgin snow.

We also see in this verse that *"His eyes were like a flame of fire."* This simply means that His gaze will penetrate anything. The eyes like blazing fire describe His severe judgment of sin (Revelation 2:18).[29] His eyes see all (Revelation 19:12; Hebrews 4:12), allowing Him to judge righteously.[30] Nothing in all creation is hidden from Jesus.

Revelation 1:15:

His feet were like burnished bronze, when it has been made to glow in a furnace, and His voice was like the sound of many waters.

His feet of burnished bronze also suggest judgment, since the brazen altar was the place where the fire consumed the sin offering. Jesus is pictured here as having come to judge the churches. Anyone who has looked upon the dazzling brilliance of metal in a furnace can form an idea of the image presented here. Brass or bronze is also symbolic of sin, and here we see it glowing hot. This is a very clear reference to judgment.[31] The feet of glowing metal also reflect a common Old Testament symbol of God's glory, such as found in Daniel 10:6.[32]

---

29   Ibid.

30   Wiersbe, Warren W.: *The Bible Exposition Commentary.* Wheaton, Ill.: Victor Books, 1996, c1989, S. Re 1:9.

31   Ibid.

32   Op. Cit., Richards, Larry: *The Bible Reader's Companion;* S. 907.

"His voice was like the sound of many waters' suggests two things: (1) the power of His Word is like the sea; His voice is a voice of power and authority that commands. Christ is speaking with authority to His Church. (2) All the *'streams'* of divine revelation are converging in Christ. See Psalm 29 and Ezekiel 43:2."[33]

Revelation 1:16:

In His right hand He held seven stars, and out of His mouth came a sharp two-edged sword; and His face was like the sun shining in its strength.

Jesus' *"right hand"* is representative of authority. Whoever these stars represent, Christ controls them. We will deal with the identity of these stars in verse 20. The *"two-edged sword"* is the penetrating quality of the Word of God that strikes deep into our souls. This describes Him as a king who is both merciful and judgmental. We see that there are times when the Word of God is used in this book as a weapon.[34]

"His face was like the sun shining in its strength" (see Malachi 4:2). In Revelation 22:16, He is the bright and morning star, for He will appear for His church when the hour is the darkest, just before the wrath of God comes upon the earth.[35]

---

33 Wiersbe, Warren W.: *Wiersbe's Expository Outlines on the New Testament.* Wheaton, Ill.: Victor Books, 1997, c1992, S. 797.

34 Isaiah 11:4, 49:2 and also Revelation 2:12, 16, and 19:19–21.

35 Op. Cit., Wiersbe.

But, however we understand the elements of this description, the overall impact of this revelation of Jesus is clear. "There is glory. There is holiness. There is awesome majesty. And there is terror."[36]

Revelation 1:17-18:

> *When I saw Him, I fell at His feet like a dead man. And He placed His right hand on me, saying, "Do not be afraid; I am the first and the last,* [18] *and the living One; and I was dead, and behold, I am alive forevermore, and I have the keys of death and of Hades.*

John went into shock and lost consciousness over all of this. I am not surprised. Can you imagine experiencing all this right out of the blue? The awesome resurrection glory of Jesus Christ was too much for John as a human being.

> *Jesus Christ is the only religious leader who has come back to life after dying. So believers in Him do not need to fear death. He lives so we will live also.*

Jesus was the first to overcome death and rise from the grave. He is the only religious leader in history to be able to do that. Consequently He is the only one who can offer

---

36   Ibid.

eternal life in Heaven to anyone. He can do this because He overcame the power of death by rising from the grave. Jesus also tells John that he need not be afraid, that He is always with us from the moment of birth until the moment of death. Then in verse 18 we see that Christ has the keys to death and Hades. **Keys** are symbols of authority. Death has its gates and Christ has the keys to those gates. Based on our choice Christ decides who goes to Heaven and who goes to Hell. We as Christians know that Jesus Christ has abolished death and He has brought life and immortality to light through the Gospel. We know that because He lives, we shall live also. For us who believe, the bitterness of death is forever past. John had nothing to fear and neither does anyone else who believes in Christ. Here Christ established that He alone has the keys of death and Hades, that is, authority over death and the place of the dead.

Revelation 1:19:

"Therefore write the things which you have seen, and the things which are, and the things which will take place after these things."

John is commanded to write down what he has just seen in this vision as well as what he is about to see. "Write it down, John; because there is no way you will remember it all."

Revelation 1:20:

"As for the mystery of the seven stars which you saw in My right hand, and the seven golden lampstands: the seven stars are the angels of the seven churches, and the seven lampstands are the seven churches."

7 stars = 7 angels of the 7 churches

7 lamp stands = 7 churches

In the original Greek, the word translated here as **angel meant messenger or agent**.[37] There are a number of interpretations among scholars as to who the stars are. So after carefully reviewing many of them, and considering what we have also covered so far, it seems most likely that they are in some way the leaders or guiding forces in these churches. I cannot quite imagine that Jesus would ask John to write a letter to a number of angels telling them what to do. However, angels could be assigned to carry the message to John as well as make certain the message is understood by those churches. So from this point forward we will consider these seven stars to be the leaders of these seven churches. By identifying the churches as lampstands, John is seeing that Jesus' message has its roots in Judaism.

Now before going on to chapter two I would like to give anyone who is not yet assured of eternity in Heaven an opportunity to secure a place there. You can be saved right now, at this very moment, if you so desire. You do not have to

---

37   Op. Cit., Strong's. P.38.

go home and write out a "to do list." You do not have to start doing good things to earn your salvation or earn your way into Heaven. You do not have to do any self-punishment and you do not have to jump through any hoops. You can have it right now, this moment! If you want salvation and eternal life right now, all you have to do is ask for it. It is a free gift from God. You can pray the following prayer or use your own words to confess your sin and ask Christ to cover that sin:

> "Dear God,
>
> I know I'm not capable of attaining your perfect standard. I've made mistakes, and those mistakes are what you call sin. I've broken your laws and commandments by thought, word, and deed. I've fallen short of your standard of perfection and I've missed the mark. I need your forgiveness! Right here and now I repent of my sins, all of them, past, present, and future. I ask you, Jesus Christ, who had no sin of your own and came into the world and died so that I could be forgiven, to be my Savior and risen Lord. Take over my heart right now! I pray this not because I'm worthy, but because I'm needy! In your name, Lord Jesus, I ask these things. Amen."

If you prayed this prayer and believe these things in your heart, you have now entered into the kingdom of God and your eternity in Heaven is assured. Scripture tells us that once we have that salvation we will never lose it (Romans 8), no matter what we do. Praise be to God if you have received Him now. Some people doubt the assurance of their own salvation, that they might lose it. Assuming that it was a true conversion, that the person sincerely asked forgiveness for their sins, repented of them, and expressed their faith that Jesus could cover those sins, and invited Him into their lives as Savior, they will never lose that salvation, nor will the Holy Spirit ever leave them.

Well it is usually at this point that someone will say, "Well what about Paul in 1 Corinthians 9:27 (NLT) where he says: *'I discipline my body like an athlete, training it to do what it should. Otherwise, I fear that after preaching to others I myself might be disqualified.'* So if Paul is worried about losing his salvation, how can I be so sure I will not lose mine?" Well the simple answer here is that Paul is not concerned about losing his salvation in this verse. This is just another instance where pulling a single verse out of the context of its chapter will result in misunderstanding. So let us back up a few verses and get the complete picture.

1 Corinthians 9:24-27 (NLT):

Don't you realize that in a race everyone runs, but only one person gets the prize? So run to win! [25] *All athletes are disciplined in their training. They do it to win a prize that will fade away, but we do it for an eternal prize.* [26] *So I run with purpose in every step. I am not just shadowboxing.* [27] *I discipline my body like an athlete, training it to do what it should. Otherwise, I fear that after preaching to others I myself might be disqualified.*

You see Paul's opponent in this race was his own body and its appetites, its lust of the eye and lust of the flesh. That is what Paul intends to discipline. Paul is deeply aware of the need to control his bodily desires because the last thing he wants to do after preaching to others is give in to sexual as well as other temptations. Such temptations were a constant problem for Paul. After all, he was a man, and these same temptations exist today for both men and women who serve as preachers, teachers, evangelists and Christian leaders in today's church. So Paul's concern expressed in verse 27 is that he might stumble into sinful conduct while running the race and therefore be disqualified from receiving the best reward attainable in Heaven.[38] Paul wants to win first prize. Paul therefore disciplines his body just as any long-distance runner would to make sure it could endure the rigors of the race and thereby receive the prize.

Philippians 3:13-14:

[13] *Brethren, I do not regard myself as having laid hold of it yet; but one thing I do: forgetting what lies behind and reaching forward*

---

38 Carson, D. A.: *New Bible Commentary:* 21st Century Edition. 4th ed. Leicester, England; Downers Grove, Ill., USA: Inter-Varsity Press, 1994, S. 1 Co 9:24.

to what lies ahead, [14] *I press on toward the goal for the prize of the upward call of God in Christ Jesus.*

James 4:7-10:

[7] *So let God work his will in you. Yell a loud no to the Devil and watch him scamper.* [8] *Say a quiet yes to God and he'll be there in no time. Quit dabbling in sin. Purify your inner life. Quit playing the field.* [9] *Hit bottom, and cry your eyes out. The fun and games are over. Get serious, really serious.* [10] *Get down on your knees before the Master; it's the only way you'll get on your feet.* (THE MESSAGE)

Sometimes Paul even denied himself things that he had a personal right to enjoy if such action would allow for a greater good to be accomplished.[39] This race might be equated to a coast to coast marathon run. Paul was doing very well in the race and was inviting many along the way to join him. But his preaching alone did not guarantee him a victorious finish. He held out the possibility that even he could be disqualified for the prize. Paul wants to be allowed by God to continue in the race. If you have ever been to a track meet you may have seen a runner disqualified for some infraction of the rules. That runner is immediately disqualified and not allowed to continue in the race. He is therefore not eligible to win any

---

39 Walvoord, John F.; Zuck, Roy B.; Dallas Theological Seminary: *The Bible Knowledge Commentary: An Exposition of the Scriptures.* Wheaton, IL: Victor Books, 1983-c1985, S. 2:525.

prize. That is very discouraging if you have been training for a long time for this big day and then you blow it. Paul's life and ministry could be cut short by the disciplinary disapproval of God if he gave in to the sinful desires of his flesh. God had disciplined such behavior in the past.[40]

1 Corinthians 10:6-10 (NLT):

These things happened as a warning to us, so that we would not crave evil things as they did,[7] or worship idols as some of them did. As the Scriptures say, "The people celebrated with feasting and drinking, and they indulged in pagan revelry."[8] And we must not engage in sexual immorality as some of them did, causing 23,000 of them to die in one day. Nor should we put Christ to the test, as some of them did and then died from snakebites.[10] And don't grumble as some of them did, and then were destroyed by the angel of death.

We see further evidence of God's discipline in 1 Corinthians 11:30-32 (NLT): *"That is why many of you are weak and sick and some have even died. But if we would examine ourselves, we would not be judged by God in this way. Yet when we are judged by the Lord, we are being disciplined so that we will not be condemned along with the world."* And in 1 Corinthians 5:5 (NLT): *"Then you must throw this man out and hand him over to Satan so that his sinful nature will be destroyed and he himself will be saved on the day the Lord returns."* Paul was concerned

---

40   Ibid.

that some people might give in to temptation and not be able to say with him one day, *"I have fought the good fight, I have finished the race"* (2 Timothy 4:7), but would find themselves cut off in the middle of the contest by the disciplinary action of God.[41]

The Christian does not run the race in order to get to Heaven. That would be a salvation by works, and as true believers know, our salvation comes only because of God's grace as a free gift. He/she is in the race because he/she has been saved through faith in Jesus Christ. Only Greek citizens were allowed to participate in the games, and they had to obey the rules both in their training and in the manner of performing. Any contestant found breaking the training rules was automatically disqualified.[42] If we want to serve the Lord and win His reward and approval, we must pay the price. The whole emphasis is on *rewards,* and Paul did not want to lose his reward.[43] As we will learn there are different levels of rewards in Heaven, so why not strive for the highest reward. Remember, whatever reward you receive will last forever and that is a very long time. Only one runner could win the olive-wreath crown in the Greek games, but *every* believer can win an incorruptible crown when he/she stands before the Judgment Seat of Christ. This crown is given to those

---

41   Ibid.
42   Ibid.
43   Ibid

who discipline themselves for the sake of serving Christ and winning lost souls. They keep their bodies under control and keep their eyes on the goal.[44]

> "There is something to be said for disciplined eating, exercising, and resting, and a Spirit-directed balanced life. We smugly congratulate ourselves that we do not smoke or use alcohol, but what about our overeating and overweight? And many Christians cannot discipline their time so as to have a consistent devotional life or Bible-study program. Paul had one great goal in life: to glorify the Lord by winning the lost and building up the saints. To reach this goal, he was willing to pay any price. He was willing even to give up his personal rights! He sacrificed immediate gains for eternal rewards, immediate pleasures for eternal joys."[45]

Now we will take a little closer look at Revelation 1:20 to find some more detail on what the stars represented to the people of the first century. **Stars were symbols of authority**. *"I see him, but not right now, I perceive him, but not right here; A star rises from Jacob a scepter from Israel, Crushing the heads of Moab, the skulls of all the noisy windbags; I see Edom sold off at auction, enemy Seir marked down at the flea market, while Israel walks off with the trophies. A ruler is coming from*

---

44   Ibid.

45   Ibid.

Jacob who'll destroy what's left in the city" (Numbers 24:17-19, THE MESSAGE).

Daniel 12:3:

"'Men and women who have lived wisely and well will shine brilliantly, like the cloudless, star-strewn night skies. And those who put others on the right path to life will glow like stars forever. (THE MESSAGE)

In each church there was one pastor or ruling minister, to whom all the rest were subordinate. This pastor, bishop, or overseer, had the special care over that flock: on him the prosperity of that congregation in a great measure depended, and he was to answer for all those souls at the judgment seat of Christ.[46] The reference here therefore is that these letters are being sent to the leaders of these churches. *"Therefore, I exhort the elders among you, as your fellow elder and witness of the sufferings of Christ, and a partaker also of the glory that is to be revealed, ²shepherd the flock of God among you, exercising oversight not under compulsion, but voluntarily, according to the will of God; and not for sordid gain, but with eagerness; ³nor yet as lording it over those allotted to your charge, but proving to be examples to the flock* (1 Peter 5:1-3).

---

46 John Wesley, *Explanatory Notes upon the New Testament*, (London: Wesleyan-Methodist Book-Room, *n.d.*), WORD*search* CROSS e-book, under: "Chapter 1".

REVELATION
CHAPTER TWO

MESSAGES TO EPHESUS, SMYRNA, PERGAMUM, AND THYATIRA

THE SEVEN CHURCHES were located on a major Roman road. A letter carrier would leave the island of Patmos (where John was exiled), arriving first at Ephesus. He would travel north to Smyrna and Pergamum, turn southeast to Thyatira, and continue on to Sardis, Philadelphia, and Laodicea—in the exact order in which the letters were dictated.

Chapters two and three contain the letters to the seven churches that we discussed in chapter one. As we begin looking at each of these letters I want to be clear in emphasizing that these letters were written to real churches that had been established during the last part of the first century. They were dictated by Jesus Himself to let the folks know how they were doing as representatives of God in the world. Please keep that clearly in mind.

All churches today fit to one degree or another into one or more of these seven first century Church categories. These letters were direct messages to these churches from Jesus. Just imagine how you might feel today if you went to your computer, opened up your e-mail and found a message directly from Jesus telling you what He thought of the way you conducted yourself as a so-called Christian and advised that you did not have straight A's on your report card. In fact, there were some subjects in which you were failing. Then in the "comments" section listed some changes you had better make before it is too late and telling you what He wanted you and your church to do.

So you had better pay attention. If you attend a certain church regularly you should be able to identify similarities in one or more of these letters. When you do that, it is your responsibility and obligation to contact your pastor or elders in order to plan for making the necessary changes to your church. The big question here is whether the pastors and elders would lead the church to comply with the commands. The one like a Son of Man in the midst of the churches sees what is missing.

Verses 1-7: Letter to the Church at Ephesus (the loveless church)

Revelation 2:1-7:

*To the angle [*messenger, agent]*[1][2] *of the church in Ephesus write: The One who holds the seven stars in His right hand* [we saw this in chapter one],[3] *the One who walks among the seven lampstands says this: 2 I know your deeds and your toil and perseverance, and that you cannot endure evil men, and you put to the test those who call themselves apostles, and they are not, and you found them to be false. 3And you have persevered and endured for my name's sake, and have not grown weary. 4 'But I have this against you, that you have left your first love. 5 'Therefore remember from where you have fallen, and repent and do the deeds you did at first; or else I am coming to you and will remove your lampstand out of its place—unless you repent. 6 'Yet this you do have, that you hate the deeds of the Nicolaitans, which I also hate. 7 'He who has an ear, let him hear what the Spirit says to the churches. To him who overcomes, I will grant to eat of the tree of life which is in the Paradise of God.'*

Jesus agrees that they've worked hard, that they didn't allow false doctrine to be taught, nor did they put up with wicked people. It sounds like a great church, does it not? It was alive, dedicated, patient, disciplined, and knowledgeable. But Jesus saw past all the religious legalism of this church. You see, the

---

1 Brackets mine.
2 Young, Robert, *Young's Analytical Concordance,* Grand Rapids, Michigan, Associated Publishers, P.38.
3 Brackets mine.

church at Ephesus had a heart condition. Now look at verse 4, what is *"first love?"* It is the kind of commitment to Christ that so often is seen in people right after they first accept Christ as their Savior. They are openly excited about their new-found relationship with Jesus. It is the "honeymoon love" of a husband and wife. In **Jeremiah 2:2** God says to His people*: "Go and shout this message to Jerusalem. This is what the Lord says: I remember how eager you were to please me as a young bride long ago, how you loved me and followed me even through the barren wilderness"* (NLT). While it is true that mature married love deepens and grows richer, it is also true that it should never lose the excitement and wonder of those "honeymoon days." When a husband and wife begin to take each other for granted, and life becomes routine, then the marriage will suffer.[4]

These Ephesians, as well as many in our present day churches who are like the Ephesians, stopped loving Christ the way they once had. This church did it back then and we have many churches today that have the same problem. They were doing a lot of things right, but they got so wrapped up in the day-to-day activities of the church that they forgot the most important thing, loving Christ.

They were carefully keeping the rules and had lost sight of why they were doing it. They lost sight of the fact that

---

4   Wiersbe, Warren W.: *The Bible Exposition Commentary.* Wheaton, Ill.: Victor Books, 1996, c1989, S. Re 2:1.

they should all have been doing these things out of love for Christ and not to make themselves feel spiritual. Teaching the correct doctrine and following all the rules simply are not enough. Like Martha, we can be so busy working for Christ that we have no time to love Him (Luke 10:38–42). Christ is more concerned about how much we love Him than He is about what we do for Him. Labor is no substitute for love. To the public, the Ephesian church was successful; to Christ, it needed open heart surgery.[5]

Revelation 2:5:

'Therefore remember from where you have fallen, and repent and do the deeds you did at first; or else I am coming to you and will remove your lampstand out of its place—unless you repent.'

> Realize something is wrong in your life?
> Confess it
> Be sorry
> Change your behavior.

Then after you realize something is wrong, you need to confess that problem, be sorry for what you have done, and then change your behavior. Similar commands concerning the need to love God are inserted frequently in the New

---

5   Wiersbe, Warren W.: *Wiersbe's Expository Outlines on the New Testament.* Wheaton, Ill.: Victor Books, 1997, c1992, S. 801.

Testament.[6] Christ stated that one's love for God should be greater than his love for his closest relatives, including his father, mother, son, and daughter (Matthew 10:37). Paul added that love for God should even be above one's love for wife or husband (1 Corinthians 7:32-35).[7] Jesus is telling them to remember how it was at the beginning, what the church was like when it was first started. They must first remember what it was like to do the right thing before they can begin to repent and change. Jesus tells them to repent and go back to the way they were doing things in the beginning.

Christ went on to warn them that if they did not follow His instructions, He would come and take away their *lampstand.* The lampstand represented *the light* they provided to the surrounding community as representatives of Jesus here on earth. If they refused to obey what Christ was telling them, they would lose their privilege to be a lampstand because the light they were to shine would have been extinguished. Christ would therefore close this church taking away all the privileges which He had provided them. The removal of the lampstand from its place can signify nothing less than the end of Christ's recognition of the church as a church of

---

6   Matt. 22:37; Mark 12:30; Luke 10:27; John 14:15, 21, 23; 21:15-16; James 2:5; 1 Peter 1:8.

7   Walvoord, John F.; Zuck, Roy B.; Dallas Theological Seminary: *The Bible Knowledge Commentary: An Exposition of the Scriptures.* Wheaton, IL: Victor Books, 1983-c1985, S. 2:934.

His. It will be abandoned by Christ just as the Temple of Jerusalem was abandoned by God prior to its destruction (Ezekiel 11:22–23; Matthew 23:38); so grave is the sin of lovelessness in a Christian church.[8]

Jesus therefore sees a lack of love in one of His churches as sufficient cause for shutting it down. If a church does not demonstrate the love of God through Christ, it will not be capable of expressing God's basic nature to those He created to know Him. That warning applies to churches and people that display the same kind of behavior today. "After the 5th century both the church and the city declined. The immediate area of Ephesus has been uninhabited since the 14th century."[9]

Revelation 2:6:

'Yet this you do have, that you hate the deeds of the Nicolaitans, which I also hate.

So after Jesus criticized them in verses four and five, He comes back with a compliment in verse six. The Nicolaitans that Christ referred to followed the teaching of *Balaam*[10] (also

---

8   Carson, D. A.: *New Bible Commentary:* 21st Century Edition. 4th ed. Leicester, England; Downers Grove, Ill., USA: Inter-Varsity Press, 1994, S. Re 2:1.

9   Op Cit., Walvoord, John F.; Zuck, Roy B.

10   Balaam: Non-Israelite prophet whom Balak promised to pay a generous amount of money if he'd place a curse on the invading army of Israelites; 2 Peter 2:12-15.

referred to in Revelation 2:14). The Greek name *"Nicolaus"* means "destroyer of the people." The Nicolaitans were a group of extremists who sheltered themselves under the name of Christianity. They promoted hateful doctrines and were guilty of hateful deeds. The church fathers considered them founders of "**libertine Gnosticism**," which remained active beyond the second century.[11] A Libertine was a person in the Greco-Roman world who had been a slave but had secured release from that status by purchasing freedom or working to achieve it. When Jewish slaves in the world of that time, especially from the city of Rome, won their freedom, many of them went to Jerusalem. Consequently, a synagogue was established there for them.[12]

Gnosticism is a generic term for a variety of religious movements during the first centuries of the Christian era. Although the theology, ritual practice, and ethics of these groups differed considerably, all claimed to offer salvation through *knowledge* (gnosis) and this knowledge was often provided by a false god,[13] a god that people made up to conform to the lifestyle they wanted to live. Christ commends the church at Ephesus for hating such wicked doctrines and practices. False teaching of any kind is unacceptable in Christ's Church and will result in judgments and condemnation,

11   Op. Cit., Achtemeier.
12   Op. Cit., *Harper's Bible Dictionary.*
13   Op. Cit., Achtemeier, S. 349.

Revelation 22:18-19: *"I testify to everyone who hears the words of the prophecy of this book: if anyone adds to them, God will add to him the plagues which are written in this book; [19] and if anyone takes away from the words of the book of this prophecy, God will take away his part from the tree of life and from the holy city, which are written in this book."*

The church at Ephesus is commended for hating the *"deeds"* of the Nicolaitans, and later in chapter 2 the church of Pergamos is blamed for allowing people in the church to hold such *"doctrines"* (Revelation 2:15). They were seemingly a class of professing Christians who sought to introduce into the church a false freedom for satisfying the lustful desires of the flesh.[14]

John's commendation of this church included hating the deeds of the Nicolaitans, who ate food that had been sacrificed to idols and committed all kinds of immoral acts. We may think that people today do not eat food offered to idols, so this does not apply to us. But in a way we do. *We worship many things in our world* other than God and Jesus Christ. The vast majorities of people worship the things of the world and mostly ignore God and Jesus Christ. We worship money, sex, power, fame, television, food, sports, and many other things. That is no different than eating food that

---

14   Easton, M.G.: *Easton's Bible Dictionary.* Oak Harbor, WA: 1996, c1897.

has been sacrificed to idols. We are worshipping idols; same thing, different century.

Revelation 2:7:

'He who has an ear, let him hear what the Spirit says to the churches. To him who overcomes, I will grant to eat of the tree of life which is in the Paradise of God.'

Some who read this verse may ask, *"What must I do to be given this eternal life?"* The answer is: *"To reach out in faith and accept a gift."* There is nothing to do beyond that.

Now let us look at 1 John 5:4-5: *"For whatever is born of God overcomes the world; and this is the victory that has overcome the world—our faith. Who is the one who overcomes the world, but he who believes that Jesus is the Son of God?"* The reason why God's commandments are not burdensome is that obedience to them enables the saint to overcome the world. Jesus won the victory over the world and God in us (the Holy Spirit) gives us the victory.[15] *"These things I have spoken to you, so that in Me you may have peace. In the world you have tribulation, but take courage; I have overcome the world"* (John 16:33). *"But as many as received Him, to them He gave the right to become children of God, even to those who believe in His name, who were born, not of blood nor of the will of the flesh nor of the will of man, but of God"* (John 1:12-13). *"Jesus won the victory over the world and God in us (the Holy Spirit) gives us the victory"* (1

---

15   *Word Pictures in the New Testament.*

John 4:4).[16] Now look at 1 Corinthians 15:57: *"But thanks be to God, who gives us the victory through our Lord Jesus Christ."* Additional verses that may help clarify the meaning here can be found in: 1 John 2:13-14; 1 John 5:4-5; Revelation 2:11, 17, 26; 3:5, 12, 21; 5:5; 12:11; 15:2; 17:14; 21:7.

Christ has "overcome" the world. Christ has achieved the victory. We overcome not by our efforts but through our faith in Christ and so we cannot lose our salvation because of the things we do. Faith is what overcomes and as long as our faith is true faith in what Christ did for us on the cross, we will never lose it because the Holy Spirit within us will not let go of us. We hope that helps clarify the meaning here. So let us see if we can sum this up.

Those who invite Christ into their lives through faith in what He accomplished on the cross (being the only acceptable sacrifice for the forgiveness of sins) will be received into God's family by being born again in the Spirit. This is made clear in the following verses: John 1:12-13; 16:33; 1 John 5:4-5; 4:4; 1 Corinthians 15:57. This involves the Holy Spirit being given to live within believers. The Holy Spirit then empowers those people who have received Christ through faith to resist sin, which is the same thing as **overcoming** the world.

Now in Revelation 2:7 we also see Jesus warning this church that they had better listen because He is not kidding. Basically Christ is telling all of us to listen to what He is saying. Christ

---

16   Ibid.

gave the Ephesian church a promise to those who would listen. *"The tree of life,"* first mentioned in Genesis 3:22, was in the Garden of Eden. Later it reappears in the New Jerusalem where it bears abundant fruit (Revelation 22:2). Those who eat of it will never die (Genesis 3:22). This promise applies to all Christians. *The paradise of God* (Revelation 2:7)is probably a name for Heaven.[17] Apparently it will be identified with the *New Jerusalem* in the eternal state. John describes the New Jerusalem as it will appear in the eternal state in chapters 21 and 22 of Revelation, the final, ultimate consummation of all things. John's description of the city in these verses emphasizes its beauty and majesty. Some of these elements might have symbolic meaning, but John did not elaborate on their interpretation. The New Jerusalem will be the future residence of the saints of all ages as well as the faithful angels.[18] [19]

This encouragement to true love reminded them again of God's gracious provision for salvation in time and eternity. Love for God is not developed by legalistically observing commands, but by responding to one's knowledge and appreciation of God's love.[20]

17   Luke 23:43; 2 Cor. 12:4—the only other references to paradise.
18   Zuck, Roy B.: *A Biblical Theology of the New Testament.* Electronic ed. Chicago: Moody Press, 1994; 1996, S. 241.
19   Ibid, S. 242.
20   Walvoord, John F.; Zuck, Roy B.; Dallas Theological Seminary: *The Bible Knowledge Commentary: An Exposition of the Scriptures.* Wheaton, IL: Victor Books, 1983-c1985, S. 2:934.

Verses 8-11: Letter to the Church at Smyrna
(the persecuted church)

Revelation 2:8-11:

"And to the angel of the church in Smyrna write: The first and the last, who was dead, and has come to life, says this: [9] *'I know your tribulation and your poverty (but you are rich), and the blasphemy by those who say they are Jews and are not, but are a synagogue of Satan.* [10] *'Do not fear what you are about to suffer. Behold, the devil is about to cast some of you into prison, so that you will be tested, and you will have tribulation for ten days. Be faithful until death, and I will give you the crown of life.* [11]*'He who has an ear, let him hear what the Spirit says to the churches. He who overcomes will not be hurt by the second death.'"*

Verse 8, of course, describes Christ. Jesus is telling them that He was there before all other gods and He will be there long after they are all gone. This second letter was addressed to the church at Smyrna, a large and wealthy city 35 miles north of Ephesus. Like Ephesus, it was a seaport. In contrast to Ephesus, which today is a deserted ruin, Smyrna, now called Izmir, is still a large seaport with a present population of about 200,000. Christ described Himself as the First and the Last, who died and came to life again. Christ is portrayed as the eternal One (Revelation 1:8, 17; 21:6; 22:13) who suffered death at the hands of His persecutors and then was resurrected (brought back to life) from the grave (Revelation

1:5). These events in the life of Christ were especially relevant to the Christians at Smyrna who, like Christ in His death, were experiencing severe persecution.

The name of the city, Smyrna, means *"myrrh,"* an ordinary perfume. It was also used in the anointing oil of the tabernacle and in embalming dead bodies.[21] While the Christians of the church at Smyrna were experiencing the bitterness of suffering, their faithful testimony was like myrrh or sweet perfume to God.[22]

Revelation 2:9:

'I know your tribulation and your poverty (but you are rich), and the blasphemy by those who say they are Jews and are not, but are a synagogue of Satan.'

Jesus starts by saying they have been made rich by their faithfulness through persecution. He is telling them that because of their faithfulness they can be certain that they are storing up treasures in Heaven. They are going to be rewarded for that faithfulness. Those that claimed to be Jews by birthright were not true Jews in their heart, and it is in the heart that Christ wants us to be circumcised. He wants

---

21   Exodus 30:23; Psalm. 45:8; Song of Solomon 3:6; Matthew 2:11; Mark 15:23; John 19:39.

22   Walvoord, John F.; Zuck, Roy B.; Dallas Theological Seminary: *The Bible Knowledge Commentary: An Exposition of the Scriptures*. Wheaton, IL: Victor Books, 1983-c1985, S. 2:934.

all of us to cut away the old way of life and receive Christ as Savior. Listen to what Paul says about this in Romans 2:28-29 NLT: *"For you are not a true Jew just because you were born of Jewish parents or because you have gone through the ceremony of circumcision. No, a true Jew is one whose heart is right with God. And true circumcision is not merely obeying the letter of the law; rather, it is a change of heart produced by God's Spirit. And a person with a changed heart seeks praise from God, not from people."*

Those who deny Christ embrace this world, which is the same as worshiping the god of this world, Satan. It is worth noting here that Christ has nothing bad to say to these faithful, suffering Christians. This is certainly in contrast with Christ's evaluations of five of the other seven churches in chapters 2 and 3. "Smyrna's sufferings, though extremely difficult, had helped keep them pure in faith and life."[23] They thought they were poor, but they were rich beyond their wildest dreams. This was in direct contrast to the church in Laodicea which we will meet in chapter 3, thinking themselves rich when they were actually poor (Revelation 3:17). The believing Christians in the church at Smyrna were being persecuted by false Christians, referred to in this verse as the synagogue of Satan (John 8:44; Philippians 3:2).

It must have been a great comfort to these believing Christians in Smyrna to know that Christ Himself cared

---

23   Ibid.

enough about them to be familiar with all of their sufferings. Besides suffering persecution, they were also enduring extreme poverty.[24] Though extremely poor, they were rich in the wonderful promises Christ had given them. Second Corinthians 6:1-10 (NLT) describes so well what enduring for Christ means to a believer:

1 As God's partners, we beg you not to accept this marvelous gift of God's kindness and then ignore it.2 For God says, "At just the right time, I heard you. On the day of salvation, I helped you." Indeed, the "right time" is now. Today is the day of salvation. 3 We live in such a way that no one will stumble because of us, and no one will find fault with our ministry.4 In everything we do, we show that we are true ministers of God. We patiently endure troubles and hardships and calamities of every kind.5 We have been beaten, been put in prison, faced angry mobs, worked to exhaustion, endured sleepless nights, and gone without food.6 We prove ourselves by our purity, our understanding, our patience, our kindness, by the Holy Spirit within us, and by our sincere love.7 We faithfully preach the truth. God's power is working in us. We use the weapons of righteousness in the right hand for attack and the left hand for defense 8 We serve God whether people honor us or despise us, whether they slander us or praise us. We are honest, but they call us impostors.9We are ignored, even though we are well known. We live close to death, but we are still alive. We have been beaten, but we have not been killed.10 Our hearts ache, but

---

24 ptōcheiain contrast with *penia*, the ordinary word for *"poverty."*

we always have joy. We are poor, but we give spiritual riches to others. We own nothing, and yet we have everything.

James 2:5 (NLT):

5 Listen to me, dear brothers and sisters. Hasn't God chosen the poor in this world to be rich in faith? Aren't they the ones who will inherit the Kingdom he promised to those who love him?

When I read these passages I realize how shallow my faith can become and how necessary it is for me to take a closer look at the sincerity of my commitment and faith on a regular basis. Perhaps I need to stop feeling sorry for myself when I do not have enough money to pay my bills or when people criticize and condemn me when I try to present them with the truth about Christ.

Just think about what a tremendous promise and hope this letter to Smyrna is to people who are living in poverty and starvation. Think what hope it offers to those who have very little and are always struggling to make ends meet, to pay their bills each month, and to put food on the table for their families. These people are faithful to Christ but just cannot seem to keep their heads above water. Such people must occasionally wonder if God cares about their individual situations. Jesus is telling such people that they may be poor and suffering now, but in eternity they are going to have riches and plenty that they are not even capable of imagining in their present condition. A few years of suffering here on earth will become an eternity of wealth and peace forever and ever.

Now the people at Smyrna were being persecuted not only by non-Jewish pagans but also by hostile Jews and Satan himself. They must have felt like they were looking down the barrel of a shotgun. Apparently the local Jewish synagogue was called the synagogue of Satan (Revelation 3:9). Satan, by the way, is mentioned in four of the seven letters: Revelation 2:9, 13, 24; 3:9. In the history of the Church the most severe persecution has come from other faith groups.

In verse 9 Jesus says: "I know the blasphemy of those that say they are Jews, but are not." At this time the religious group that was persecuting the church at Smyrna and pretending to be the only true people of God, may have said that they were the only church of God in the world, when indeed *they were the synagogue of Satan.* As Christ has His Church in the world, so the devil has his synagogue. Those groups which are founded on opposition to the truths of the Gospel, and which promote false teaching, impurity, and rites and ceremonies created by people which never entered into the purposes of God, these are all synagogues of Satan. Satan rules over them, he works in them, his interests are served by them, and he receives honor from them. For the synagogues of Satan to pretend to be the Church or Israel of God[25] is no less than blasphemy (the act of insulting or showing contempt or lack

---

25 "Israel of God" refers to the true believers in Israel whose numbers were increased by the addition of the Gentiles who turned from idols to serve the living and true God. (Edward J. Young, *The Book of*

of reverence for God). You can take it to the bank that God is not pleased when His name is made use of to establish and promote the interests of Satan; and He will righteously judge those who continue to do so.[26] You do not have to just take my word for this. Read Hebrews 10:26-31 (NLT):

[26] *Dear friends, if we deliberately continue sinning after we have received knowledge of the truth, there is no longer any sacrifice that will cover these sins.* [27] *There is only the terrible expectation of God's judgment and the raging fire that will consume his enemies.* [28] *For anyone who refused to obey the law of Moses was put to death without mercy on the testimony of two or three witnesses.* [29] *Just think how much worse the punishment will be for those who have trampled on the Son of God, and have treated the blood of the covenant, which made us holy, as if it were common and unholy, and have insulted and disdained the Holy Spirit who brings God's mercy to us.* [30] *For we know the one who said, "I will take revenge. I will pay them back." He also said, "The Lord will judge his own people."* [31] *It is a terrible thing to fall into the hands of the living God.*

There are cults and organizations in our present day that are now bringing persecution upon the Christians and Jews

Isaiah—Volume 3: Chapters 40 to 66.Grand Rapids, MI: William B. Eerdmans, 1972. WORD*search* CROSS e-book, 218.)

26 Henry, Matthew: *Matthew Henry's Commentary on the Whole Bible: Complete and Unabridged in One Volume*. Peabody: Hendrickson, 1996, c1991, S. Re 2:8.

that will be just as bad, if not worse than it was in the first century and many other times in history right up to the time in which we are living. What and who are they? I'd like to reveal all of this information to you but if I did the major focus of this book might be lost in political differences.

But I can tell you this: The corruption, greed, and immorality that have become so commonplace in almost all areas of human behavior are causing pain and suffering to one degree or another for the greatest majority of people in this world. Evil is the engine driving the train. I believe the opportunity to turn this free-fall around may be gone forever if honest, God-fearing men and women do not turn to Christ and pray for His forgiveness, mercy, and grace. God may have already begun the countdown to the seven-year Tribulation. No nation can exist and thrive without Jesus as their foundation! Many throughout history have tried and failed. The United States did it better than anyone else in history for about 200 years and then step by step walked away from the faith on which its founders built the country. But try to convince the people of the world this basic truth and you'll encounter hatred, ridicule, and persecution that you may have never thought existed.

Our only hope is a worldwide revival, a turning to God so that He will heal us (2 Chronicles 7:14). Prayer is needed on the part of all believers and without it we are probably going to suffer the punishment God has warned us about repeatedly in the Bible.

The slander of the Jews of Smyrna is characteristic of the Jewish bitterness against Christians in that city. These Jews would have taken any opportunity of informing against the Christians to the Roman government. In fact their hatred of Christians was such that they would not hesitate to make up false charges against these Christians and report them to the Roman government as well.[27]

Revelation 2:10-11:

Do not fear what you are about to suffer. Behold, the devil is about to cast some of you into prison, so that you will be tested, and you will have tribulation for ten days. Be faithful until death, and I will give you the crown of life. He who has an ear, let him hear what the Spirit says to the churches. He who overcomes will not be hurt by the second death.

Jesus tells them they have nothing to fear, not even death. If you die your faithfulness has guaranteed your eternal life with Jesus Christ in Heaven. That is the reward. Most people think of death as a terrible thing, and it will be for those who do not accept Christ as the only one who is able to cover the penalty for their sins. However, for those who do receive Christ as their personal Savior, the day they die will be the

---

27 Carson, D. A.: *New Bible Commentary:* 21st Century Edition. 4th ed. Leicester, England; Downers Grove, Ill., USA: Inter-Varsity Press, 1994, S. Revelation 2:8.

best day of their lives. If you are saved there is no reason to fear death.

I am reminded of the first time I saw the Grand Canyon. All of a sudden there it was, as far as the eye could see, a huge fingerprint of the Master Creator. It literally took my breath away. Other than my wife I have not seen anything more beautiful before or since. I imagine that is kind of how it will be when in an instant we leave life on this earth and immediately find ourselves in Heaven with Jesus.

The ten days here could refer to a literal ten days or it could refer to a short period of time. Some have taken these words *"for 10 days"* as a symbolic representation of the entire persecution of the church. Others think it refers to ten persecutions under Roman rulers. The most probable meaning is that it anticipated a limited period of time for suffering.[28] Scott finds precedence in Scripture that ten days means a limited period of time.[29] It is also important here to understand that the word for *"crown,"* in the Greek, means *"joy"* or *"victory."* Whoever serves Christ faithfully throughout their life will receive that crown. They will receive the joy

---

28 Walvoord, *Revelation*, pp. 61-2.

29 Walter Scott, *Exposition of the Revelation of Jesus Christ*, p# 69. He cites Genesis 24:55; Nehemiah 5:18; Jeremiah 42:7; Daniel 1:12; Acts 25:6. Alford holds the same position, citing Numbers 11:19; 14:22; 1 Samuel 1:8; Job 19:3 (*The Greek Testament*, 4:567).

of life, the joy of being with Jesus in Heaven throughout eternity.[30]

"He who overcomes" refers again to believers, to those who have accepted Jesus as their Savior. The *First Death,* as we will see later, is physical death, the death of the body. The *Second Death* is spiritual death, the eternal death spent in the Lake of Fire. If you have accepted Jesus as your Savior you will only die once. You will go through the process of physical death but in so doing it will be like walking through a door. The moment you die you will find yourself immediately in the kingdom of Heaven (Luke 23:43). If you do not accept Christ as Savior, the First Death is the physical death at which time the body dies and you immediately go to Hell where you will await eternal judgment. When that judgment occurs you are cast into the Lake of Fire for eternity and that is considered the Second Death (spiritual death; Revelation 2:11; 20:14).

Jesus wanted this message to go to these suffering Christians so they might have courage as well as hope for the future: *"Do not be afraid* (literally "stop being afraid") *of what you are about to suffer."* This tells them that although their severe trials were to continue, that they would receive further persecution by imprisonment and additional suffering for ten days, but then everything would one day be all right.

---

30 Robertson, A.T.: *Word Pictures in the New Testament.* Oak Harbor, 1997, S. Re 2:10.

Jesus goes on to say that He is going to allow Satan to test them. Why would He do that? The problem of human suffering, even for a limited time, has always troubled faithful Christians. Suffering can be expected for the ungodly, but why should the godly suffer? The Scriptures give a number of reasons. Suffering may be (1) disciplinary, as we see in Hebrews 12:1-13 (NLT):[31] *Therefore, since we are surrounded by such a huge crowd of witnesses to the life of faith, let us strip off every weight that slows us down, especially the sin that so easily trips us up. And let us run with endurance the race God has set before us. ² We do this by keeping our eyes on Jesus, the champion who initiates and perfects our faith. Because of the joy awaiting him, he endured the cross, disregarding its shame. Now he is seated in the place of honor beside God's throne. ³ Think of all the hostility he endured from sinful people; then you won't become weary and give up. ⁴ After all, you have not yet given your lives in your struggle against sin. ⁵ And have you forgotten the encouraging words God spoke to you as his children? He said, "My child, don't make light of the Lord's discipline, and don't give up when he corrects you. ⁶ **For the Lord disciplines those he loves,**[32] and he punishes each one he accepts as his child." ⁷ As you endure this divine discipline, remember that God is treating you as his own*

31 Walvoord, John F.; Zuck, Roy B. ; Dallas Theological *Seminary: The Bible Knowledge Commentary: An Exposition of the Scriptures.* Wheaton, IL: Victor Books, 1983-c1985, S. 2:935.

32 Emphasis added.

children. Who ever heard of a child who is never disciplined by its father? [8] *If God doesn't discipline you as he does all of his children, it means that you are illegitimate and are not really his children at all.*[9] *Since we respected our earthly fathers who disciplined us, shouldn't we submit even more to the discipline of the Father of our spirits, and live forever?* [10] *For our earthly fathers disciplined us for a few years, doing the best they knew how. But God's discipline is always good for us, so that we might share in his holiness.* [11] *No discipline is enjoyable while it is happening—it's painful! But afterward there will be a peaceful harvest of right living for those who are trained in this way.* [12] *So take a new grip with your tired hands and strengthen your weak knees.* [13] *Mark out a straight path for your feet so that those who are weak and lame will not fall but become strong.*

Suffering may also be (2) preventive, as Paul's thorn in the flesh found in <u>2 Corinthians 12:7-10 (NLT)</u>:[33]

So to keep me from becoming proud, I was given a thorn in my flesh, a messenger from Satan to torment me and keep me from becoming proud. [8] *Three different times I begged the Lord to take it away.*[9] *Each time he said, "My grace is all you need. My power works best in weakness." So now I am glad to boast about my weaknesses, so that the power of Christ can work through me.* [10] *That's why I take pleasure in my weaknesses and in the insults,*

---

33   Walvoord, John F.; Zuck, Roy B.; Dallas Theological Seminary: *The Bible Knowledge Commentary: An Exposition of the Scriptures.* Wheaton, IL: Victor Books, 1983-c1985, S. 2:935.

hardships, persecutions, and troubles that I suffer for Christ. For when I am weak, then I am strong.

Suffering may also be for (3) the learning of obedience as in Romans 5:3-5 (NLT):[34]

We can rejoice, too, when we run into problems and trials, for we know that they help us develop endurance. [4] And endurance develops strength of character, and character strengthens our confident hope of salvation. [5] And this hope will not lead to disappointment. For we know how dearly God loves us, because he has given us the Holy Spirit to fill our hearts with his love.

And lastly suffering can lead to (4) the providing of a better testimony for Christ as in Acts 9:15-16 (NRSV) regarding the calling of Paul:[35]

But the Lord said to him, "Go, for he is an instrument whom I have chosen to bring my name before Gentiles and kings and before the people of Israel; [16] I myself will show him how much he must suffer for the sake of my name.

In their suffering the believers at Smyrna were encouraged to be faithful, even to the point of death. While their persecutors had the ability to kill them, it would only result in their receiving the crown of life. Later Polycarp, having become the bishop of the church in Smyrna, was martyred,

---

34   Ibid.

35   Ibid.

and undoubtedly others were also killed.[36] *"The crown of life"* is one of several crowns promised to Christians.[37] The crown of life is also mentioned in James 1:12 (NLT): *"God blesses those who patiently endure testing and temptation. Afterward they will receive the crown of life that God has promised to those who love him."*

Believers are encouraged to be faithful by contemplating what awaits them after death, namely, eternal life, the crown of life.[38]

The Second Death is a frightening prospect because it refers to the Lake of Fire, the eternal Hell. Such a doom is to die twice. The Smyrneans are reminded that to die through human wrath is small potatoes compared with suffering the judgment of God.[39] The enemy may kill the body, but the saint (one who has accepted Christ as Savior) need never fear the second death. (Revelation 20:14; 21:8).

36   Robert Jamieson, A. R. Fausset, and David Brown, *A Commentary Critical, Experimental and Practical on the Old and New Testaments.* Grand Rapids: Wm. B. Eerdmans Publishing Co., 1945. 6:662.

37   1 Cor. 9:25; 1 Thessalonians. 2:19; 2 Timothy 4:6-8; 1 Peter 5:4; Revelation 4:4.

38   Ibid.

39   Carson, D. A.: *New Bible Commentary*: 21st Century Edition. 4th ed. Leicester, England; Downers Grove, Ill., USA: Inter-Varsity Press, 1994, S. Re 2:8.

"Those who are born twice will die only once.
Those born only once will die twice"[40]

Verses 12-17: The Letter to the Church in Pergamum (the lenient church)

Revelation 2:12-17:

"And to the angel of the church in Pergamum write: The One who has the sharp two-edged sword says this: 13 'I know where you dwell, where Satan's throne is; and you hold fast My name, and did not deny My faith even in the days of Antipas, My witness, My faithful one, who was killed among you, where Satan dwells. 14 'But I have a few things against you, because you have there some who hold the teaching of Balaam, who kept teaching Balak to put a stumbling block before the sons of Israel, to eat things sacrificed to idols and to commit acts of immorality. 15 'So you also have some who in the same way hold the teaching of the Nicolaitans. 16 'Therefore repent; or else I am coming to you quickly, and I will make war against them with the sword of My mouth. 17 'He who has an ear, let him hear what the Spirit says to the churches. To him who overcomes, to him I will give some of the hidden manna, and I will give him a white stone, and a new name written on the stone which no one knows but he who receives it.'"

---

40   Wiersbe, Warren W.: *Wiersbe's Expository Outlines on the New Testament.* Wheaton, Ill: Victor Books, 1997, c1992, S. 802.

This is a church that is involved with compromise (tolerance). In other words, it is a church that does not stand firm on the Word of God. If the surrounding culture puts enough pressure on this church, they will bend in order to satisfy the people of this world.

Look back at verse 12 if you would. Pergamum (Pergamus) was a great political and religious center and all the main roads of Western Asia met there. It had many great buildings, including a library with 200,000 volumes, second only to the library in Alexandria. The Kingdom of Pergamum became a Roman province in 130 B.C. Pliny termed it the most illustrious city of Asia. Parchment (χαρτα Περγαμενα [charta Pergamena]) derived its name from Pergamum. It was a rival of Ephesus in the temples to Zeus, Athena, and Dionysos. The city was also home to the temple of Asklepios, the god of healing, called the god of Pergamum, with a university for medical study.[41] Asklepios was worshipped in the form of a living serpent fed in the temple; and on the coins minted by the town he often appears with a rod encircled by a serpent, the same image representing a medical practitioner today. The city has been described as a sort of union of a pagan cathedral-city, a university-town, and a royal residence, frequented during a succession of years by kings who all had a passion for "the good life" and the pleasures of the flesh and

---

41   Robertson, A.T.: *Word Pictures in the New Testament.* Oak Harbor: 1997, S. Re 2:12.

plenty of money to enjoy it to the maximum.[42] Pergamum was the first city in Asia (A.D. 29) with a temple for the worship of Augustus (Octavius Caesar), the Roman Emperor. Pergamum is therefore a center of emperor-worship "where Satan dwells" according to Revelation 2:13.[43]

The sword which is mentioned in verse 12 refers to Christ's judicial authority, His right to judge.[44] There are those scholars who also suggest that the sword represents Jesus' ability to separate the believers from unbelievers, to punish the unbelievers and reward the believers.[45] That it is the sword of salvation as well as the sword of death.[46]

Revelation 2:13:

I am fully aware that you live in the city where Satan's throne is, at the center of satanic worship; and yet you have remained loyal

42 Vincent, Marvin Richardson: *Word Studies in the New Testament.* Bellingham, WA. 2002, S. 2:446.

43 Op. Cit., Robertson, S. Re 2:12.

44 Keener, Craig S.; InterVarsity Press: *The IVP Bible Background Commentary:* New Testament. Downers Grove, Ill.: InterVarsity Press, 1993, S. Re 2:12.

45 Henry, Matthew: *Matthew Henry's Commentary on the Whole Bible:* Complete and Unabridged in One Volume. Peabody: Hendrickson, 1996, c1991, S. Re 2:12.

46 Walvoord, John F.; Zuck, Roy B.; Dallas Theological Seminary: *The Bible Knowledge Commentary: An Exposition of the Scriptures.* Wheaton, IL: Victor Books, 1983-c1985, S. 2:936.

to Me, and refused to deny Me, even when Antipas, my faithful
witness, was martyred among you by Satan's devotees.

This passage refers to the *"mystery cults"* of Babylon that
set up their headquarters in Pergamum. It also includes the
emperor worship that played a key role in this demon infested
city.[47] A group of compromising people led by Satan and his
henchmen had gradually infiltrated into this church, and
Jesus Christ hated their doctrines and their practices.[48] Make
no mistake Satan's throne is not in Hell. It is in this world. He
is not sitting on a throne in Hell ruling there, but rather his
kingdom is in the world in which we live. When this letter
was written to the church at **Pergamum,** it was from this city
that Satan's power was being unleashed. This city became the
center of his operation.

All citizens were expected to participate in public
religious ceremonies or they would be suspected of disloyalty
against the state; but Christians could not take part in such
ceremonies or festivals or eat the meat served there which
had been sacrificed to false gods (idols). They were therefore
labeled as a group of people who were disloyal to the emperor.
Once one Christian was martyred, a legal precedent was set

---

47   *Wiersbe, Warren W.: Wiersbe's Expository Outlines on the New Testament.*
     Wheaton, Ill.: Victor Books, 1997, c1992, S. 802.

48   Wiersbe, Warren W.: *The Bible Exposition Commentary.* Wheaton, Ill.:
     Victor Books, 1996, c1989, S. Re 2:12.

for the execution of Christians throughout the empire, and that is exactly what happened.[49]

The church at Pergamum was feeling the heat of this same kind of evil and in many ways it was giving in to it. But there were those within the church that remained loyal to Christ and waged an uncompromising battle right there at the throne of Satan. So Jesus complimented them. We do not know exactly who Antipas was, but he was very likely one of the leaders of the church, perhaps even their pastor. Antipas is described as being a *"faithful witness,"* an attribute he shared with Christ (Revelation 1:5). Satan's work and throne are seen throughout Revelation chapter 2 (2:9, 10, 13, 24; and also 3:9) and are connected to the Old Testament characters of Balaam (2:14) and Jezebel (2:20). Satan's attempt to destroy the Church will be described in his full scale frontal attack recorded in Revelation 4–20.[50] This passage tells us that there were people in this church that remained faithful even when Antipas was murdered right in front of them. The faithfulness of some of the people in that church should be an example as well as a challenge to each of us today.

49   Keener, Craig S.; InterVarsity Press: *The IVP Bible Background Commentary: New Testament.* Downers Grove, Ill: InterVarsity Press, 1993, S. Re 2:13.

50   Hughes, Robert B.; Laney, J. Carl; Hughes, Robert B.: *Tyndale Concise Bible Commentary.* Wheaton, Ill.: Tyndale House Publishers, 2001 (The Tyndale Reference Library), S. 737.

The works of Christians can best be evaluated when the circumstances under which they did those works are taken into account. This church's location makes its good works particularly noteworthy. It is located in the same city as Satan's headquarters. Jesus is saying that He considers carefully all the advantages and opportunities we have for serving in the places where we live or travel. He also considers carefully all of the temptations and discouragements we face in those places, and makes gracious allowances for them. This people dwelt where Satan's seat was located, where he kept his court. His kingdom includes the whole world and his throne can be found wherever we find the most evil of conditions. His seat is in some places that are infamous for sexual sin, evil, crime, and cruelty.[51]

What in the world has happened today to Christian faithfulness, to uncompromising values and standards established by God and our Savior Jesus Christ? **Antipas** was apparently a man who would rather die than compromise. So were a number of others in this evil environment. Many of us would rather compromise than change the simplest pattern of our selfish lives. What would be your reaction if the president, prime-minister, or grand high exalted mystic ruler walked into your church and told you that you can no

---

51   Henry, Matthew: *Matthew Henry's Commentary on the Whole Bible: Complete and Unabridged in One Volume.* Peabody: Hendrickson, 1996, c1991, S. Re 2:12.

longer teach that Christ is the only way to salvation, and that disobedience would result in death?

Revelation 2:14-15:

'But I have a few things against you, because you have there some who hold the teaching of Balaam, who kept teaching Balak to put a stumbling block before the sons of Israel, to eat things sacrificed to idols and to commit acts of immorality. So you also have some who in the same way hold the teaching of the Nicolaitans.'

We have seen that name, "Nicolaitans," before in the letter to Ephesus. Apparently Christ is not real pleased with that group. Here we see that the sin of Pergamum was the same as that of Balaam. It was the toleration of evil. The church had remained loyal to Christ but was tolerating those who held to the teachings of Balaam. In order to fully understand the letter to the church at Pergamum we need to understand what exactly was meant by the "teaching of Balaam." The story of Balaam appears in **Numbers 22:1–25:9**. I suggest you turn to your Bibles and read this passage.

Balaam, a non-Israelite prophet, was one of many prophets of eastern religions who worshiped all the gods of the land. Many of these false teachers had a considerable amount of power and influence. When they pronounced a blessing or a curse, it was considered as true prophecy. When Moses led his people across the wilderness, God commanded him not to attack Edom or Moab (Deuteronomy 2:4-9). He did not. When Edom attacked, "Israel turned away from him" (Numbers 20:21). As the great nation of Israelites traveled north on the east side of the Jordan River, King Balak, of Moab feared Israel would attack him. He had seen the conquests of Israel (Numbers 21) and was afraid his people would be overcome too. Balak sought a strategy other than battle to stop Moses. He decided to use a prophet to curse Israel. He realized that physical force would never defeat the Jews, so he resorted to spiritual deception by hiring Balaam to curse Israel. Balak sent his messengers with bribes to obtain Balaam's services. He offered Balaam a good price for doing the job. Balaam asked God's permission to curse Israel. Can you believe such boldness? Permission was refused. Balak's messengers went home and reported failure. Read the passage to find the rest of the story.

Balaam gives a wonderful history of Israel in these visions, all the way from their election as a nation to their exaltation in the kingdom. We may apply these truths, of course, to the New Testament believer, who has been chosen of God, justified, given a rich inheritance in Christ, and promised future glory.

Had Balaam stopped with his visions from God, he would have been safe, but he wanted the money and the honor that Balak promised. So he told the king how to defeat Israel. So His plan was simple: invite the Jews to share in the heathen sacrificial feasts and corrupt them with idolatry and lust. The ceremonies involved in Baal worship were very wicked, and

Balaam knew that the Jewish men would be tempted to join with the Moabite women. This is exactly what happened. What the armies of the other nations could not do, the women of Moab and Midian were doing. If Satan cannot overcome God's people as a lion (1 Peter 5:8), then he comes as a serpent. Beware of the friendliness of God's enemies. In this day and age when people are telling Christians to become friendly with their spiritual enemies, we need more courageous men and women who will take a stand for separation and righteousness.

Of course, Balaam thought that Israel's sins would destroy the nation. This is *"the error of Balaam"* mentioned in Jude 11. Revelation 2:14 mentions *"the teaching of Balaam."* The teaching of Balaam was his counsel to Balak that he invite the Jews to mix with the Gentiles, marry Moabite women, and share in their evil feasts. Such a "doctrine" is nothing but compromise. This is the great danger today: Christians individually and churches (and denominations) collectively are forgetting their calling to be separate and are joining themselves to the world. This can only mean judgment.[52]

What Balaam could not accomplish with a curse he did through seductive means. In the New Testament, Peter warned against false teachers and described their destruction (2 Peter 2:12-19). He further said that they bore a curse as

---

52   Wiersbe, Warren W.: *Wiersbe's Expository Outlines on the Old Testament.* Wheaton, IL: Victor Books, 1993, S. Nu 22:1.

experts in greed. Peter wrote that they left the right way and followed the way of Balaam. In Revelation 2:14 the church at Pergamum was complimented for faithfulness under persecution but also warned that some followed after Balaam in offering meat to idols and in immorality.[53] The choice before them was simple: **Repent** and find eternal life, or persist in tolerating evil and invite God's anger (verses 16, 17).[54]

When those who call themselves Christians commit adultery, close their eyes to homosexuality, cheat in business, or lower their moral standards to suit the situation, they fit into the Pergamum mentality. Why do churches allow such behavior within their congregations? It is simply because they can draw more people into their fellowship if they are tolerant of the personal lifestyles of those people. Before long, if you get enough of that, you have a church that does not reflect the pure standards of God, and God is not going to bless that kind of a church. In fact, God is going to punish that kind of a church. *"You adulteresses, do you not know that friendship with the world is hostility toward God? Therefore,*

---

53 Hatfield, Lawson G., *Holman Illustrated Bible dictionary, Word Search Bible Electronic Edition.* "Balaam."

54 Willmington, H. L.: *Willmington's Bible Handbook.* Wheaton, Ill.: Tyndale House Publishers, 1997, S. 795. For other references to Balaam, see Deuteronomy 23:4–5, Joshua 24:9–10, Nehemiah 13:2, Micah 6:5; 2 Peter 2:15–16, Jude 11, and Revelation 2:14.

whoever wishes to be a friend of the world makes himself an enemy of God" (James 4:4). In other words, if you choose to accept cultural norms of morality that are the opposite of God's Word, then you choose to be an enemy of God. God does not compromise His truth and neither should we. Nicolaitans were comparable to those following the teaching of Balaam (Joshua 13:22). They advocated extreme indulgence in sin. Uncleanness, immorality, and orgies were encouraged based upon a perverted understanding of God's grace (Romans 6:1). There are many organizations and cults in our world today that promote the same kind of behavior. I do not know that the evil that exists today is worse than it was in the first century, but there certainly is a lot more of it.

A number of various forces are working daily to lead us all to a one-world government. If you don't do your own investigating to find truth you probably won't ever find it because the media is now very much an ally in the one-world movement. If you see a world government established in your lifetime you can know that the Tribulation is about to begin. We'll discuss this in much more detail as we move along.

"Money finds money and power finds power from one generation to the next, and a continuing cycle takes place."[55] I hope you can readily see that there has been a steady growth in the power of evil for hundreds of years, and the treasure chests of the evil will continue to grow along with the power

---

55   Ibid.

that kind of money can buy, until the time is right and God begins the seven-year Tribulation. You can take that to the bank! Now back to Revelation.

Revelation 2:16 (TLB):

Change your mind and attitude, or else I will come to you suddenly and fight against them with the sword of my mouth.

Christ tells them to repent, to change their mind and attitude. What is it necessary to repent from? It is necessary to repent from sin and Jesus is telling them that if they do not repent and do something about this, He will come to them and punish them. The church as a body and each member of the church body are not to tolerate evil in any form.

Revelation 2:17:

Let everyone who can hear, listen to what the Spirit is saying to the churches: Everyone who is victorious shall eat of the hidden manna, the secret nourishment from Heaven; and I will give to each a white stone, and on the stone will be engraved a new name that no one else knows except the one receiving it.

Christ is saying that they should listen up and not miss this message that is coming directly from Him. Just as Israel received manna from Heaven as its food during the forty years God caused them to wander in the desert, true believers will be given Jesus Christ, the bread that will give them a continuing food supply, as we see in John 6:51: *"I am the living bread that came down out of Heaven; if anyone eats of this bread he shall live forever."*

"Hidden manna" (bread) speaks of the person and the death of Christ as He is revealed in the Word of God. In fact, Jesus said that He Himself was the Bread. Here are Jesus' words in John 6:32-35:

Jesus then said to them, "Truly, truly, I say to you, it is not Moses who has given you the bread out of heaven, but it is My Father who gives you the true bread out of heaven. 33" For the bread of God is that which comes down out of heaven, and gives life to the world." 34 Then they said to Him, "Lord, always give us this bread." 35 Jesus said to them, "I am the bread of life; he who comes to Me will not hunger, and he who believes in Me will never thirst."

The believer needs to feed on Christ—this is a must for spiritual growth. Such feeding is done by reading the Bible and thinking prayerfully about what we've read. In our world today Christ is hidden from view; He is no longer known or understood as He once was. Oh how people misrepresent Him and abuse Him![56] We also see in verse 17 that every believer will get a *white stone.* One interpretation of this verse that seems quite likely is that in the days when the book of Revelation was written it was common that a victor in the athletic games would receive a white stone rather than a gold, silver, or bronze medal. The white stone was the victor's

---

56   Op Cit., McGee, Rev. 2:17

admission ticket to the festival that was held for the winners after the games. He alone could use it as his pass.

Could it be that the meaning here is that the believer will receive the ticket to the eternal victory celebration in Heaven?[57] There was a *"new name"* written on the stone that no one knows except the one who receives it. This is some kind of a personal message from Christ to the ones He loves and it is given as an admission pass into eternal glory. I will know mine and you will know yours if you are truly saved, and we will know that the Lord wrote them for each of us alone. This is such a beautiful message because it is telling us that Christ loved us so much, not just as a group of believers, but each one of us individually. He has something very special planned for each individual believer and He will know them personally in Heaven.[58]

Another very likely explanation is that the people of Asia Minor to whom John was writing had a custom of giving to intimate friends a *tessera*, a cube or rectangular block of stone or ivory with words or symbols engraved on it. It was a secret, private possession of the one who received it. Well, Christ says that He is going to give to each of His own a stone with a new name engraved upon it. It may not be that it will be a new name for you and me but that it will be a new name for

57   Op Cit., MacArthur, Audio Tape Series on Revelation, Rev. 2:17.
58   Ibid.

Him.[59] We will find out when we get to Heaven. If you do not know Jesus Christ as your personal Savior, then the *"hidden manna"* is not for you; the *"white stone"* is not yours. All you have is the sword of judgment.

The Letter to the Church at Thyatira (The compromising church)

Revelation 2:18-29:

"And to the angel of the church in Thyatira write: The Son of God, who has eyes like a flame of fire, and His feet are like burnished bronze, says this: [19] *'I know your deeds, and your love and faith and service and perseverance, and that your deeds of late are greater than at first.* [20] *But I have this against you, that you tolerate the woman Jezebel, who calls herself a prophetess, and she teaches and leads My bond-servants astray so that they commit acts of immorality and eat things sacrificed to idols.* [21] *I gave her time to repent, and she does not want to repent of her immorality.* [22] *Behold, I will throw her on a bed of sickness, and those who commit adultery with her into great tribulation, unless they repent of her deeds.* [23] *And I will kill her children with pestilence, and all the churches will know that I am He who searches the minds and hearts; and I will give to each one of you according to your deeds.* [24] *But I say to you, the rest who are in Thyatira, who do not hold this teaching, who have not known the deep things of Satan, as they call them—I place no other burden on you.* [25] *Nevertheless*

---

59   Op. Cit., McGee, Revelation 2:17.

what you have, hold fast until I come. [26] *He who overcomes, and he who keeps My deeds until the end, to him I will give authority over the nations;* [27] *and he shall rule them with a rod of iron, as the vessels of the potter are broken to pieces, as I also have received authority from My Father;* [28] *and I will give him the morning star.* [29] *He who has an ear, let him hear what the Spirit says to the churches.'"*

Although this church had some good points, it also tolerated evil. This letter shows the depth of sin that compromise ultimately leads to. This church tolerated immorality and is, unfortunately, the kind of church that is common today. God promises that He will judge this church severely, sparing only those that do not hold to its teaching (verse 24). God expects His Church to be as pure as a virgin. He wants sin to be dealt with in the Church, not accommodated or tolerated.

Revelation 2:18:

"And to the angel of the church in Thyatira write: The Son of God, who has eyes like a flame of fire, and His feet are like burnished bronze, says this:"

The longest message was sent to the smallest church in the smallest city. Thyatira was about 40 miles southeast of Pergamum and was located in an area noted for its abundant crops and the manufacture of purple dye. It was a military town as well as a commercial center with many trade guilds. Today we would call them unions. Now wherever guilds were found, idolatry and immorality—the two great enemies of the early church—were almost always present as well. At that time each guild had its own god, a kind of guardian-like god that supposedly gave himself to taking care of the members of each individual guild. The members worshipped that god. "Associated with that worship was immoral behavior as is the practice in most pagan[60] systems. The city also was home to a special temple to Apollo, the *'sun god.'* Lydia, the purple-seller of this city, having been converted at Philippi, was probably the woman who first carried the Gospel to her native town of Thyatira"[61] (Acts 16:14-15).

It was John's job in this letter to deliver a message of warning and judgment from Jesus to this congregation, which explains the description of Jesus' eyes and feet.[62] So right at the beginning of this letter we see Christ ready to judge sin. Christ is introduced as the Son of God, whose eyes are like blazing fire and whose feet are like burnished bronze. This description of Christ is similar to what we saw in Revelation 1:13-15, but here He is called the *Son of God* rather than the *Son of Man*. Because of the warning of judgment in these letters, Christ apparently wanted to make it clear that He was God and was the only One that had the authority to

---

60 Someone who does not worship God/Christ

61 MacArthur John, *Audio Tape Series*, Revelation 2:20.

62 Wiersbe, Warren W.: *The Bible Exposition Commentary*. Wheaton, Ill.: Victor Books, 1996, c1989, S. Re 2:18.

judge sins. The words *"burnished bronze,"* which describe His feet, translate a rare Greek word *chalkolibanō,* also used in Revelation 1:15. It seems to have been an alloy of a number of metals that took on a brilliant shine when polished.[63] Feet like fine brass are suggestive of Jesus' purity and holiness. For brass to shine as described here, all the impurity must be processed out of the metal. He judges therefore with perfect wisdom so that we can be assured everyone will be treated with absolute fairness and justice.[64] This description of the glorified Christ is used in both the Old and New Testaments to signify judgment.[65, 66]

The description of Jesus' eyes speaks of His piercing, penetrating, perfect knowledge. He is able to look into the hearts and minds of every human being and determine all of their inner thoughts and motives. He knows exactly what is in your heart and the hearts of everyone in your church, and *He is not going to tolerate you or your church if you or they tolerate sin.*

---

63 Walvoord, John F.; Zuck, Roy B.; Dallas Theological Seminary: *The Bible Knowledge Commentary: An Exposition of the Scriptures.* Wheaton, IL: Victor Books, 1983-c1985, S. 2:937.

64 Henry, Matthew: *Matthew Henry's Commentary on the Whole Bible: Complete and Unabridged in One Volume.* Peabody: Hendrickson, 1996, c1991, S. Re 2:18

65 Op. Cit., Richards, Larry: *The Bible Reader's Companion*, S. 908

66 Daniel 10:6; Revelation 1:14, 15; Revelation 2:18; Revelation 19:12.

Revelation 2:19:

I know your deeds, and your love and faith and service and perseverance, and that your deeds of late are greater than at first.

The deeds mentioned in verse 19 are significant, especially in light of the fact that judgment will be delivered according to one's deeds as is explained in Revelation 20:12-14 (NLT):

I saw the dead, both great and small, standing before God's throne. And the books were opened, including the Book of Life. And the dead were judged according to what they had done, as recorded in the books. [13] *The sea gave up its dead, and death and the grave gave up their dead. And all were judged according to their deeds.* [14] *Then death and the grave were thrown into the lake of fire. This lake of fire is the second death.*

Now do not misunderstand either of these verses to say that a person's salvation is determined by how many good works they do. You will see when we get to chapter 20 that those being judged are those who do not have their name in the Book of Life, which is the book containing the names of all who have believed in Jesus Christ as their Lord and Savior. The Lord will then have a separate judgment for all believers who will be given their rewards based on the things they did as a result of their faith and commitment to Christ. Salvation comes only as a free gift of grace from God through a person's faith in Jesus. But here we see that the church at Thyatira was growing in its service for Jesus (*"you are now doing more than you did at first"*).[67]

Jesus is saying that many of them are faithful and consistent and that they should hang in there. Out of that kind of love they are serving each other, and they are getting better at this all the time. That is the kind of compliment you would think would set people apart as absolutely without a flaw. The people in this church worked hard, faithfully, and patiently, but unfortunately beneath that healthy, relational exterior there was a cesspool.

You see there are people who truly care about and love one another even in the most liberal churches, and they do not want to see any conflict develop that might hamper the church's growth and overall friendliness. Even thieves can care about one another. People who are involved in illegal business dealings or politics can care about one another, but they are still committing sin in the eyes of God. People who are kind, moral, loving, and serving can appear to be doing all that God requires, but if they allow sin to take root and flourish in the lives of people around them and do not discourage that behavior, they are targeted for judgment by God. And if they allow such behavior without speaking out against it, they are equally involved in that sin, and such behavior could

---

67   Carson, D. A.: *New Bible Commentary:* 21st Century Edition. 4th ed. Leicester, England; Downers Grove, Ill., USA: Inter-Varsity Press, 1994, S. Re 2:18.

also be evidence that the person is not truly saved. James 4:17: *"Remember, it is sin to know what you ought to do and then not do it"* (NLT).

Revelation 2:20:

'But I have this against you, that you tolerate the woman Jezebel, who calls herself a prophetess, and she teaches and leads My bond-servants astray so that they commit acts of immorality and eat things sacrificed to idols.'

The desire of God for His Church is a beautiful balance of holiness and love, but love without holiness can descend into immorality. So we can love each other and care for each other and do all kinds of great things for each other, but if we do not maintain that pure standard of holiness that God has set up for us, if we start compromising a little bit here and a little bit there, the ultimate result is going to be immorality in our lives and in our church. We have to remove this in order to keep ourselves pure and our church pure and we have to be very careful of who we associate with and where they stand.

Revelation 2:20 introduces us to Jezebel, the only woman mentioned in the seven letters of Revelation chapters 2 and 3. This refers to wicked Queen Jezebel, wife of Ahab, king of Israel. We need some background so that we might understand just what Jezebel was like. We can only understand how evil she truly was by the hatred Jesus had for what was going on in the church at Thyatira. In order to do that let us go to the book of 1 Kings. You can read the complete story for yourself in 1 Kings 16:29–17:7; 18:1–19:3; 21:1–26; 2 Kings 9:1–13, 30–37 and I strongly encourage you to do so. We will only summarize the highlights here.

Jezebel, the daughter of Ethbaal, king of Tyre and Zidon, married King Ahab of Israel and then encouraged him to do things that were evil in God's eyes. He built a temple for Baal and set up other forms of idol worship. Scripture tells us that Ahab *"did more to provoke the anger of the Lord"* than any other king had done. Ahab reigned for a total of twenty-two years, from 874 to 853 B.C.[68]

Now Jezebel, Ahab's bride, was one of Satan's most notorious puppets for implementing outrageous acts of evil. She was a devoted follower of the Phoenician god, Baal, and she supported some 850 prophets of Baal and Asherah. **Jezebel had as her ultimate goal the elimination of worship of the God of Israel, Jehovah** and executing His servants. Obadiah saved a hundred of them, at the risk of his own life. Jezebel herself maintained four hundred priests of Astarte. When the prophets of Baal perished at Carmel, at the word of Elijah, she sought to avenge herself on him. Afterwards, she secured the vineyard of Naboth for her husband by perjuries and murder; and her tragic death, the fitting close of a bloody life, took place, according to the prediction of Elijah, near the scene of this crime. Her name has become a means

---

68 *International Standard Bible Encyclopedia.*

of emphasizing the evil that exists in the worst of women, and is used by John to describe the extent of evil that exists in this woman (Revelation 2:20) in the church of Thyatira.[69]

Now just who were these two gods, Baal and Asherah that we come across so often in scripture? There were many different gods who were called *"Baal"* with some kind of subtitle added, such as *"Baal-Peor."*[70] The word Baal signifies lord, not so much in the sense of ruler, as possessor or owner. The name was given to the principal male deity of the Phoenicians, corresponding to Bel or Belus of the Babylonians. The female deity associated with Baal was Astarte.[71]

The worship of Baal was accompanied with splendid ceremonies. Priests and prophets were dedicated to serving him (2 Kings 10:19). Incense (Jeremiah 7:9) and prayers (1 Kings 18:26) were offered to him. The worshipers threw themselves to the ground before the idol and kissed it (1 Kings 19:18), perhaps at the same time kissing Baal's hand that was elevated toward the sun. "The *'high places of Baal'* (Hebrew *bamotha'al*), was an elevation somewhere in the Transjordan plateau, probably near Mount Nebo, which was important to the worship of Baal. Ancient worshipers

---

69   *A Dictionary of the Holy Bible.*

70   *AMG's Encyclopedia of Bible Facts.*

71   Freeman, James M.; Chadwick, Harold J.: *Manners & Customs of the Bible. (Rev. ed.).* North Brunswick, NJ: Bridge-Logos Publishers, 1998, S. 167.

felt that high places elevated them closer to their gods. Each locality had its special Baal, and the various local *"Baals"* were summed up under the name of *"Baalim,"* or *"lords."*

As punishment for all their evil acts, God had all the descendants of Jezebel and Ahab killed. That is exactly what Jesus is saying He will do to the children (followers) of Jezebel in the church at Thyatira in Revelation chapter 2. So we do not see any symbolism in **Revelation 2:21-23**, where Jesus says:

'I gave her time to repent, and she does not want to repent of her immorality. [22] *'Behold, I will throw her on a bed of sickness, and those who commit adultery with her into great tribulation, unless they repent of her deeds.* [23] *'And **I will kill her children with pestilence**, and all the churches will know that I am He who searches the minds and hearts; and I will give to each one of you according to your deeds.'*

Whether this refers to death in this life or eternal death in the Lake of Fire is not certain, but it could mean both. Jesus will, one way or another kill this false prophetess and her followers if they do not repent. On a scale from 1 to 10 with 10 being the most evil, Jezebel would have been a 10+. She promoted Baal worship in Israel. She was guilty of whoredom and witchcraft (2 Kings 9:22) as well as idolatry, murder, and deceit, and she cast a dark shadow over both Israel and Judah for what must have been a very long thirty-three years. And the church at Thyatira was following her example and leadership. This false prophetess in the church was using *false teaching* to deceive God's people. She gave them permission to sin (see 2 Peter 2 and Jude). She would not repent even though God gave her the opportunity. Please remember that it is never too late for a church or an individual to repent and return to the Lord.[72] You now possibly know more about Jezebel than you ever thought you would, and perhaps than you ever wanted to know, so let us get back to the church in Thyatira.

This worship that Jezebel taught required worshipping idols, participating in idol feasts, celebrations, and immoral orgies. We all too often see today that people are required to do things on the job or as members of an organization that are against God's will. When that happens, such people can be directly associated with the same things that were a problem in the church at Thyatira. Doing such things then, as well as now, would obviously be impossible for a true Christian. If you were employed in the wool industry in Thyatira, you had to belong to a guild. And in order to have good standing in the guild you would need to engage in guild activities. If you did not, you could lose your job.

That kind of seduction worked then and it works today. We find people rationalizing behavior because they think in some way it can result in good. The people at Thyatira probably went to church on Sunday and worshipped. Then

---

72   Wiersbe, Warren W.: *Wiersbe's Expository Outlines on the New Testament*. Wheaton, Il: Victor Books, 1997, c1992, S. 803.

during the week they would do whatever their job required. That is not what God had in mind for His followers then and it is not what He wants us to do either. This woman referred to as Jezebel may have suggested to them that they all needed their jobs because they had to support their families as well as the work of the church in the world. So when their guild had an idol feast, she would encourage them to go to it. The philosophy this woman promoted was something like this: "It's OK to do some of these immoral things because in the long haul it benefits the church. After all, we're under grace and it's the spirit that concerns God, not the flesh. These physical things don't really affect your spiritual dimension, so don't worry about doing them." What is the fate of those who follow her false teaching? Let us look at those verses again.

Revelation 2:21-23:

'I gave her time to repent, and she does not want to repent of her immorality. ²² 'Behold, I will throw her on a bed of sickness, and those who commit adultery with her into great tribulation, unless they repent of her deeds. 23 'And I will kill her children with pestilence, and all the churches will know that I am He who searches the minds and hearts; and I will give to each one of you according to your deeds.'

Jezebel intentionally misled the members of this church to take part in the sexual immorality that accompanied pagan religion and to eat food sacrificed to idols. What was acceptable socially in Thyatira society was condemned by Jesus, but church leaders had allowed it to infect the church. This immoral behavior had been going on for some time (verse 21). Now it is entirely possible, as was mentioned earlier, that the church in Thyatira may have first heard the gospel from Lydia, converted through Paul's ministry in Acts. Luke writes about it in Acts 16:13-15.

It is rather curious that a woman would first bring the gospel message of Jesus to Thyatira and then another woman would corrupt and disgrace that message by changing it to allow for some sinful behavior, much like Ahab's wife, Jezebel, corrupted Israel (1 Kings 16:31-33). Calling her sin adultery, which could involve sexual promiscuity (having several sexual partners) or even worship of false gods and acceptance of false teaching, Christ promised judgment and great suffering, not only upon Jezebel but also upon anyone who followed her teaching. Jesus also promised He would strike her children dead, meaning that not only would her followers suffer but some would be killed for the evil they committed. The judgment would be so unforgettable that all the churches would know that Christ is the One who searches hearts and minds.[73] God is certainly consistent. We have seen how He punished evil in the days of Jezebel and Ahab and

---

73   Walvoord, John F.; Zuck, Roy B.; Dallas Theological Seminary: *The Bible Knowledge Commentary: An Exposition of the Scriptures.* Wheaton, IL: Victor Books, 1983-c1985, S. 2:937.

their children, and how He promised to do the same thing to this Jezebel-like leader and her followers in the church at Thyatira. What do you think Jesus will do to teachers and followers who are doing the exact same thing in the Church today? Christ makes it pretty clear in chapter 22.

Revelation 22:18-19:

I testify to everyone who hears the words of the prophecy of this book: if anyone adds to them, God will add to him the plagues which are written in this book; [19] *and if anyone takes away from the words of the book of this prophecy, God will take away his part from the tree of life and from the holy city, which are written in this book.*

Jesus found a lot of dirt under the carpet in the church at Thyatira. And no amount of loving and sacrificial works can compensate for tolerating evil. The church was permitting a false prophetess to manipulate the people in a way that caused them to compromise the truth. Now it is quite likely that this woman was not actually called **"Jezebel."** The name is symbolic for an evil and **false prophetess.** It is the symbolic name of a woman who pretended to be a prophetess, and who claimed a Christian had the right to eat things sacrificed to idols.[74] This seductive teaching of Jezebel was similar to the *"doctrine of Balaam"* that Jesus had condemned earlier in the

---

74   Strong, James: *The Exhaustive Concordance of the Bible:* Showing Every Word of the Test of the Common English Version of the Canonical

church of Pergamos (Revelation 2:14). She taught believers how to compromise with the religion of the Roman Empire and the practices of the guilds, so that Christians would not lose their jobs or their lives.[75]

We have Christian churches teaching the same thing today. They teach people not to offend homosexuals, not to offend abortionists, not to offend Muslims, nor Hindus, nor Mormons, but rather be tolerant of everyone's beliefs. They teach that we all worship the same god and that we just have different paths that lead to Him.

If you are at all familiar with Church history you may recall that during the Middle Ages, directly preceding the Protestant Reformation of the early 1500's, the Roman Catholic Church took on many of the characteristics of the church at Thyatira to which the letter here in Revelation 2 is directed.

It is interesting to compare the churches at Ephesus and Thyatira. The Ephesian church was losing its love for Jesus, yet it was faithful in judging teachers who taught false doctrine. The people in the church at Thyatira were just the opposite. They were growing in their love, but at the same time were tolerating the teaching of false doctrine. Neither

---

Books, and Every Occurrence of Each Word in Regular Order. Electronic ed. Ontario: Woodside Bible Fellowship. 1996, S. G2403.

75   Wiersbe, Warren W.: *The Bible Exposition Commentary*. Wheaton, Ill.: Victor Books, 1996, c1989, S. Re 2:18.

of these extremes should be allowed to gradually work its way into the church, because once it gets in it becomes like a cancer spreading rapidly. What I mean by that is that if the church is pure but allows just one person to deviate slightly from teaching the truth without calling them to accountability, then there will soon be another, and then a third, and before long half of the church will have accepted *false doctrine. "Speaking the truth in love"* (Ephesians 4:15) is the way to maintain purity in any church! Church discipline is also a part of this equation where necessary and we will talk about that in just a little while.

Not only was the church at Thyatira tolerant of evil, but it was proud and unwilling to repent. Jesus gave this false prophetess time to repent, yet she refused. He was also giving her followers the opportunity to repent. Jesus' eyes of fire had searched out their thoughts and motives, and He would make no mistakes in judgment.[76] In fact, Jesus threatened to use this church as an example to *"all the churches"* that they were not to tolerate evil. Jezebel and her children (followers) would be sentenced to tribulation and death. Idolatry and compromise are, in the Bible, pictured as fornication[77] and unfaithfulness to the marriage vows. Listen to what God said through Jeremiah and then Hosea:

---

76 Ibid.

77 Fornication- Sexual intercourse between an unmarried man and an unmarried woman.

Jeremiah 3:6-10 (NLT):

During the reign of King Josiah, the Lord said to me, "Have you seen what fickle Israel has done? Like a wife who commits adultery,[78] Israel has worshiped other gods on every hill and under every green tree.[7] I thought, 'After she has done all this, she will return to me.' But she did not return, and her faithless sister Judah saw this.[8] She saw that I divorced faithless Israel because of her adultery. But that treacherous sister Judah had no fear, and now she, too, has left me and given herself to prostitution.[9] Israel treated it all so lightly—she thought nothing of committing adultery by worshiping idols made of wood and stone. So now the land has been polluted.[10] But despite all this, her faithless sister Judah has never sincerely returned to me. She has only pretended to be sorry. I, the Lord, have spoken!"

As we continue reading in Hosea please be thinking not only of what God said in Jeremiah, but also what Jesus told the church at Thyatira in verses 22 and 23. In effect, God did to Israel in the Old Testament exactly what Jesus, in the New Testament, said would be done to an unfaithful church who also prostituted itself to false gods and false teaching.

---

78 Adultery – Betrayal; cheating; intercourse between a married man and woman who are not married to each other, or one may be married and the other not.

Hosea 9:1-3, 7-9, 13, 17 (NLT):

[1] *O people of Israel, do not rejoice as other nations do. For you have been unfaithful to your God, hiring yourselves out like prostitutes, worshiping other gods on every threshing floor.* [2] *So now your harvests will be too small to feed you. There will be no grapes for making new wine.* [3] *You may no longer stay here in the Lord's land. Instead, you will return to Egypt, and in Assyria you will eat food that is ceremonially unclean...* [7] *The time of Israel's punishment has come; the day of payment is here. Soon Israel will know this all too well. Because of your great sin and hostility, you say, "The prophets are crazy and the inspired men are fools!"* [8] *The prophet is a watchman over Israel for my God, yet traps are laid for him wherever he goes. He faces hostility even in the house of God.* [9] *The things my people do are as depraved as what they did in Gibeah long ago. God will not forget. He will surely punish them for their sins...* [13] *I have watched Israel become as beautiful as Tyre. But now Israel will bring out her children for slaughter."...* [17] *My God will reject the people of Israel because they will not listen or obey. They will be wanderers, homeless among the nations.*

What do you think Jesus is going to do to the twenty-first century Church for turning away from Him and being *unfaithful?* Do you think all the disasters that have occurred over the last ten years are just a coincidence? Perhaps, but maybe that is the same thing Israel and Judah thought when God kept firing warning shots across their bow. Then one day, because the people refused to repent and turn again to Him, even after God had given them so many opportunities, He had enough and allowed the country to be ravaged and the people sent away into exile. Do you think He will do any less to the United States, Canada, Europe or any other place in the world that rejects Him? Remember God is the same yesterday, today, and tomorrow. That suggests to me that He will punish people the same as He has done in the past. If you have an ear, listen to what God has said to His people in the past. Then repent or suffer the same consequences.

Jezebel's bed of sin would become a bed of sickness! To *"kill with death"* means *"to kill with pestilence"* (see NASB). Jesus would judge the false prophetess and her followers once and for all.[79]

Now why should the evil conduct and teaching of this false prophetess be blamed on the church of Thyatira? Because that church allowed her to seduce the people of that city. But how could the church help it? They did not have, as a church, civil power to banish or imprison her. True, but what they did have as a church was the authority to exercise church discipline against her and censure her for a time, as Paul instructs us to do in 1 Corinthians 5:1-13 (NLT): *"I can hardly believe the report about the sexual immorality going on among you—something that even pagans don't do… You must call a meeting of the church. I will be present with you in spirit, and so*

79 Wiersbe, Warren W.: *The Bible Exposition Commentary.* Wheaton, Ill.: Victor Books, 1996, c1989, S. Re 2:18.

will the power of our Lord Jesus.[5] *Then you must throw this man out and hand him over to Satan so that his sinful nature will be destroyed and he himself will be saved on the day the Lord returns.*
[6] *Your boasting about this is terrible. Don't you realize that this sin is like a little yeast that spreads through the whole batch of dough?*[7] *Get rid of the old "yeast" by removing this wicked person from among you. Then you will be like a fresh batch of dough made without yeast, which is what you really are. Christ, our Passover Lamb, has been sacrificed for us.*[8] *So let us celebrate the festival, not with the old bread of wickedness and evil, but with the new bread of sincerity and truth.* [9] *When I wrote to you before, I told you not to associate with people who indulge in sexual sin.*[10] *But I wasn't talking about unbelievers who indulge in sexual sin, or are greedy, or cheat people, or worship idols. You would have to leave this world to avoid people like that.*[11] *I meant that you are not to associate with anyone who claims to be a believer yet indulges in sexual sin, or is greedy, or worships idols, or is abusive, or is a drunkard, or cheats people. Don't even eat with such people.* [12] *It isn't my responsibility to judge outsiders, but it certainly is your responsibility to judge those inside the church who are sinning.*[13] *God will judge those on the outside; but as the Scriptures say, "You must remove the evil person from among you."*

Matthew 18:15-17 (NLT):

"If another believer sins against you, go privately and point out the offense. If the other person listens and confesses it, you have

won that person back.[16] *But if you are unsuccessful, take one or two others with you and go back again, so that everything you say may be confirmed by two or three witnesses.*[17] *If the person still refuses to listen, take your case to the church. Then if he or she won't accept the church's decision, treat that person as a pagan or a corrupt tax collector.*

The fact that they neglected to use the power they had—made them share equally in her (Jezebel's) sin. This Jezebel proposed that it was all right to declare that Caesar was indeed a god, and that it was not necessary to be so exclusive in their worship of Jesus Christ. In addition she advocated that casual sex should not be a matter of concern. There are many so-called Christians today who believe that Jesus may not be the only way to salvation and eternal life. We have churches and Christians today that are tolerant of all kinds of sinful patterns of behavior. We have people in churches today that are tolerant of people no matter what their behavior or what they believe or teach. We have people in churches today that do not care about the doctrine that is taught as long as it increases the attendance of the church. Far too many people who go to church and call themselves Christians have no regard for holy standards, holy truth, or holy living. If anyone says anything critical about their right to live the kind of lifestyle that they want to live, or believe just what they want to believe, they take exception and often become angry, even taking legal action in some instances.

Any Christian who sits in front of a television and watches four or five hours of programming each night, goes to a lot of movies promoting violence, sex, dishonesty, and satanic themes, and listens to talk shows that promote the *life is all about me* philosophy, and much of the other nonsense in the public media, is subjecting themselves to immorality. And it is going to get a hold on them. In these verses Jesus is issuing a dire warning. His message to them and also to us is that if we do not pay attention to what He is saying, the result is sickness and death.

Then Jesus goes on to say at the end of Revelation 2:23 that He will give everyone exactly what they deserve. In other words, if you have hated others, if you have cheated others, whether in thought, word, or deed, you will get that same treatment right back from God. How would you like God to treat you exactly the way you treat others? How many of you would like to get from God just what you deserve because of your behavioral pattern? I do not think I would look forward to such treatment. And remember, your deeds reflect your relationship with God. Your deeds reflect your spiritual condition.

However, if you have accepted Christ as your Savior, your sin is covered by His blood and you will not receive such punishment. Christ has already paid the price that we would have to pay if our sins were not covered. Because of what Christ has done, God does not see the sins of believers and they will not be punished.

There are many people who find it difficult to accept the **doctrine of grace.** These people find it very difficult to understand how they can simply receive salvation as a gift from God, that there is not anything they have to do to earn it. In fact, many people do not want that kind of salvation because they want to prove how good they are and how much better they are than other people. This attitude of course is not in accordance with the teaching of the Holy Scripture, the Word of God. We all have the opportunity to receive that salvation as a free gift from Him *if* we will accept it. God does not want us to try to be better than others. He wants us to serve others and to humble ourselves before Him (Micah 6:8). That humbling factor is a requirement because without humility you cannot admit that you are a sinner in need of a Savior.

> *God says:*
> *Don't try to be better than others.*
> *Do serve others and*
> *Humble yourself before God.*

Revelation 2:24-25:

'But I say to you, the rest who are in Thyatira, who do not hold this teaching, who have not known the deep things of Satan, as they call them—I place no other burden on you. [25] *'Nevertheless what you have, hold fast until I come.'*

There were people in this church who, in spite of the heavy influence to be tolerant of the openly sinful practices of other members, remained faithful and obedient to the commands and the will of God. God will reward and bless those people and in these verses He is giving due recognition to such faithfulness. In verse 25 Jesus is telling the people that are subjected to the evil going on in this church that they are going to have to hold on for dear life. They are going to have to hold on to their faith and not be misled by the false teaching that is being allowed and accepted by the leadership of this church. They need to hang on even though the influence is powerful. Such faithfulness will be rewarded.

Many faithful followers will leave a church when they detect false teaching beginning to creep in and there is certainly a sound scriptural basis for doing so if, and only if, the other members of the church do not respond to attempts to have them repent, and if being in the clear majority they prevent any carrying out of church discipline.[80] But one should take this matter to prayer before making a decision. Christ may want true believers to remain in the church if there is a way to bring those who have gone astray back into the fold. Whatever false teaching was going on at that time, however, there were churches then which, like the church of

---

80   See Ephesians 5:7-21; 1 Corinthians 5:9-13.

Thyatira, had some believers who held fast to the truth of the teaching of the Bible.[81]

Verse 25 also gives us a hint of the Rapture of the Church: "*hold fast until I come.*" The Rapture of course is when Jesus removes all believers from the earth just before the final disasters fall on those who refuse to believe in Him as their Savior (1 Thessalonians 4:13-18).

Moving on to **Revelation 2:26-27,** we read:

To everyone who overcomes, who to the very end keeps on doing the things that please me, I will give power over the nations. [27] And he shall rule them with a rod of iron, as the vessels of the potter are broken to pieces, as I also have received authority from My Father.

Believers who obey are going to be given authority. They will reign with Christ in an earthly millennial kingdom.[82] We will learn a lot more about this millennial (thousand year) kingdom later in this study. This promise was originally made way back in Psalm 2 by God the Father to God the Son.

---

81 Walvoord, John F.; Zuck, Roy B.; Dallas Theological Seminary: *The Bible Knowledge Commentary: An Exposition of the Scriptures.* Wheaton, IL: Victor Books, 1983-c1985, S. 2:937.

82 For 1000 years.

Psalm 2:8-9:

[8] *Ask of me, and I will make the nations your heritage, and the ends of the earth your possession. [9] You shall break them with a rod of iron, and dash them in pieces like a potter's vessel.*

Jesus is saying that there is a time coming during the millennial kingdom when any wrongdoing will be dealt with severely. And we are going to be right there ruling with Him, protecting His people, protecting holiness and righteousness in the Kingdom.[83] The believers in Thyatira are promised authority over the nations which probably refer to the fact that God's people, will live and reign with Christ (see Revelation 20:4). When Jesus sets up His kingdom on earth, it will be a righteous kingdom with perfect justice. He will rule with a rod of iron (Psalm 2:8–9). Rebellious men will be like clay pots, easily broken to pieces by His swift judgment.[84] In some way, which we are not given any more details about, Jesus is going to give us authority to rule in the same way such authority was given to Him by His Father.

Revelation 2:28:

And I will give him the morning star.

---

83   Revelation 1:6; 3:21; 1 Corinthians 6:2.
84   Wiersbe, Warren W.: *The Bible Exposition Commentary*. Wheaton, Ill.: Victor Books, 1996, c1989, S. Revelation 2:18.

The morning star is Jesus.[85] The Sun is a star, and as it breaks upon the horizon in the morning it brings light to the darkness. Is that not what Christ brought to the world?

> "The identity of the star is settled when Christ says, *'I am the morning star'* (Revelation 22:16). It is another way of saying, *'I am the light of the world.'*[86] The central concept found in the symbol is that of Christ as light shining in darkness.[87] With the birth of the Messiah, the morning star arose—the gospel light dawned.[88] The phrase points to Christ's glory, as the source of light, and to His grace in the sharing of life. Christ not only described Himself as the morning star but also declared that He gives the morning star to those who overcome (Revelation 2:28)."[89]

When the world is in its darkest hour, Christ will appear in the dark sky in blazing glory and bring the light of His truth to the world. Those who overcome will in some way be given Jesus. We cannot know exactly what this means but possibly

---

85 Revelation 22:16; 2 Peter 1:19.

86 John 8:12; 9:5: 12:46.

87 Luke 2:32; John 1:4, 7–9; 3:19; 12:35; 2 Corinthians 4:6; Ephesians 5.:14; 1 Pt 2:9; 1 John 2:8; Revelation 21:23.

88 Isaiah 9:1–2; Matthew 4:15–16.

89 Elwell, Walter A; Comfort, Philip Wesley: *Tyndale Bible Dictionary.* Wheaton, Ill.: Tyndale House Publishers, 2001 (Tyndale Reference Library), S. 911.

it means we are going to be just like Him. We will not be God as He is, but our resurrected bodies may be perfect in every way just as His is, and we may be thereby capable of doing all the things He can do. Whatever it means, I bet it will be something we find out of this world.

Revelation 2:29:

'He who has an ear, let him hear what the Spirit says to the churches.'

We have seen this before and it means the same thing as it did before. *"You had better listen and pay attention;"* this message comes directly from Jesus. The conclusion of each of the letters to the churches calls everyone to listen and understand what the Spirit is saying to the churches. These letters are also directed to all churches and all people who live in the world today. Listen, because *this is the only way you can avoid eternity in Hell.* If you do not listen and repent, you are going to hate yourself in the morning.

REVELATION CHAPTER THREE

MESSAGES TO THE CHURCHES IN SARDIS, PHILADELPHIA, AND LAODICEA

The Letter to the Church at Sardis
(The dead church)

Revelation 3:1-6:

"To THE ANGEL of the church in Sardis write: He who has the seven Spirits of God and the seven stars, says this: 'I know your deeds, that you have a name that you are alive, but you are dead. [2] *'Wake up, and strengthen the things that remain, which were about to die; for I have not found your deeds completed in the sight of My God.* [3] *'So remember what you have received and*

heard; and keep it, and repent. Therefore if you do not wake up, I will come like a thief, and you will not know at what hour I will come to you. [4] *'But you have a few people in Sardis who have not soiled their garments; and they will walk with Me in white, for they are worthy.* [5] *'He who overcomes will thus be clothed in white garments; and I will not erase his name from the book of life, and I will confess his name before My Father and before His angels.* [6] *'He who has an ear, let him hear what the Spirit says to the churches.'*

The Holy Spirit is described here as the seven Spirits of God. We have seen before that this does not mean there are seven spirits, but rather refers to the perfection of the Holy Spirit,

> "One unique aspect of the portrayal of the Holy Spirit in the book of Revelation is the reference to the 'seven spirits of God' (Revelation 1:4; 3:1; 4:5; 5:6). Since John referred to the Spirit in the singular elsewhere in Revelation 1:10; 2:7, 11, 17, 29; 3:6, 13, 22; 4:2; 17:3; 21:10, there is no reason to think that he held to a plurality of Spirits. The seven spirits are mentioned in relation to the seven stars (3:1), the seven lamps (4:5), and the seven horns and seven eyes (5:6). It is therefore probable that the number seven is representative of perfection, and the 'sevenfold Spirit' at Revelation 1:4; 3:1; 4:5; and 5:6 is an acceptable interpretation. The connection of the number seven with the Spirit may also be referring to Isaiah 11:2,

where the Spirit is described in terms of attributes: 'The Spirit of the Lord will rest on him [Jesus]—the Spirit of wisdom and of understanding, the Spirit of counsel and of power, the Spirit of knowledge and of the fear of the Lord.' These attributes (beginning with the 'Spirit of the Lord') add up to seven."[1]

Why do you suppose Jesus introduces Himself this way, as the sevenfold Spirit? I believe what He is saying here is that the One (Jesus) who writes this letter is the One who ministers in His Church through the Holy Spirit who guides and directs faithful pastors and elders. If anyone in the church is teaching false doctrine it is the pastor's and the elder's responsibility. If it has been going on for some time, those in the church who are faithful should begin the steps involved in church disciplinary procedure beginning with the pastor.[2]

Why would Jesus begin the letter to Sardis like this? Probably as a reminder of what they had given up. A dead church would not have the benefit of the living power of the Holy Spirit, nor would it have leaders who were godly and who made evident the life and power of God, both of which were absent in the church at Sardis. *The Holy Spirit is the key to living the Christian life.* If believers are faithful to Jesus, He

1   Zuck, Roy B.: *A Biblical Theology of the New Testament. Electronic ed.* Chicago: Moody Press, 1994; Published in electronic form by Logos Research Systems, 1996, S. 202.

2   Matthew 18:15-17 (See p. 78, top).

will give us life and give it abundantly[3] (John 10:10). Ignore Him and our lives will be as dead as those who lay in the vast cemetery marked by hundreds of burial mounds, some seven miles from Sardis, but visible from that city.[4]

This is a very important point. No matter what a church does outwardly, if they do not have godly leaders who are led by the power of the Spirit, they are *dead*. Unfortunately many churches today are going through all the motions but they are not following or submitting to the guidance of the Holy Spirit.

As in Revelation 1:20, the seven stars, representing the pastors of the churches, were also held in the hands of Jesus through the Holy Spirit. Christ was holding seven stars in His right hand and walking among the seven golden lampstands. The "stars" were the angels or messengers of the churches and the "lampstands" were the seven churches.[5]

---

3   In large quantities.

4   Richards, Larry: *The Bible Reader's Companion*. Wheaton, Ill.: Victor Books, 1991, S. 910.

5   The pastor or messenger of the church was addressed as the angel (*angelos*). The word's principal use in the Bible is in reference to heavenly angels (William F. Arndt and F. Wilbur Gingrich, *A Greek-English Lexicon of the New Testament*. Chicago: University of Chicago Press, 1957, pp. 7-8). But it is also used to refer to human messengers (cf. Matthew 11:10; Mark 1:2; Luke 7:24, 27; 9:52). John Walvoord and Roy Zuck, ed., *The Bible Knowledge Commentary: An Exposition*

There is really nothing that Jesus can commend this church for, so He jumps right into the condemnation. This church was contaminated by the world. Like so many churches today it was basically populated by unsaved people playing church. They did have, however, a superficial (without depth of character) reputation as a church even though they were dead.

Some people think they can play church and have a church without the basic truths of the Gospel. The Gospel says that Christ is God and He became man and came to earth so that we could receive salvation. He atoned[6] for our sins on the cross. He was resurrected and overcame the grave. He rose from the dead so that we might do the same. Without that kind of faith the Holy Spirit could not be the guiding force in that church and thus the designation, *dead.*

Revelation 3:2:

'Wake up, and strengthen the things that remain, which were about to die; for I have not found your deeds completed in the sight of My God.'

---

of the Scriptures by Dallas Seminary Faculty, (Colorado Springs, CO: Cook Communications, 1985), WORD*search* CROSS e-book, 933.

6   Atonement, the means by which the guilt-punishment chain produced by violation of God's will is broken, aswell as the resulting state of reconciliation ('at-onement') with God. *Harper's Bible Dictionary.*

The first thing this church has to do is "*strengthen the things that remain*" before they lose everything else. Strengthen the foundation before the building falls down. In the past their behavior fell far short of Jesus' expectations in the areas of love, faithfulness, perseverance, and commitment.[7] Christ tells them that their behavior is not acceptable. The things that they are doing to try to demonstrate their goodness and holiness are not acceptable to Christ. Those deeds are not sufficient to gain Christ's approval. That is not the way to receive salvation. Jesus is telling them that their deeds may be acceptable to the people around them who see them as good-hearted, beneficial, and kind, but they are not acceptable to Christ. These people are therefore living a lie.

Did you ever talk to someone who said something like, "Oh, a loving God would never send anyone to Hell. I'm really a pretty good person. I do some nice things for people. I give to the Salvation Army. I go to church a couple of times a month. I put some money in the offering plate regularly. I believe that God will recognize that." There are a lot of people who feel that way.

What are these people doing? Again, they are living a lie and it is not going to get them anywhere, except maybe into Hell.

---

7   Richards, Larry: *The Bible Reader's Companion*. Wheaton, Ill.: Victor Books, 1991, S. 910.

Revelation 3:3:

'So remember what you have received and heard; and keep it, and repent. Therefore if you do not wake up, I will come like a thief, and you will not know at what hour I will come to you.

Christ is warning here of a sudden judgment if Sardis does not repent. We are going to come back to this verse a little later on.

Revelation 3:4:

'But you have a few people in Sardis who have not soiled their garments; and they will walk with Me in white, for they are worthy.

Because some people in the church of Sardis refused to deny Christ and follow the false teachers from their church, Christ will replace their human garments with those that are divinely pure. The white robes Jesus is speaking of stand for holiness and purity. He is going to give them perfect holiness and perfect purity in the future. They will walk with Christ throughout eternity because they are worthy, not in the same sense as God and Christ (Revelation 4:11; 5:9), but in the sense that they will be sinless.[8] Jesus died to make them sinless before God and now they are being rewarded.

Let us take a closer look at the command in this letter. Christ is telling them that if they want the church to survive,

---

8   Robertson, A.T.: *Word Pictures in the New Testament.* Oak Harbor, 1997, S. Revelation 3:4.

this is how they can go about it. So this letter gives a blueprint for revival. Jesus is telling them that in order to revive a dead church, action has to be taken by the remnant of believers that remain in that church. What follows are steps that need to be taken: Verse two tells them to **(1)** *"Wake up!"* They are told that they cannot be indifferent any longer to what is going on in their church. This is a call to reverse the current attitude of indifference. They appear to be asleep. So Jesus tells them to "Wake up!" If a church is to have renewal, people must realistically assess what is happening and get involved. This is probably one of those churches where 20% of the people do 80% of the work.

Next, Jesus goes on to tell them to **(2)***strengthen those things that remain* which are almost dead. There are still a few people in this church who are living according to the will of God. So lock onto the spiritual values of those true believers and build on them.

Jesus then tells them to **(3)***remember what they received and heard.* They are to go back to the Bible, back to the truth of the Word they once believed and followed. He is telling them to rebuild the church on a foundation of sound doctrine and cast aside the man-made doctrine that has taken over their church. Then they are told to **(4)***obey* that Word and not to be distracted by the world. Finally, they are to **(5)***repent!* Repent means to turn away from what you have been doing with remorse and sorrow.

These five steps are essential for revitalizing a dead or dying church, and that is exactly what Jesus is calling them to do.

Francis Schaeffer studied the decline of Western civilization, and he came to the conclusion that **secular humanism** is responsible for our problems because **secular humanists believe the individuals have the right to choose what is best for themselves** regarding such things as abortion, homosexuality, prisoners' rights, socialism, world government, and **they all deny the existence of God**. *Every communist and every socialist is a secular humanist,* and although every humanist is not a communist or socialist, every communist or socialist is a secular humanist.

"The beliefs of secular humanism were all written into the second *Humanist Manifesto* where **eleven concepts** were presented that changed the world. *Humanist Manifesto II* proclaimed that secular humanists:

1. **"Reject traditional religious beliefs, and seek new human purposes and goals.** Humanists proclaim there is *no divine purpose for the human species... No deity will save us; we must save ourselves."*

2. **Reject as both illusory and harmful the "promises of immortal salvation or fear of eternal damnation"** which are the basis of both Judaic and Christian beliefs.

3. **Believe that moral values derive from human experience.** Ethics are "autonomous and situational,"

and that we should "strive for the good life, here and now." Thus humanists believe that individuals determine what is right and wrong.

4. **Believe that *reason and intelligence* will guide mankind to a better world.**

5. **Stress individual freedom without moral restraints.**

6. **Recognize"...*the right to birth control, abortion, and divorce*," and that"...*the many varieties of sexual exploration should not in themselves be considered evil.*"** Thus humanists condone homosexuality and other forms of sexual perversion.

7. **Support concepts of individual freedom** such as 'an individual's right *to die with dignity, euthanasia, and the right to suicide.*'

8. **Advocate democracy and participatory democracy rather than a republican form of government.**

9. **Advocate the separation of church and state and the separation of ideology and state.** This program was designed to remove both God and prayer from public schools.

10. **Alternative advocate economic systems and the need to democratize the economy.** Humanists promote socialism.

11. **Advocate the "elimination of all discrimination based upon race, religion, sex, age, or national origin," and "the right to universal education."** They

also oppose sexism or sexual chauvinism [prejudice].[9] This requires government control over every aspect of our lives."[10]

There are several others, but I think you are pretty much getting the drift of what secular humanism is all about. Most of the concepts that the secular humanists are trying to convince the world to buy into are advocated in the *"Humanist Manifestos I and II,"* have been implemented, and their plan to introduce socialism, create a world government, and undermine the Judeo-Christian beliefs of our nation and our world are well on the way to completion.[11]

---

9   Brackets mine.
10   Op. Cit., Pike, *Morals and Dogma*, 51. Bold face type is from Pike; normal type are comments on the items listed.
11   Secular Humanism—Excluding God from Schools & Society. Secular Humanism is an attempt to function as a civilized society with the exclusion of God and His moral principles. During the last several decades, Humanists have been very successful in promoting their beliefs. John J. Dunphy, in his award winning essay, *The Humanist* (1983), illustrates this strategic focus, "The battle for humankind's future must be waged and won in the public school classroom by teachers who correctly perceive their role as the proselytizers of a new faith: A religion of humanity—utilizing a classroom instead of a pulpit to carry humanist values into wherever they teach. The classroom must and will become an arena of conflict between the old and the new— the rotting corpse of Christianity, together with its adjacent evils and

Revelation 3:5-6:

'He who overcomes will thus be clothed in white garments; and I will not erase his name from the book of life, and I will confess his name before My Father and before His angels. ⁶ 'He who has an ear, let him hear what the Spirit says to the churches.'

Those who remain faithful shall be *dressed in white*, a sign of triumph and victory. This could well have reference to the spiritual bodies believers will be given in Heaven according to <u>2 Corinthians 5:1-5</u>.[12] *"For we know that when this earthly tent we live in is taken down (that is, when we die and leave this earthly body), we will have a house in heaven, an eternal body made for us by God himself and not by human hands. ² We grow weary in our present bodies, and we long to put on our heavenly bodies like new clothing. ³ For we will put on heavenly bodies; we will not be spirits without bodies. ⁴ While we live in these earthly bodies, we groan and sigh, but it's not that we want to die and get rid of these bodies that clothe us. Rather, we want to put on our new bodies so that these dying bodies will be swallowed up by life.*

---

misery, and the new faith of humanism." Is this what's happening? John Dewey, remembered for his efforts in establishing America's current educational systems, was one of the chief signers of the 1933 *Humanist Manifesto*. It seems the Humanists have been interested in America's education system for nearly a century. They have been absolutely successful in teaching children that God is imaginary and contrary to "science." Copyright © 2002–2015 Secular-Humanism.com

12   Op. Cit., Robertson, Revelation 3:5.

⁵ *God himself has prepared us for this, and as a guarantee he has given us his Holy Spirit.*"

Believers are assured of everlasting life in Heaven and in addition they will receive special rewards when they get there. For the true believers, whose faith has overcome the world, they are going to experience perfect holiness. Someday they will be clothed in the brilliance of eternal purity and holiness. We see here these recurring promises of eternal blessing and salvation for all those who believe.

What is the *"Book of Life?"* *"Book of Life"* in the book of Revelation refers to a heavenly record with the names of Christians who remain faithful. It is used first in the letter to Sardis (Revelation 3:5) where Jesus, identified as *"the Lamb"* is keeper of the book. If a person's name is found in the book, admittance is granted to the New Jerusalem (20:15; 21:27). If one's name is not written there, the judgment is final destruction. Absolute confidence in God's care for His own is affirmed by the words *"written before the foundation of the world"* (13:8; 17:8).[13] You see if a person is a true believer, they will remain faithful. The Holy Spirit will not allow them to fall away. If a person believes they are a Christian but do not believe that faith in Christ as their Savior is their only ticket to Heaven, then they are not truly saved and will not, because

---

13   Elwell, Walter A.; Comfort, Philip Wesley: *Tyndale Bible Dictionary.* Wheaton, Ill.: Tyndale House Publishers, 2001 (Tyndale Reference Library), S. 233.

they cannot, remain faithful without the power of the Holy Spirit to help them. Do those verses validate the Doctrine of Predestination? I do not believe so, but that is the subject for a separate study.

When some people read this verse they also ask, "Does this mean that Jesus might erase my name from the Book of Life?" Of course not, that is not what this verse is suggesting at all. The verse says, "I will not." What do you suppose makes someone think He might when Christ just said He will not? Romans 8:26-39 makes it very clear that He will not. There is no way that a Christian can lose his/her salvation once he or she has it. It is just not going to happen if their salvation is for real.

The Letter to the Church in Philadelphia (The Obedient Church)

Revelation 3:7-13:

"And to the angel of the church in Philadelphia write: He who is holy, who is true, who has the key of David, who opens and no one will shut, and who shuts and no one opens, says this: [8] *'I know your deeds. Behold, I have put before you an open door which no one can shut, because you have a little power, and have kept My word, and have not denied My name.* [9] *'Behold, I will cause those of the synagogue of Satan, who say that they are Jews and are not, but lie—I will make them come and bow down at your feet, and make them know that I have loved you.* [10] *'Because you have kept the word of My*

*perseverance, I also will keep you from the hour of testing, that hour
which is about to come upon the whole world, to test those who dwell
on the earth.*[11] *'I am coming quickly; hold fast what you have, so
that no one will take your crown.* [12] *'He who overcomes, I will make
him a pillar in the temple of My God, and he will not go out from
it anymore; and I will write on him the name of My God, and the
name of the city of My God, the new Jerusalem, which comes down
out of heaven from My God, and My new name.* [13] *'He who has an
ear, let him hear what the Spirit says to the churches.'"*

The city was named for a king of Pergamum, *Attalus
Philadelphus*, who had built it. *"Philadelphus"* is similar to
the Greek word *philadelphia*, meaning *"brotherly love."*[14] That
term is used several times in the Scripture.[15] Philadelphia is
a missionary church. It is a church that is faithful. This is
a letter that is written to a church that needs no warnings,
chastening, or threatening. This church was faithful, godly,
loyal, and effective.

---

14 Walvoord, John F.; Zuck, Roy B.; Dallas Theological Seminary: *The
Bible Knowledge Commentary: An Exposition of the Scriptures.* Wheaton,
IL: Victor Books, 1983-c1985, S. 2:939.

15 Romans 12:10; 1 Thessalonians 4:9; Hebrews 13:1; 1 Peter 1:22; 2
Peter 1:7[twice]; Revelation 3:7.

Revelation 3:7:

"And to the angel of the church in Philadelphia write: He who is holy, who is true, who has the key of David, who opens and no one will shut, and who shuts and no one opens, says this."

God is holy! What does that mean? He is totally and completely isolated from sin, which makes Him totally unlike us. God cannot even look upon sin. He cannot stand sin in His presence. That is why someone had to pay a price to cover our sin. Our sin was bought by the blood of a perfect sinless sacrifice in order to make us acceptable before God. God was willing to take the form of the man, Jesus, come to earth and be that sinless perfect sacrifice for us. The shed blood of Jesus is the only thing that will get us into Heaven. Through that blood we who believe in Him have no sin, which gives us a free pass to receive a new sinless body with which we are allowed to enter Heaven.

Without Jesus paying the price for our sin, no one could enter Heaven because there can be no sin in Heaven where God lives. Let us take this even a step further. God is holy and so is Jesus holy. Holy is also a common title for Jesus. We see it in Mark 1:24, Luke 1:35, John 6:69, and Acts 3:14. In Revelation 3:7 Jesus is identifying Himself as the Holy One; He is identifying Himself as God. The Lord Jesus shares the holy, sinless, and pure nature of God. Jesus is God. He is the Holy One and because He is holy He also cannot tolerate sin. He also identifies Himself in this verse as the One who is true. In the original Greek we find the word, "*alethinos*" meaning *"very God,"* as distinguished from the false gods and from all those who say that they are what they are not. Jesus is real and genuine. Furthermore, He is the visual example of who God is and all that is meant in the names of God: Jesus is *Light,* John 1:9 (NLT):*"The one who is the true light, who gives light to everyone, was coming into the world."* Jesus is Bread and Jesus said, *"I tell you the truth, Moses didn't give you bread from heaven. My Father did. And now he offers you the true bread from heaven* (John 6:32 NLT). Jesus is the Vine, John 15:1 (NLT): *I am the true grapevine, and my Father is the gardener.*

1 John 2:8 (NLT):

Yet it is also new. Jesus lived the truth of this commandment, and you also are living it. For the darkness is disappearing, and the true light is already shining.

In the midst of a world where so much is false, perverted, and filled with error, Jesus is the one source of truth. He is truth in all that He says and all that He does. He alone can be completely trusted.[16] This holy and true God looks at this church at Philadelphia and He can only compliment them. He is telling this church that He is absolutely holy and can only speak what is true; and that His perfect holiness

---

16   John 1:9; 1John 2:8; John 6:32; John 15:1; John 17:3; 1Thessalonians 1:9.

and truth has examined them and finds there is absolutely nothing to criticize.

Jesus is further described in verse seven as One who has the key of David. A key is a very simple symbol in Scripture. Whenever you see a key you can equate it with authority. Whoever has the key has control and this term, *"The key of David,"* is a direct reference back to Isaiah 22:22: *"Then I will set the key of the house of David on his shoulder, when he opens no one will shut, when he shuts no one will open."*

This verse is speaking about Eliakim, the son of Hilkah. At the time, Hezekiah was king and he had a treasure house. Eliakim was given the key to that royal treasury. This royal treasury was the treasury of David, which began with David's reign as the first king of the royal line of Israel, and the accumulated treasury of David (1011 B.C.–970 B.C.) kept growing until the time of Hezekiah 726 B.C.–698 B.C. when it was loaded with incredible riches.[17]

Eliakim had the key which meant that he had the authority or control over the treasury. He could open its riches and he could lock them up. The one who possessed *the key of David* had control over the royal treasury. Now **David is the type for Christ**. David was the supreme ruler of the Kingdom of Israel and Jesus is the supreme ruler of the kingdom of Heaven. This is not always an easy concept to understand so

---

17   Wiersbe, Warren W.: *The Bible Exposition Commentary*. Wheaton, Ill.: Victor Books, 1996, c1989, S. Re 3:7.

let us spend just a few minutes on this. We will start with a definition of the word.

Type properly means a *"model"* or *"pattern"* or *"mold"* into which clay or wax was pressed, that it might take the figure or exact shape of the mold. The word *"type"* is generally used to denote a resemblance between something present and something future, which is called the ***antitype***.[18] The reference to David is often used in Scripture when the writer is pointing to Christ. This is undoubtedly to tell the reader in general terms what the coming Messiah, Christ, would be like. For example, Jeremiah 30:9 NLT: *For my people will serve the Lord their God and their king descended from David—the king I will raise up for them.*

Ezekiel 37:24 NLT: *"My servant David will be their king, and they will have only one shepherd. They will obey my regulations and be careful to keep my decrees."* The house of David is the typical designation of the kingdom of Jesus Christ and we read in Psalm 122:5: *"Here stand the thrones where judgment is given, the thrones of the dynasty of David."* The holding of the keys, the symbols of power, thus belong to Christ as Lord of the kingdom and Church of God.[19] Here Jesus is telling us that He is the One who has the key of David, He is the One who can open the treasure house and pour out on us royal

---

18 *Easton's Bible dictionary.*

19 Vincent, Marvin Richardson: *Word Studies in the New Testament.* Bellingham, WA: 2002, S. 2:464.

riches. Jesus has the key to all the riches in this world and in Heaven. He will give those riches only to those who deserve them.[20]

Jesus Christ alone has the authority to open the door for people to get into the kingdom. Jesus is of course referring here to salvation. We saw in Revelation 1:18 that Jesus had the keys to Hell and death, and here He has the key to salvation and blessing. He can send people to Hell or he can open the door and send them to Heaven. That, after all, is why Jesus came. So that He could open the treasure house and let us in.

Jesus is describing Himself as the One who opens and no one will shut, and the One who shuts and no one can open. That simply means that whatever He does, that is it. If He opens the door of the kingdom to someone, then no one can shut it. If He shuts it, there is not anyone else who has the authority to open it. Without Christ you cannot have salvation. No one else can provide it and we certainly cannot earn it on our own. I believe this description could also imply that there are doors that can be opened which provide opportunities for service and evangelism. In fact, in Revelation 3:8, Jesus states that: "*I have put before you an open door which no one can shut.* "The bottom line, however, of verse 7 is that Christ is sovereign. Whatever He does and whatever He decides is the final word. No one can stand against Him.

---

20   Luke 1:32-33.

Revelation 3:8:

I know your deeds. Behold, I have put before you an open door which no one can shut, because you have a little power, and have kept My word, and have not denied My name.

In Scripture an *"open door"* describes an opportunity for ministry.[21] Jesus is opening up opportunities for them to serve and to take the Gospel message of salvation to those who may not have heard it. Jesus is saying to them, "I have examined you thoroughly and cannot find even a single flaw. You are doing everything the way I want it done."

Jesus also determines where His chosen servants will serve (Acts 16:6–10). This church had a vision to reach a lost world, and God provided them with an open door. Jesus says there are several things which characterize this church First, He says they *"have a little power."* Christ opens the door for ministry to this small church because they only have a little power. Would it not make more sense to open the door to ministry for a church that had a whole lot of power? That is exactly the point here. Jesus opens up the door of opportunity for ministry and evangelism to the church at Philadelphia because she has only a *"little strength."* Such a church is fit for such service. Look at 2 Corinthians 12 where Paul had been asking Jesus to remove the thorn from his flesh. Jesus said to him: *"My grace is all you need. My power works best in*

---

21   Acts 14:27; 1 Cor. 16:9; 2 Corinthians 2:12; Colossians 4:3.

weakness.' So now I am glad to boast about my weaknesses, so that the power of Christ can work through me" (2 Corinthians 12:9).

Being a small church with just a little power allows for God's power to be all the more evident. For God to do great works of evangelism[22] through this little church all the more points to the real power which is Christ, so that He may receive all the glory. Jesus is telling them they are not very big but they have power. Spiritual power was flowing in this church. Lives were being transformed and people were being changed. That is what happens in a church that commits itself to teaching the truth of Christ. Kind of reminds you of the slogan of Village Church of Wheaton,[23] *"The little church with a big message."*

Secondly, it was characterized by obedience, doing what God says we should do. Jesus says that they "have kept My Word." They were committed to the truth of the Bible. They did not deviate from a pattern of obedience. They did what they were expected to do. Look at John 14:23: *"Jesus answered and said to him, 'If anyone loves Me, he will keep My word; and My Father will love him, and We will come to him and make Our abode with him.'"*

These people obeyed Jesus just like believers are supposed to obey. Third, not only did they have power and obedience,

---

22 Evangelism—Active calling of people to respond to the message of grace and commit oneself to God in Jesus Christ.

23 Wheaton, Illinois.

but they also had loyalty. Jesus says in verse eight that they *"have not denied"* His name. This church was probably under some kind of pressure, perhaps even persecution from **"the synagogue of Satan"** (verse 9). That would have been a local Jewish synagogue and they probably would have been mercilessly attacking the faith of this little church, trying to get them to deny that Jesus is the Messiah. But whatever the persecution was like, this church did not deny Jesus' name. So this church had only a little power but a lot of obedience, loyalty, and endurance.

They have kept Jesus' command to endure patiently. They took the bad times, trials, difficulties, and still remained faithful. In effect Jesus is telling them they have done things the way He did things (Philippians 2:5-8). That is the way Jesus lived His life. He had patience and obedience in His relationship with His Father in all things. Jesus is telling this church, *"Well done! You have done it the way that I did it."* And Jesus continued being obedient to God until they killed Him.

2 Thessalonians 3:5 (NLT):

May the Lord lead your hearts into a full understanding and expression of the love of God and the patient endurance that comes from Christ.

Matthew 10:2 (NLT):

And all nations will hate you because you are my followers. But everyone who endures to the end will be saved.

Here we have a little church that had nothing wrong with it; nothing scandalous, nothing devastating. They were obedient, loyal, and had endurance. Because of this Jesus promises them that they have a place in His kingdom, eternal security, and no one can take those things away from them. As mentioned earlier, this verse also implies that Jesus is giving them serving opportunities and evangelistic opportunities. Jesus is going to use them as His representatives to bring salvation to the lost. And this has to be absolutely the greatest thrill that the members of any church could have.

This open door referred to in verse 8 might also mean that they have an open door to the treasure house where they can collect all the blessings that are available to them in Christ as Paul points out in Ephesians 1:3 (NLT): *All praise to God, the Father of our Lord Jesus Christ, who has blessed us with every spiritual blessing in the heavenly realms because we are united with Christ.*

Do you know there are far too many pastors in this country that can go for a year or more and never see a single new person come to know Christ as their Savior? There are probably some churches that have not seen anyone come to Christ for years, and the reason for this is that Jesus is not opening any doors for them. But when He sees a church that is loyal, obedient, and enduring, the first thing you see God do for a church like that is open the door of opportunity for evangelism. An open door, by the way, was an image the apostle Paul used a lot, and he used it when he wanted to talk about freedom for proclaiming the Gospel. In 1 Corinthians 16:9 (NLT) Paul writes:*"There is a wide-open door for a great work here, although many oppose me."* Then in 2 Corinthians 2:12 (NLT): *"When I came to the city of Troas to preach the Good News of Christ, the Lord opened a door of opportunity for me."* Finally in *Colossians 4:2-3 (*NLT*):* *"Devote yourselves to prayer with an alert mind and a thankful heart. [3] Pray for us, too, that God will give us many opportunities to speak about his mysterious plan concerning Christ. That is why I am here in chains."*

The key in verse seven opens a lot of things. It opens the kingdom; it opens the treasure house; and it opens the opportunity for ministry. If Jesus Christ gave them an open door, then He would see to it that they were able to walk through it. There is also another promise that has to be related to the opportunity for evangelism, and we find that in the next verse.

Revelation 3:9:

'Behold, I will cause those of the synagogue of Satan, who say that they are Jews and are not, but lie—I will make them come and bow down at your feet, and make them know that I have loved you.'

"Behold" in modern-day English could probably be translated, *"Wow, can you believe this?"* The Jewish synagogue here is a synagogue of Satan. They do not worship God there, but rather they worship Satan. They do not know that they worship Satan, but they do. They claim they are true Jews but they are not; they lie. They claim to be true Jews, sons of Abraham and sons of God. Genetically they are Jewish, legally Jewish, ceremonially Jewish, but spiritually they are not Jewish. Scripture says that he is a Jew who is one inwardly. Circumcision is that which is of the heart, not the flesh, Romans 2:28-29 (NLT): *"For you are not a true Jew just because you were born of Jewish parents or because you have gone through the ceremony of circumcision. ²⁹No, a true Jew is one whose heart is right with God. And true circumcision is not merely obeying the letter of the law; rather, it is a change of heart produced by God's Spirit. And a person with a changed heart seeks praise from God, not from people."*

Whatever is blocking our heart from accepting Jesus as Savior must be removed. This church at Philadelphia was being persecuted by this hostile group of Jews who hated them for teaching that Jesus is the Messiah, because, you may remember, the Jews had demanded Jesus' death. Jesus says that He is going to take this synagogue of Satan and have them bow down before this little church. Bowing down at someone's feet was the ancient posture of being a humbled, defeated enemy. Isaiah 60:14 (NLT): *The descendants of your tormentors will come and bow before you. Those who despised you will kiss your feet. They will call you the City of the Lord, and Zion of the Holy One of Israel.*

Isaiah is saying that the day is coming when the Millennium begins when a remnant (one-third) of the Jews who will survive through the Tribulation will rule over the entire world. The whole world will bow down to the Jews that have accepted Christ as their Savior during the Tribulation.

Christ could also be saying in verse 9 that the Jews in this synagogue of Satan may well get saved in this little church. Imagine that! Just think about the very likely meaning here. Christ may use a faithful church to bring nonbelievers in any apostate church (a church that has abandoned its faith in God) to salvation. That would include all kinds of churches and religions. God is promising that He will bring nonbelievers to salvation through Philadelphia type churches. Maybe it is time for your church to take an honest inventory as to whether or not you qualify to be a Philadelphia church, and if not, why not?

There is a future day coming when the whole nation of Israel is going to bow down before Christ, Romans 11:26 (NLT): *"And so all Israel will be saved. As the Scriptures say, 'The one who rescues will come from Jerusalem, and he will turn Israel away from ungodliness.'"*

Throughout Church history Jews have been converted. They too have become equal members in the Church of Christ by declaring their faith in Him. Those churches that are faithful like the church at Philadelphia are the ones Jesus gives an open door to, causing Jews to be attracted to them. The promise to Philadelphia involves much more than the promise Christ made to Smyrna. To Smyrna the promise was that "the synagogue of Satan" would not be able to get the best of them. But the promise to Philadelphia is that she will get the best of the synagogue of Satan; that she will win over some of their members. Now there is one more promise in this letter and it is significant.

Revelation 3:10:

Because you have kept the word of My perseverance, I also will keep you from the hour of testing, that hour which is about to come upon the whole world, to test those who dwell on the earth.

Christ is saying that because they have endured suffering and have not wavered, and in the midst of suffering they have not denied Jesus' name and have kept His Word, because of that Christ will keep them from the hour of testing that is about to come on the whole world. Some, in fact a great many, commentators believe this means that because they have successfully passed all their tests to try their faith, they are going to be spared the future test of the Tribulation.

So the Pre-Tribulation Rapture folks believe that obedient and faithful Christians throughout history are going to escape a final hour of testing. Now just what is it that a test provides? Well, it exposes something, does it not? It reveals what you know and it reveals your character. It reveals how you are doing. It also exposes you for what you are. The believers in the Philadelphia church had apparently already gone through some manner of testing to prove their faith in Jesus and were promised they would not have to be exposed to a time of testing that others would have to go through. I have concluded that this verse is impossible to interpret with one-hundred percent accuracy. It could mean any number of different things, so for now I am going to give you two interpretations and you can select the one you like best. I do believe, however, that there are other verses that give us better evidence of when the Rapture will occur.

Here is the first interpretation:

> "The church in Philadelphia received no rebuke from Christ. Instead they were commended and given a promise because they had been willing to endure patiently. The promise was, I will also keep you from the hour of trial that is going to come upon the whole world to test those who live on the earth. This is an explicit promise that the Philadelphia church will not endure the hour of trial which is unfolded, beginning in Revelation 6. Christ was saying that the Philadelphia church would not enter the future time of trouble; He could not have stated it more explicitly. If Christ had meant to say that they would be preserved through a time of trouble, or would be taken out from within the Tribulation, a different verb and a different preposition would have been required. Though scholars have attempted to avoid this conclusion in

order to affirm posttribulationism, the combination of the verb "keep" (terein) with the preposition *'from'* (ek) is in sharp contrast to the meaning of keeping the church "through" (dia), a preposition which is not used here. The expression "the hour of trial" (a time period) makes it clear that they would be kept out of that period. It is difficult to see how Christ could have made this promise to this local church if it were God's intention for the entire church to go through the Tribulation that will come on the entire world. If the church here is taken to be typical of the body of Christ standing true to the faith, the promise seems to go beyond the Philadelphia church to all those who are believers in Christ (cf. Walvoord, Revelation, pp. 86-8)."[24]

Here is the second interpretation:

"The believers had endured patiently, as Christ had commanded, so Christ promised to keep them from the hour of trial that would come upon the whole world to test those who live on the earth. Some believe that the phrase *'I will also keep you from the hour of trial'* means there will be a future time of great tribulation from which true believers will be spared.

24 John Walvoord and Roy Zuck, ed., *The Bible Knowledge Commentary: An Exposition of the Scriptures by Dallas Seminary Faculty*, (Colorado Springs, CO: Cook Communications, 1985), WORD*search*CROSSe-book, 939.

This is a key verse for those who subscribe to the *pre-Tribulation-Rapture* theory—that believers will be kept from the hour of trial because they will not be on the earth during that time of great tribulation. Christians will have been taken to heaven in what is called the **'Rapture'**[25]. Others believe that the verse refers to times of great distress in general, the church's suffering through the ages. Others interpret *'keep from'* to mean that the church will go through the time of tribulation and that God will keep them strong during it, providing spiritual protection from the forces of evil (7:3). The verb 'keep from' is the same Greek verb in the Lord's prayer ('Deliver us from the evil one,' Matthew 6:13 nlt). As Jesus said before his death, "I'm not asking you to take them out of the world, but to keep them safe from the evil one" (John 17:15 nlt)…

"This *'hour of trial'* is also described as the *Great Tribulation or Day of the Lord*, mentioned also in Daniel 12:2; Mark 13:19; and 2 Thessalonians 2:1-12. All the judgments recorded in the remainder of the book of Revelation take place during this time of tribulation. While believers may have to face difficulty and suffering, they will certainly be protected from God's wrath and judgment."[26]

---

25   1 Corinthians 15:51-53; 1 Thessalonians 4:15-17

26   Bruce B. Barton et al., *Life Application Bible Commentary – Revelation*, (Wheaton, IL: Tyndale, 2000), WORD*search*CROSSe-book, 43-44.

You might also want to consider Revelation 6:10, where we find the saints who have been murdered for the cause of Christ. They are under the altar crying out. *And they cried out with a loud voice, saying, "How long, O Lord, holy and true, will You refrain from judging and avenging our blood on those who dwell on the earth?"* (Revelation 6:10). Revelation 11:10 describes the two witnesses that are preaching the Word of God and are murdered, and their bodies are left to lie in the street, which makes some people very happy. *"And those who dwell on the earth will rejoice over them and celebrate; and they will send gifts to one another, because these two prophets tormented those who dwell on the earth".*

Here we find people who were tormented by the preaching of the Gospel to the degree that they celebrated and had a party when these witnesses were killed. You will find the same description in Revelation 13:8, 12, 14; 14:6; 17:2, 8. *"Those who dwell on the earth"* becomes a technical term for those whose names are not written in the book of life, those who have rejected the gospel message of Jesus Christ.

The loyal, faithful servants are going to be spared from that time. The translation of the Greek word *"from"* in Revelation 3:10 can also be translated *"out of."* Then we have 1 Thessalonians 1:9-10 where Paul is telling the Thessalonians that Jesus will deliver us from the wrath to come: *"For they themselves report about us what kind of a reception we had with you, and how you turned to God from idols to serve a living and true God, [10] and to wait for His Son from heaven, whom He raised from the dead, that is Jesus, who rescues us from the wrath to come."* The Bible further tells us in 1 Thessalonians 5:9: *"For God has not destined us for wrath, but for obtaining salvation through our Lord Jesus Christ."* If any of you can find evidence that will explain Revelation 3:10 to me without a shadow of doubt, please let me know because I have just not been able to do it, and I have given it my best!

At this point you may want to review the section on the Rapture in the "Background Information" at the beginning of this book. It discusses what the Rapture is and looks at the various theories about when it might occur.

At the time of the Rapture all saved people will be taken from the earth leaving only unsaved people, those that rejected Christ. Sometime during the period of time after the Rapture and up until the time of the Second Coming of Jesus some nonbelievers will change their mind, repent, and accept Jesus Christ as their Savior. Many of these will undoubtedly lose their lives during the latter part of the Tribulation, but will be taken immediately to Heaven upon their death. Many others will continue to reject Christ and fight against His people. Many of them will be killed and immediately go to Hell.

Revelation 3:11:

"I am coming soon. Continue strong in your faith so no one will take away your crown."

"*I am coming soon,*" means that it is soon from God's perspective. It does not seem that it could mean soon to us because after all it has been two thousand years since this was written. But a thousand years is like a day to the Lord, "*But do not let this one fact escape your notice, beloved, that with the Lord one day is like a thousand years, and a thousand years like one day*" (2 Peter 3:8).So it is soon to Jesus. He says He is coming and that all He describes in this book of Revelation is going to take place. Just before He comes all the way back to earth, He will appear in the heavens for the Rapture of the Church, all living or dead who accepted Christ as their Lord and Savior, to remove them from the hour of testing. To the church this statement, "*I am coming,*" is not a threat, but rather a cause for celebration because it is a coming to deliver the Church. It is the promise of a hopeful event as Paul begins to describe in 2 Thessalonians 2:1 (NLT): "*Now, dear brothers and sisters, let us clarify some things about the coming of our Lord Jesus Christ and how we will be gathered to meet him.*"

Then we see a command given in Revelation 3:11: "*Hold fast*" or "*continue strong.*" This means to hold on, be faithful, persevere, and endure. This is the perseverance of the saints. Only saints who are faithful to the end are saved. Now at this point someone may want to jump to their feet and say, "*Wait a minute, I thought it was the eternal power of God that secures us.*" Well, that is true, we are secure in that power. But do you know how He secures us? He secures us by giving us a persevering faith. Our security comes in the form of an undying faith. That is why John writes in 1 John 2:10: "*The one who loves his brother abides in the Light and there is no cause for stumbling in him.*"

You see the people in the Philadelphia church would have taken the persecution, they would have endured the difficulty, because true Christians are granted eternal security by God as the result of a faith that never ceases. Jesus calls us to keep on persevering in order to maintain that salvation and He provides the true believer with Holy Spirit power to ensure that we are able to remain faithful. It can be said no more clearly than it is in Colossians 1:22, 23: "*yet He has now reconciled you in His fleshly body through death, in order to present you before Him holy and blameless and beyond reproach— if indeed you continue in the faith firmly established and steadfast, and not moved away from the hope of the gospel that you have heard, which was proclaimed in all creation under heaven, and of which I, Paul, was made a minister.*"

Some may feel that Paul's statement to the Colossians raises some doubt about the assurance of our salvation. Is it possible for a believer to lose his salvation? No. The "*If*" clause does not suggest doubt or lay down a condition by which we *"keep up our salvation."* You will find in the next two paragraphs a complete explanation of the original Greek text of this verse. You may study it carefully or simply accept the fact that neither Colossians 1:23 nor Revelation 3:11 in any way suggest that there is even a slight possibility that a Christian can lose his/her salvation.

"The word *'if'* here is not *ean* (ἐαν), but *ei* (εἰ), having here the idea of *'assuming that you continue in the faith.'* This means that if a person continues to live to the best of their ability according to the Gospel as it was preached by Paul, such behavior would show that the person was saved and thus they would be presented holy and sinless before God. That is, Paul was here addressing truly born-again Colossians, not unsaved professors of Christianity who would follow the Colossian heresy. It is not being able to hold onto salvation that Paul has in mind, but whether or not a person was truly saved. If they were truly saved that would be demonstrated by their continuance to live in accordance with the gospel message. This is directed against the false teacher's claim that living according to the Gospel message they heard was not enough to receive salvation, and that they needed to do more.[27]

If you have accepted Jesus Christ as your personal Savior, knowing that He died on the cross to pay for your sins, then you should be absolutely certain that you are saved and that the Holy Spirit will never let you fall away. Paul himself had assured the Romans and all Christians that when they received Christ there is absolutely nothing that can separate them from the love of Christ (Romans 8:38-39).

---

27 Wuest, Kenneth S.: *Wuest's Word Studies from the Greek New Testament: For the English Reader.* Grand Rapids: Eerdmans, 1997, c1984, S. Col 1:21.

So read Colossians 1:22-23 above again and then read here as it could be translated literally from the original Greek text: *"Jesus has brought you back into relationship with God through the death of His physical body. You are now holy and totally cleansed of your sin. Assuming that you continue living by the faith you have in Jesus, a faith that is built on an immovable rock solid foundation, you will be able, as such a building is able, to remain immovable no matter how terrible the storms that come at it. You, like the building, are firmly established in your faith and will not be shifted away. You are secure on your foundation of faith in Jesus Christ and by the Gospel message He taught, which was proclaimed in all creation, which is under heaven, of which I, Paul, became one who ministers."*[28]

Paul creates a picture in this verse of a house supported firmly by a solid foundation. The town of Colossae was located in a region known for earthquakes, and the word translated *"moved away"* can mean *"earthquake stricken."* Paul was saying that if you are truly saved, and built on the solid foundation of Jesus Christ, then you will continue in the faith and nothing will move you. If you have heard the Gospel, trusted Jesus Christ, and He has saved you, He will never let you go.

Some of you might say, *"Well, I know someone who believed for a while and they don't believe any more."* That is because they were not really ever truly saved. Because those God saves He keeps, nothing or no one is able to remove them from that

---

28   Ibid.

position of eternal security. Look at John 6:39 (NLT): *"And this is the will of God, that I should not lose even one of all those he has given me, but that I should raise them up at the last day."*

<u>1 John 2:3-6 (NLT)</u>:

And we can be sure that we know him if we obey his command-ments.⁴ If someone claims, "I know God," but doesn't obey God's commandments, that person is a liar and is not living in the truth.⁵ But those who obey God's word truly show how completely they love him. That is how we know we are living in him.⁶ Those who say they live in God should live their lives as Jesus did.

Christ keeps them, not against their will, but He keeps them by His Holy Spirit filling them with the power to hold tightly to their faith no matter what the circumstances. He tells them to *"hang on"* with a persevering faith. Why? Again <u>Revelation 3:11</u>: *"Hold on to what you have, so that no one will take away your crown."*²⁹Let us just for a moment go back to Revelation 2:10 to review what we were told there: *"Don't be afraid of what you are about to suffer. The devil will throw some of you into prison to test you. You will suffer for ten days. But if*

---

29 The crown was a symbol of victory and reward among the Romans and Greeks (*Easton's Bible Dictionary*).The translation for several Hebrew and Greek words designating special headpieces worn in biblical times. Among all items of apparel, a person's headgear was perhaps most significant in designating social, religious, and/or political status. Having to do with achieving the highest possible ranking, prize.

you remain faithful even when facing death, I will give you the crown of life. (NLT)

In Greek that means the crow*n "which is life." The crown is eternal life.*[30] James helps clarify this for us in James 1:12 (NLT): *"God blesses those who patiently endure testing and temptation. Afterward they will receive the crown of life that God has promised to those who love him."*

THE CROWN OF ONE'S FAITH IS ETERNAL LIFE.
FAITH = CROWN = ETERNAL LIFE.
THAT IS THE REWARD.

2 Timothy 4:8 (NLT):

And now the prize awaits me—the crown of righteousness, which the Lord, the righteous Judge, will give me on the day of his return. And the prize is not just for me but for all who eagerly look forward to his appearing.

The crown
is
Eternal Life!

We will be given the best life possible when we reach our heavenly home, our eternal life will be perfectly righteous and perfectly satisfying. *"And when the Great Shepherd appears, you will receive a crown of never-ending glory and honor"* (1 Peter

---

30   Op. cit, Wuest

5:4 NLT). Our eternal glory, our eternal righteousness is all wrapped up in our **eternal life; that is our crown.**

Revelation 3:12:

"He who overcomes, I will make him a pillar in the temple of My God, and he will not go out from it anymore; and I will write on him the name of My God, and the name of the city of My God, the new Jerusalem, which comes down out of heaven from My God, and My new name."

In other words, everyone who believes that Christ has paid for their sins by His death on the cross is going to be made a permanent pillar in the house of God, which of course is Heaven. What does He mean by a pillar? He means you will have an eternal place of honor, stability, permanence, and security. What a wonderful promise.

"I will write on him the name of my God." This should give everyone goose bumps. This means that we belong to God and we are His very own possessions. That is why God wants to write His name on us. He wants us to know we have security forever in Heaven and a personal relationship with Him. We belong to God in a special way. Just as the name of Jehovah (*"Holiness to the Lord"*) was on the golden plate on the high priest's forehead (Exodus 28:36-38), so the saints in their heavenly royal priesthood shall bear His name openly.[31]

---

31 Jamieson, Robert; Fausset, A. R.; Brown, David: *A Commentary, Critical and Explanatory, on the Old and New Testaments.* Oak Harbor,

Let us look at some more verses to get a better feel for what this means. Revelation 7:3: *"Wait! Don't harm the land or the sea or the trees until we have placed the seal of God on the foreheads of his servants."* Revelation 9:4: *"They were told not to harm the grass or plants or trees, but only the people who did not have the seal of God on their foreheads."* Revelation 14:1: *"Then I saw the Lamb standing on Mount Zion, and with him were 144,000 who had his name and his Father's name written on their foreheads."* Revelation 22:4: *"And they will see his face, and his name will be written on their foreheads."*

Revelation 3:12:

"And the name of the city of my God, the New Jerusalem, which comes down out of Heaven from my God."

This means we have eternal citizenship in the capitol city of Heaven, which is the **New Jerusalem.** This is just another reinforcement of our safety, security, and glory. We will get to this later but Revelation 21:2 says: *"And I saw the holy city, new Jerusalem, coming down out of heaven from God, made ready as a bride adorned for her husband."* Then He goes on to describe this incredible city beginning in 21:10 and continuing through the end of the chapter.

Finally, we will get His new name. We will get Christ's new name. What does that mean? The new name of Christ will be *"All that He is."* We know Christ, but we only know

WA: 1997, S. Re 3:12.

what we have read and felt. We have not yet seen Him. The moment we see Him His countenance will take on utterly new dimensions. Whatever we may have called Him and understood by the name we have called Him will be replaced by the reality of what we see, and there will be a new name to describe Him, and He will give us that new name and we will be privileged to call Him by it. We will be able to see Him with the eyes of a redeemed body.

Revelation 3:13:

He who has an ear, let him hear what the Spirit says to the churches.

Do you see the power that is revealed in all of these letters thus far? These letters alone should win over an unfaithful church, as well as those individuals in a church who are unfaithful. If nothing else, these letters should frighten people into seeking after the truth that Jesus offers. The letters to the faithful churches should draw those from the unfaithful churches by the unequaled promises given them.

The Letter to the Church in Laodicea
(the lukewarm church)

We now come to the last of the letters to the seven churches and we find that this is the church that made Jesus sick. We see an unsaved church. In fact, if there were any believers in this church they are not referred to in the letter at all. *"Lukewarm"* here is a metaphor for unsaved people. Laodicea has the grim distinction of being the only church about which Christ has nothing good to say. It is total condemnation. Consequently they get the most severe criticism.

Revelation 3:14:

"To the angel of the church in Laodicea write: The Amen, the faithful and true Witness, the Beginning of the creation of God, says this:"

The Lord identifies Himself here with 3 titles: 1) The Amen. 2) The Faithful and True Witness. 3) The Beginning of the Creation of God. Let us first look at the title, *"The Amen,"* which means truth or certainty. Whatever God says is true and certain, and all of God's promises are certain and sure because of the work of Jesus. Jesus Christ is God's Amen, the One who confirmed all the promises God had made in the Old Testament.

Then He identifies Himself as *"The Faithful and True Witness."* Not only is Jesus by His work, the Amen, but every time He speaks we can know He is telling the truth. He is completely reliable. This is a good way to begin this letter because it makes clear to the people in Laodicea that Jesus knows what He is talking about. Whatever evaluation He makes of their church is absolutely accurate.

The third thing He says about Himself is that He is "The Beginning of the Creation of God." What He means by this is that He is the source of creation. He is the power by which creation began. This letter to Laodicea has much in common with Paul's letter to the church at Colossae. These cities were located very close together. Apparently there was a heresy in Colossae about Jesus, and that heresy said that He was a created being and not at all God. It is very possible that same heresy had reached Laodicea. When Jesus says here that He is "the beginning of the creation of God," He is saying basically the same thing that Paul said in Colossians 1:15-16:[32] *"He is the image of the invisible God, the firstborn of all creation. For all things were created, in the heavens and on earth, visible and invisible, whether thrones or dominions or rulers or authorities— all things have been created through Him and for Him."*

Jesus is the head of everything including the Church. Apparently there was some question about the validity of such a statement because obviously Jesus was a man. He had been born as a part of the creation, but although He was born as a man He always existed as God; and while as a man He had a beginning, as God He was the beginning. It is quite possible that the reason the church in Laodicea is unsaved is because they had a false doctrine regarding who and what Jesus was. What Jesus is saying to them in this letter is that they must understand who He is. He is the One who has confirmed all the promises and covenants of God; the One who speaks truth and nothing but the truth, to borrow a court oath, and He is the beginning of the creation.

---

32   Also see: John 1:3; 1 Corinthians 8:6; Hebrews 1:2.

Before going any further I want to mention some things about the city of Laodicea that will be important in this letter. First, the inhabitants of Laodicea had to bring water into the city by aqueduct and this water was often contaminated. Laodicea was also an extremely wealthy city and a banking center. Further it was the production center for black wool and eye salve. All three of these industries play a major part in this letter and so does the water supply.

Revelation 3:15-16:

"I know your works: you are neither cold nor hot. Would that you were either cold or hot! [16]*So, because you are lukewarm, and neither hot nor cold, I will spit you out of my mouth."*

Deeds (works) always reveal who and what a person is.

Romans 2:5-10 (NIV):

But because of your stubbornness and your unrepentant heart, you are storing up wrath against yourself for the day of God's wrath, when his righteous judgment will be revealed. [6] *God "will repay each person according to what they have done."* [7] *To those who by persistence in doing good seek glory, honor and immortality, he will give eternal life.* [8] *But for those who are self-seeking and who reject the truth and follow evil, there will be wrath and anger.* [9] *There will be trouble and distress for every human being who does evil: first for the Jew, then for the Gentile;* [10] *but glory, honor and peace for everyone who does good: first for the Jew, then for the Gentile.*

Paul makes it as clear as possible that God will judge you according to your deeds. You may say, 'Wait a minute, I thought we were saved by grace and faith" That is right, we are, but whether we are saved or not shows up in our deeds. So God says, "Because I know your deeds I therefore know your heart. I can see who you are by what you do." That is a very important statement with sweeping implications in the New Testament. A person who is a Christ followermakes it evident by their behavior. A person who is not a Christian also makes that evident by their behavior, even if they may consider themselves to be Christian.

We see in verse 16, the most serious criticism found in any of the letters: *"I will spit (vomit) you out of my mouth because you are lukewarm."* In the Christian life, there are three *"spiritual temperatures":* a heart that is on fire for God (Luke 24:32), a cold heart (Matthew 24:12), and a lukewarm heart (Revelation 3:16). The lukewarm person is rather pleased with himself or herself and does not realize his or her need. This criticism of being *"lukewarm"* takes us back to our comments about the water supply. Six miles to the north, in Hierapolis, there were some famous hot springs. People would go to these hot springs because of the healing and soothing effect of the hot water. In Colossae, ten miles south and east, there was a cold stream. The stream was always flowing with cold water which is typical of water flowing from the mountains. That kind of water is thirst quenching.

Laodicea did not have the hot, healing water of Hierapolis, nor did they have the cold, refreshing water of Colosse because by the time they piped water from either source down to their city it had become foul, tepid water that flowed for miles through underground aqueducts. It was not hot and it was not cold. This lukewarm water was absolutely useless and any visitor who came there and was not used to this stuff would put it in their mouth and immediately spit it out. One historian says that the water supply of Laodicea was derived from an artificial pipeline, bringing water which was literally lukewarm and so impure as to have an emetic (an agent that causes vomiting) effect. What is the spiritual significance of all of this? Simply that the Laodicean church made Christ vomit. **It was a sickening church.** Some churches make Jesus weep, some make Him angry, and this one made Him sick.

What do these three categories mean? What does cold mean? That is not too tough. The meaning here suggests outright rejection of Jesus Christ and His message. Jesus says they are not cold. Now there are many in the world that are cold toward Christ and His message. The Gospel is meaningless to them. They do not even want to hear anyone talk about it. They are lost, they are in the dark and they could care less.

Now, what does hot mean? It means being on fire for Christ. They are not that either. You can tell a believer by how they respond to the Word of God. They show a lot of emotion when they read it, hear it, or speak about it. If Jesus were to use the slang of today, He might say something like: *"I could take it if you were like the hot water of Heropolis because then you would be for real. I could even take it if you were like the cold water of Colosse; that is better than being the foul water of Laodicea, lukewarm."* Most were pretending to be Christians and going to church but they were not saved. They were content with self-righteous religion. They were hypocrites playing games. They were like the people described in Matthew 7:22 and 23 where Jesus says: *"Many will say to Me on that day, 'Lord, Lord, did we not prophesy in Your name, and in Your name cast out demons, and in Your name perform many miracles?'* [23] *"And then I will declare to them, 'I never knew you; DEPART FROM ME, YOU WHO PRACTICE LAWLESSNESS.'*

They are like the people described in in 2 Timothy 3:1-5 (NIV): *"But mark this: There will be terrible times in the last days.* [2] *People will be lovers of themselves, lovers of money, boastful, proud, abusive, disobedient to their parents, ungrateful, unholy,* [3] *without love, unforgiving, slanderous, without self-control, brutal, not lovers of the good,* [4] *treacherous, rash, conceited, lovers of pleasure rather than lovers of God—* [5] *having a form of godliness but denying its power. Have nothing to do with such people."*

They are nothing more than hypocrites touched in some way by Christianity but not belonging to Christ and they make Christ sick. There is no one further from the truth than a person who talks about having a relationship with God or

Christ without real faith. They are really in Satan's hands, and such false Christians are very difficult to help. People who are satisfied with their good works, satisfied with their attitude toward God, and satisfied that they attend church regularly are very difficult to convince that they are not truly saved. It would be easier to win over a prostitute, a criminal, an agnostic, or an atheist. Jesus said that it was easier to reach the Publicans and the harlots than it is the Pharisees and the Sadducees. There is more hope for the salvation of an atheist than a pompous, half-hearted, conceited hypocrite who thinks he knows the truth and yet has no clue of what the truth is other than his own preconceived[33] ideas. Like the Pharisees they do not feel the need for a Savior.

What do we see being taught in our universities today? What has the age group from 20 to 50 been fed for the last several decades? The answer is far left liberal beliefs that lack morality, self-denial, and self-discipline. The God that has so richly blessed the United States is ridiculed; there are attempts to remove faith symbols and observances from every aspect of its culture. Topics that decent people would not have even considered fifty years ago are today promoted, encouraged, and winked at. People doing such things would have been ridden out of town on a rail when I was growing up, and rightly so. Today, however, the system is blamed

---

33 Preconceived: To form (as an opinion) prior to actual knowledge or experience

for their behavior and they are afforded special treatment, consideration, and tolerance. We are talking about such practices such as loss of respect for human life (skyrocketing murder rate, sex trafficking, abortion, euthanasia), blatant rudeness and disrespect, rampant self-centeredness, sexual immorality of so many varieties that it takes too much space to list them all, loss of a sense of right and wrong, and a host of others. We can little afford for such things to continue because God is in the process, or possibly even has already withdrawn His hand of protection from the United States.

When a society reaches a point where they do not recognize **evil** for what it is, it is thereby no longer possible to recognize what is good. Where there is no concept of good or evil, there is no opportunity for hope. Chaos will result and the culture will have no direction. It will be everyone for themselves. Can you imagine what life would be like among a community of people living in such a manner? Your life and property would not be worth a plugged nickel, and your anxiety level would be off the chart.

The only answer for a country is to have enough faith in God that as Christian citizens we join together in prayer regularly (2 Chronicles7:14), and combine that prayer with: 1) A knowledge of God's will through reading His Word in the Bible daily. 2) A constant awareness of God throughout our day. That means 24/7. 3) Full obedience and submission to God's Word. Without these things there is nothing to strengthen or to provide the necessities any country requires to be free and prosperous. Calvin Coolidge was once quoted as saying, *"The strength of the United States* [or any country][34] *is the strength of its religious convictions."* He was so right.[35] I only hope we all wake up to this fact before it is too late.

I believe affluence can be a curse! When people were not quite so affluent, they seemed to be more appreciative of what little they had and were far less inclined to do anything and everything for the sake of money. The church at Laodicea is a sad reminder of many churches in the world throughout the history of the Christian era, and serves as an illustration of people who participate in outward religious worship without the inner commitment. How many people have gone along with the rituals of the church service without a true state of being born again into the family of God? How many church members are far from God, yet by their membership in the church have satisfied their own hearts and have been lulled into a sense of false security? Do you feel secure in your salvation? If you do, do you have the right reason for feeling that way? The quality of being **lukewarm** assumes the dimension of being utterly intolerable to God. This is what Christian churches are like throughout most of the world today. Listen to what God has to say to them:

---

34 Brackets added.
35 Citizen Link Website, *Focus on the Family*, November 8, 2007.

Revelation 3:17:

You say, 'I am rich; I have acquired wealth and do not need a thing.' But you do not realize that you are wretched, pitiful, poor, blind and naked.

It does not matter what you say, it is what you do. It is all about whether or not you do the will of God. So here we see the unsaved religionists who want to name the name of God and the name of Christ and show you everything they have done. Jesus says they are deceiving themselves when they say that they are rich and have become wealthy and have need of nothing. That kind of reminds me of the rich young ruler in Matthew.

Matthew 19:16-24 (NIV):

Just then a man came up to Jesus and asked, "Teacher, what good thing must I do to get eternal life?" [17] "Why do you ask me about what is good?" Jesus replied. "There is only One who is good. If you want to enter life, keep the commandments." [18] "Which ones?" he inquired. Jesus replied, "'You shall not murder, you shall not commit adultery, you shall not steal, you shall not give false testimony, [19] honor your father and mother,' and 'love your neighbor as yourself.'" [20] "All these I have kept," the young man said. "What do I still lack?" [21] Jesus answered, "If you want to be perfect, go, sell your possessions and give to the poor, and you will have treasure in heaven. Then come, follow me." [22] When the young man heard this, he went away sad, because he had great wealth. [23] Then Jesus said to his disciples, "Truly I tell you, it is hard for someone who is rich to enter the kingdom of heaven. [24] *Again I tell you, it is easier for a camel to go through the eye of a needle than for someone who is rich to enter the kingdom of God."*

This was a test of priorities for this man. Obviously, based on his decision, he demonstrated that his money was his god. He failed the test. Laodicea was a city of tremendous material wealth and it gave the people a sense of false security. They were famous for their wealth and apparently the church thought that it was wealthy too. That feeling of wealth apparently spilled over into the church giving them a false sense of spiritual wealth as well. Let me go a step further here. Most scholars think the heresy at the church of Colosse was a form of Gnosticism which means *"to know."* [36] In other words there were people there who believed they had found the ultimate spiritual truth. Christ was not enough for them; they believed they had gone beyond Christ. To them Christ was just a rung on the ladder on the way to the top. That is why Paul writes in

Colossians 2:1-8:

1 For I want you to know how great a struggle I have on your behalf, and for those who are at Laodicea, and for all those who have not personally seen my face, 2 that their hearts may be encouraged, having been knit together in love, and attaining to all the wealth

---

36   Wood, D. R. W.: *New Bible Dictionary.* InterVarsity Press, 1996, c1982, c1962, S. 417.

*that comes from the full assurance of understanding, resulting in a true knowledge of **God's mystery**,[37] that is, Christ Himself, 3 in whom are hidden all the treasures of wisdom and knowledge. 4 I say this in order that no one may delude you with persuasive argument. 5 For even though I am absent in body, nevertheless I am with you in spirit, rejoicing to see your good discipline and the stability of your faith in Christ. 6 As you therefore have received Christ Jesus the Lord, so walk in Him, 7 having been firmly rooted and now being built up in Him and established in your faith, just as you were instructed, and overflowing with gratitude. 8 See to it that no one takes you captive through philosophy and empty deception, according to the tradition of men, according to the elementary principles of the world, rather than according to Christ.*

Paul is saying: do not let anybody spoil you through philosophy and empty deceit into thinking that there is anything more elevated than Christ. That same heresy had most likely found its way into the Laodicean church. These people are saying, "We are the ascended ones." This is a familiar, typical, unsubstantiated line from people who consider themselves "open-minded" and "enlightened." They aim their cannons at people who believe the Bible means what it says and that it is God's Word to people and declare, "You mindless literalists,[38] all of you people who just

---

37 Emphasis added.

38 A term used to belittle individuals who follow the historical-grammatical method of biblical interpretation, the method used by

believe the simplicity of the Bible have no sophistication, no advanced education, you have not attained to the ascendant knowledge." They had spiritual pride, they were rich, they had become spiritually wealthy, they had attained the ascended knowledge, and they had gone beyond that simple belief about Christ that these uneducated Christians believed. They think they are spiritually rich and they have been able to do this completely by their own abilities.

They also feel they "have need of nothing." That is a self-righteous works system. "I've attained it all; I've reached the elevated level." These are the hardest people to reach with the truth of Christ; the self-appointed intellectual, the unsaved hypocrites, who stay in the church and pollute the purity of God's Word. Liberal churches flood the United States as well as the rest of the world. Churches that are full of people who think they have ascended beyond Christ. They do not see Christ as the Creator God, but rather have an infatuation with their own intellect and assume that they have been elevated beyond the simplicity of fundamental truth. They have developed a self-righteous works system that makes them think they are the cream of the crop spiritually and need absolutely nothing. When you come to them with the simple Gospel, they are amused. By the way these are the ones that are on the "broad road," in the words of Jesus.

---

those who also believe in biblical inerrancy (no mistakes in the Bible).

Matthew 7:13,14:

13 "Enter by the narrow gate; for the gate is wide, and the way is broad that leads to destruction, and many are those who enter by it. 14 "For the gate is small, and the way is narrow that leads to life, and few are those who find it.

It is a road of religion on which they have posted signs:

> **Heaven**
> Just around the Bend

But the road actually ends up in Hell. They are the ones that build their houses on sand, Matthew 7:24-27: *"Therefore everyone who hears these words of Mine, and acts upon them, may be compared to a wise man, who built his house upon the rock. 25 "And the rain descended, and the floods came, and the winds blew, and burst against that house; and yet it did not fall, for it had been founded upon the rock. 26 "And everyone who hears these words of Mine, and does not act upon them, will be like a foolish man, who built his house upon the sand. 27 "And the rain descended, and the floods came, and the winds blew, and burst against that house; and it fell, and great was its fall."*

So Jesus says to them in Revelation 3:17, "You say you have all this spiritual stuff and you don't know anything. The truth is you are wretched and miserable. Why? Because you are poor, and blind and naked." Here we see it clearly. The "lukewarm" condition is "lostness." It is the sickening condition of thinking you are spiritually rich when you are bankrupt; thinking you are beautiful when you are wretched; imagining that you should be envied when you actually need to be pitied; believing you see everything clearly when you see nothing. You are stone blind; feeling that you are clothed in spiritual finery, when in actuality you are stark naked. That is why Jesus tells them in Revelation 3:18: "*I advise you to buy from Me gold refined by fire, that you may become rich, and white garments, that you may clothe yourself, and that the shame of your nakedness may not be revealed; and eye salve to anoint your eyes, that you may see.*"

If we turn to <u>1 Peter 1:3-9</u> we might get a clearer understanding of what Jesus tells them they need. They need faith! "*Blessed be the God and Father of our Lord Jesus Christ, who according to His great mercy has caused us to be born again to a living hope through the resurrection of Jesus Christ from the dead, 4 to obtain an inheritance which is imperishable and undefiled and will not fade away, reserved in heaven for you, 5 who are protected by the power of God through faith for a salvation ready to be revealed in the last time. 6 In this you greatly rejoice, even though now for a little while, if necessary, you have been distressed by various trials, 7 so that the proof of your faith, being more precious than gold which is perishable, even though tested by fire, may be found to result in praise and glory and honor at the revelation of Jesus Christ; 8 and though you have not seen Him, you love Him, and though you do not see Him now, but believe in*"

Him, you greatly rejoice with joy inexpressible and full of glory, 9 obtaining as the outcome of your faith the salvation of your souls."

In Revelation 3:18 we see the industry of Laodicea coming into play. Jesus says, *"I advise you, I'm giving you some counsel."* Although He has already told these people that they make Him sick, His grace compels Him to give them an invitation. He could have turned them into ashes by the breath of His mouth but instead, once again, He shows how gracious He is. He says, *"You need to buy from me."* What does He mean "to buy?" It is the same kind of buy as in Isaiah 55:1: *"Ho! Everyone who thirsts, come to the waters; And you who have no money come, buy and eat. Come, buy wine and milk Without money and without cost."*

Some people would read this verse and say, *"I thought salvation was a free gift from God and here Jesus Himself says that we must in some way pay for it."* No, that is not what Jesus is saying at all. This is God's offer of mercy. It is the kind of thing you can buy when you do not have any money. In other words it is free for the taking. All you can offer in payment is your own wretched condition and that is payment enough for Jesus. **He will gladly exchange His righteousness for your shame.** Jesus is telling them to give Him their lives; that is the price; all that you are for all that He is.

What a bargain! For anyone willing to do that, Jesus will give them gold refined by fire that will make them rich. This is pure gold refined by fire, no impurities. They thought they were rich in spiritual truth. But in reality they were bankrupt.

Jesus tells them that He will give them spiritual gold and riches and that He will give them what is pure and valuable and priceless, which is a true and tested faith. Jesus is simply telling them to come to Him and He will give them the kind of true faith that will result in salvation. *"You lust and do not have; so you commit murder. You are envious and cannot obtain; so you fight and quarrel. You do not have because you do not ask"* (James 4:2).

The goods of Christ are freely given, yet they have their price—renunciation of self and of the world.[39] Then Jesus tells them to buy white garments, so that they may clothe themselves. Isaiah taught that God wants to clothe us with the robe of His righteousness.

Isaiah 61:10:

I will rejoice greatly in the LORD, my soul will exult in my God; for He has clothed me with garments of salvation, He has wrapped me with a robe of righteousness, as a bridegroom decks himself with a garland, and as a bride adorns herself with her jewels.

First Jesus tells them that He will give them saving faith and then He tells them He will give them righteousness. Next Jesus says: *"I want you to get some eye salve for your eyes so that you can really see."* The Laodiceans found this powder that when placed on the eyes had a very soothing, therapeutic, and

---

39   Vincent, Marvin Richardson: *Word Studies in the New Testament.* Bellingham, WA: 2002, S. 2:471.

medicinal effect. So what they would do is place this powder in some coarse dough and place that coarse dough in their eyes and somehow seal it so it could remain there for a period of time. Jesus is saying, in effect, *"You think that eye salve can make you see better, but in reality you do not see at all. But if you come to me I'll give you the ability to truly help you see."*[40]

Salvation is the gold that makes people spiritually rich in faith. Salvation is the white robe that covers our sinful nakedness. Salvation is the eye salve that gives us knowledge of God and of His truth. What exactly is it that Jesus is offering? He is offering everlasting faith, everlasting righteousness, everlasting understanding, and everlasting life. Jesus is saying, "you are poor, you are blind, and you are naked. Let Me fix that." All these things come together when a person repents and offers himself or herself to Jesus.

Revelation 3:19:

'Those whom I love, I reprove and discipline; be zealous [eager] *therefore, and repent.'*

In verse 19 we see a direct appeal; this tells us what our attitude is to be toward the apostate church. This is not an easy verse to interpret. Some people immediately think that Jesus must be talking to believers because He says, *"Those*

---

40   Jamieson, Robert; Fausset, A. R.;Brown, David: *A Commentary, Critical and Explanatory, on the Old and New Testaments.* Oak Harbor, WA: S. Re 3:18.

whom I love." That is not necessarily so. In fact the most referred to verse in Scripture, John 3:16, says: *"For God so loved the world.* "The context here in verse 18 indicates that these people needed the gold of true spiritual riches, the garment of true righteousness, and the sight of true spiritual understanding. That should make it pretty clear that these people are not saved.

Verse 20 tells us that Christ is still on the outside trying to get in. So we must assume here in verse 19 that these people are unbelievers. Jesus loves the world. So He says, *"Those whom I love, I reprove*[41] *and discipline."* He is telling us here that He loves unbelievers so much and wants them to repent and come to faith so they may become sons and daughters of the king.

The word *reprove* can also mean to *"convict"* or *"expose"* (Matthew 15:18; Ephesians 5:11). So God is saying that He loves the world enough to expose the sin of the world to sinners, and to make sinners feel guilt over their sin so that they might recognize the need for forgiveness for that sin. This is simply the nature of Jesus. God and Jesus love everyone and provide each person an opportunity to have their sin forgiven and have eternal life in Heaven if they are willing to come to Him for that forgiveness.[42]

---

41 Reprove:To scold or correct gently or with kindly intent; to express disapproval of *(MW Collegiate Dictionary).*

42 *HCSB Reverse Interlinear Bible.*

The word *"discipline"* is used also in Luke 23:16 and 22. There its usage means to punish and that is how it is translated. In 2 Timothy 2:25 it is used again as a form of punishment that is inflicted on unbelievers. It is translated, "correcting those who are in opposition," so that they may come to salvation. God will reprove, or treat with contempt, the unsaved. He will punish the unsaved even though He loves them. God gives everyone free-will to decide whether they will follow Him or not. It would not be possible for you to feel true love if the person giving the love did not have the opportunity to choose whether they would love you or not.[43]

Those He loves He will convict, expose to judgment, and punish. He is referring here not only to a convicting work that leads to salvation in some cases, but to an ultimate punishment that leads to damnation. He is saying, "Don't think that because I'm a loving God I'm not going to punish you; I will." God has no desire to do that; He has no pleasure in the death of the wicked (Ezekiel 18:23 and 32). So the meaning we should get here in these words is one of compassion, and that feeling carries on throughout this whole letter. God is showing His love for these people in an unsaved church.

In light of all this He says, *"Be zealous therefore, and repent."* There can be no salvation without repentance. If you are going to be zealous let it be in the pursuit of repentance. The offer of salvation always requires repentance. Repentance means that

---

43   Op. Cit., Jamieson

you realize you are guilty. You realize you are a hopeless sinner in the presence of God if you do not have Christ as a Savior. You realize that although God has affection for you and He loves you as He loves the whole world, you are on the brink of judgment. You realize the cause of this condition is your sin and that you alone cannot do anything about that. So you turn from it.

It is not always easy to do that but the message to the lukewarm, unsaved church is clear in commanding they be zealous and repent. There is an invitation here that indicates Jesus' attitude toward the apostate (abandonment of one's religious faith) church is not one of indifference. He is telling them that they are part of the world He loves, but they are also part of those He is going to send to Hell unless they repent. He extends a tender invitation in verse 20.

Revelation 3:20:

'Behold, I stand at the door and knock; if anyone hears My voice and opens the door, I will come in to him and will dine with him, and he with Me.'

There is yet another way we could interpret this verse. Perhaps Jesus is knocking at the door of His Church hoping to be let in. There are so many churches like this today all over the world, and Jesus is no longer welcome to enter them. To paraphrase Jesus I believe we could say something like this: "You are supposed to be a part of the body of the Church of Christ. Why do you refuse to let me in? I want you to repent, so open the door and let me in. Is there anyone here who will open the door?" You know it only takes one Christian to be in a church and Christ is there. Is it possible that there was not a single Christian in the Laodicean church? Can there be churches where not one single person is a real Christian? The answer to that is, yes. Just look around at the number of churches that are watering down the Bible, embracing all the immoralities of the culture and multiple ways of obtaining salvation. No true Christian could remain in such a church because these things are repulsive to God, and if you want to make God really angry teach that such things are okay to teach in His Church!

Do you belong to such a church? If you do, you have a difficult decision. You can kick the dust off your feet and go to a Bible-teaching church that emphasizes evangelism, or you can stay and challenge those who are corrupting those who do not know the truth that the Bible teaches. Perhaps there is a handful of people like you and you decide to mount a direct frontal attack on the pastor and leaders of the church. In such a case you will have opened the door and allowed Jesus to come in. He will stand beside you to purge the church of false teaching. However there may simply be too many people who have hardened their hearts against Jesus and refuse to repent. In the process, however, you will most likely be influential with some people who will see the truth, repent, and invite the real Jesus into their lives as Lord and Savior. I would not suggest you attempt indefinitely to continue trying to make others see the light. I would suggest perhaps a year would be enough time and if there can be no clear direction toward resolution I suggest your group shake the dust off your feet and go elsewhere or even plant a new church.

Matthew 10:14-15:

"Whoever does not receive you, nor heed your words, as you go out of that house or that city, shake the dust off your feet. [15] Truly I say to you, it will be more tolerable for the land of Sodom and Gomorrah in the day of judgment than for that city."

Do not be silent in the face of false doctrine. If just one person stands up to resist false teaching, then Christ will be in the church. When He says He will dine with him that is just another way of saying He will have fellowship with them. A shared meal in ancient times was a symbol of fellowship.

Then the final promise in **Revelation 3:21:**

'He who overcomes, I will grant to him to sit down with Me on My throne, as I also overcame and sat down with My Father on His throne.'

Again paraphrasing what Jesus is saying in more contemporary language might sound something like this: *"If you'll let me in I'll not only have fellowship with you now, and at the marriage supper, and in the Kingdom, and throughout eternity, but here's another thing: I'll grant you a place with me on my throne as I also overcame and sat down with my Father on His throne."* How could anyone in their right mind refuse such an offer? Jesus does not just say that He will let us into Heaven and allow us to enjoy its benefits. He says, *"I'll take you to the throne and that's where you will sit."*

Jesus is going to lift up believers and place them on His throne and His throne is the same as the Father's throne. What does He mean by that? Is He just talking about a literal seat where we are all going to be piled up? No, He is saying, *"You're going to judge the world, you're going to sit with me and have authority, and rule and reign."* We are going to sit on that throne as kings and priests (Revelation 1:6). What a tremendous promise. This is without doubt the most incredible promise imaginable. You and I, worthless sinners before God on this earth, will sit with Christ on His throne which is also the Father's throne in Heaven. Absolutely unbelievable! When God says He will exalt[44] you that is exactly what He means.

Revelation 3:22:

"He who has an ear, let him hear what the Spirit says to the churches."

Who would not want to listen to this? If they do, Christ will fellowship with them and identify Himself with them and take them to His Father's throne. The day will come,

---

44 Exalt: To enhance the status of; *synonyms* dignify, distinguish, ennoble, erect, glorify, honor, magnify, boost, build up, elevate, lift, promote, raise, upgrade, uplift; enhance; extol, laud, praise (*MW Collegiate Dict.; MW Collegiate Thesaurus*).

however, when this opportunity no longer exists. He (Jesus) will return in power and glory, leading the armies of Heaven, no longer awaiting the decisions of men. But then by His own power and majesty He will take control, judging those who did not invite Him to come in.

We have seen seven churches described in this last book of the Bible. Fast forwarding to our day all seven of these churches are represented in our current churches and each possesses its own challenge. There are pure churches like Smyrna and Philadelphia, there are also churches like Ephesus that have left their first love and need to return to it. There are modern day churches like Pergamos that have tolerated sin and refuse to deal with it. Such churches are beginning to become more and more numerous in our present culture. These churches simply do not want to deal with sin.

Then there are churches like Thyatira that are in full blown compromise with the world. There are churches like Sardis that are mostly dead and have only a few believers left. Then there are the apostate (false) churches. But in every case Christ says to them with all their defects, "Please Repent! Please take the steps necessary to make things right." This is the capacity Jesus has for love, continually calling His Church to purity and holiness, and that should be our challenge as well.

How can we reach those who think they are saved but are not? How can we reach those who are not saved and do not believe the Bible? The best way to help all of these people is to pray for them. Pray, pray, pray, and pray some more; unceasingly, fervently, and from our hearts ("P-U-S-H, **pray u**ntil **s**omething **h**appens"⁴⁵). Pray for God to place them in situations which can draw them to His truth, and pray for the Holy Spirit to draw them and for them to respond in a positive way.

There are other ways that God may use you to bring others to the point of salvation, but the best way to insure they are brought to that place is to pray. Pray when you are alone and pray in groups with fellow believers.

So ends God's admonitions to the Church, as expressed to the seven churches in Asia. From your Box Seat you have seen the opening of the Book of Revelation. You have been introduced to the Prologue and have been given a foundation for understanding many of the key concepts and doctrines. You have seen an overview of the history of the land of Israel.

In the coming volumes you are yet to find out what transpires during the final days of earth's history. Volume 2 will first give you a glimpse into the throne room of God and introduce you to the only being that can open the scroll sealed with seven seals. Then it will also go into detail about what will occur as each of those seals is opened. You don't want to miss it! See you in Volume 2: *Tribulation Begins.*

—Ron Teed

---

45   Theme of a sermon preached by Rev. Emmanuel Ala-adjetey of Ghana while visiting in the United States.

BIBLIOGRAPHY

6,000 Plus Illustrations for Communicating Biblical Truths, (Omaha, Nebraska: Christianity Today, 1997), WORD*search* CROSS e-book.

Achtemeier, Paul J. *Harper's Bible Dictionary, 1ˢᵗ ed.* Harper & Row, Publishers; Society of Biblical Literature: San Francisco: Harper & Row, 1985, S. 864.

Allen, James. *What the Bible Teaches: Revelation.* Kilmarnock, Scotland: John Ritchie Ltd., 1997, 424.

The Apocalypse [reprint]., Grand Rapids: Kregel, 1987.

Austel, Hermann J. "Zechariah," in *Baker Commentary on the Bible,* Walter A. Elwell (Ed.). Grand Rapids, MI: Baker Books, 1989, WORD*search* CROSS e-book, 700

Baker Commentary on the Bible

Barclay M. Newman. *A Concise Greek-English Dictionary of the New Testament,* (Stuttgart: German Bible Society, 1993), WORD*search* CROSS e-book, 76.

Barnes, Albert. *Barnes' Notes on the New Testament*

Barnes, Albert. *Notes on the New Testament Explanatory and Practical.* WORD*search* CROSS e-book, Under: "Revelation of John 8".

Barnes, Albert. *Barnes' Notes on the New Testament;* Revelation 1:13.

Barton, Bruce B. et al. *Life Application Bible Commentary—Revelation.* Wheaton, IL: Tyndale, 2000), WORD*search* CROSS e-book.

Betts, T. J. and Chad Brand, Charles Draper, Archie England, eds. *Holman Illustrated Bible Dictionary*, (Nashville: Holman Bible Publishers, 2003), s.v. "," WORD*search* CROSS e-book.

Boa, Kenneth and William Kruidenier. "Romans 11:1-36– Israel's Future Vindicates the Gospel," in *Holman New Testament Commentary—Romans.* Max Anders (Ed.) Nashville, TN: Broadman & Holman, 2000. WORD*search* CROSS e-book.

Boice, James Montgomery, (Ed.). *An Expositional Commentary—The Minor Prophets, Volume 2: Micah-Malachi.* Grand Rapids, MI: Baker Books, 2002. WORD*search* CROSS e-book.

Brand, Chad, Draper, Charles & England, Archie (Eds.). *Holman Illustrated Bible Dictionary*, (Nashville: Holman Bible Publishers, 2003), s.v. WORD*search* CROSS e-book.

Bruce, Barton B. et al. *Life Application New Testament Commentary.* Wheaton, IL: Tyndale House, 2001. WORDsearch CROSS e-book.

Bullinger, E.W. (1837-1913). *"The Sixth Vision On Earth,"* in *Commentary on Revelation.* Chicago: F.H. Revell, 1909; repr. Grand Rapids, MI: Christian Classics Ethereal Library, 2003. WORD*search* CROSS e-book.

Butler, Trent C., (Ed.) "Tribulation," in *Holman Bible Dictionary.* Nashville, TN: Holman Bible Publishers, 1991. WORD*search* CROSS e-book.

Carson, D. A. *New Bible Commentary: 21st Century Edition.* 4th ed. Leicester, England; Downers Grove, Ill., USA: Inter-Varsity Press, 1994.

Clarke, Adam. *A Commentary and Critical Notes.* New York: Abingdon-Cokesbury Press, 1826. WORD*search* CROSS e-book.

Cole, R. Dennis. *New American Commentary—Volume 3b: Numbers.* Nashville, TN: Broadman & Holman, 2000. WORD*search* CROSS e-book.

Comfort, Philip and Walter A. Elwell. *The Complete Book of Who's Who in the Bible.* Wheaton, IL: Tyndale House Publishers, 2004. WORD*search* CROSS e-book.

Comfort, Philip W. *Cornerstone Biblical Commentary—Volume 11: Matthew and Mark.* Carol Stream, IL: Tyndale House, 2005. WORD*search* CROSS e-book.

Dake, Finis Jennings. *"Temples in History and Prophecy, Five"* in *Dake's Topical Index,* WORDsearch CROSS e-book.

Dake, Finis Jennings. *Dake's Annotated Reference Bible*: Containing the Old and New Testaments of the Authorized or King James Version. WORDsearch CROSS e-book.

Easley, Kendell. "Revelation 17–Earth's Last Great City" in *Holman New Testament Commentary—Revelation*, Max Anders (Ed.) Nashville, TN: Broadman & Holman, 1998. WORD*search* CROSS e-book.

Easton, George. "Prince," in *Illustrated Bible Dictionary: And Treasury of Biblical History, Biography, Geography, Doctrine, and Literature*. London: T. Nelson and Sons, 1897. WORD*search* CROSS e-book.

Easton, M.G. *Easton's Bible Dictionary*. Oak Harbor, WA: 1996, c1897.

Easton, M.G., M.A., D.D. *Illustrated Bible Dictionary And Treasury of Biblical History, Biography, Geography, Doctrine, and Literature*. T. Nelson and Sons, London, Edinburgh and New York.

Easton, Matthew George. "Knop," in *Illustrated Bible Dictionary: And Treasury of Biblical History, Biography, Geography, Doctrine, and Literature*. London: T. Nelson and Sons, 1897. WORD*search* CROSS e-book.

Easy-to-Read Commentary Series—Daniel: In God I Trust. Holiday, FL: Green Key Books, 2004. WORD*search* CROSS e-book.

Easy-to-Read Commentary Series—Revelation: Tribulation and Triumph. Holiday, FL: Green Key Books, 2004. WORD*search* CROSS e-book.

Easy-to-Read Commentary Series—The General Epistles: A Practical Faith. Holiday, FL: Green Key Books, 2004. WORD *search* CROSS e-book.

Elwell, Walter (Ed.). *Baker Commentary on the Bible.* Grand Rapids, MI: Baker Books.

Elwell, Walter A. and Philip W. Comfort. *Tyndale Bible Dictionary.* Wheaton, IL: Tyndale House Publishers, 2001. WORD*search* CROSS e-book.

Elwell, Walter A., (Ed.). *Evangelical Dictionary of Theology*, Second ed. Grand Rapids, MI: Baker Book House, 2001. WORD*search* CROSS e-book.

Elwell, Walter A., (Ed.). *"Apocalyptic,"* in *Evangelical Dictionary of Theology*, Second ed. Grand Rapids, MI: Baker Book House, 2001. WORD*search* CROSS e-book.

Encarta ® World English Dictionary © & (P) 1998-2005 Microsoft Corporation.

Evans, William; Coder, S. Maxwell. *The Great Doctrines of the Bible.* Enl. ed. Chicago: Moody Press, 1998, c1974.

Fleming, Don. *The AMG Publishers Concise Bible Dictionary.* Copyright © 1990, 2004 by Database © 2007 WORD*search* Corp.

Fruchtenbaum, Arnold G. *The Footsteps of the Messiah.* San Antonio, Texas: Ariel Ministries, 2002.

Geisler, Norman L. & Howe, Thomas A. *The Big Book of Bible Difficulties: Clear and Concise Answers from Genesis to Revelation.* Grand Rapids, MI: Baker Books. WORD*search* CROSS e-book.

Grenz, Stanley J., Guretzki, David & Nordling, Cherith Fee. "Day of the Lord," in *Pocket Dictionary of Theological Terms.* Downers Grove, IL: InterVarsity Press, 1999. WORD*search* CROSS e-book.

Hendriksen, William. *Baker New Testament Commentary— Exposition of the Gospel According to Matthew.* ©1973 by Database © 2008 WORD*search* Corp.

Ironside, H. A. *H. A. Ironside Commentary—Daniel.* San Diego, CA: Horizon Press, 1911. WORD*search* CROSS e-book.

Jamieson, Robert; Fausset, A. R. & Brown, David. *A Commentary, Critical and Explanatory, on the Old and New Testaments.* Oak Harbor, WA: Inc., 1997.

Kaiser, Walter C. Jr. *A History of Israel.* Nashville, Tennessee: Broadman & Holman, 1998. WORD*search* CROSS e-book.

Keener, Craig S. *The IVP Bible Background Commentary: New Testament.* Downers Grove, Ill.: InterVarsity Press, 1993.

Keener, Craig S. *The IVP New Testament Commentary Series– Matthew.* Downers Grove, IL: Inter Varsity Press.

Kistemaker, Simon J. *Baker New Testament Commentary— Exposition of the Book of Revelation,* (Grand Rapids, MI:

Baker Academic, 2001), WORD*search* CROSS e-book, 308.

Kittel, Gerhard; Friedrich, Gerhard; & Bromiley, Geoffrey William. *Theological Dictionary of the New Testament.* Grand Rapids, MI.: W.B. Eerdmans, 1995, c1985.

Larkin, Clarence. *Rightly Dividing the Word.* Philadelphia: Clarence Larkin Estate, 1921. WORDsearch CROSS e-book.

Louw, Johannes P. & Nida, Eugene Albert. *Greek-English Lexicon of the New Testament: Based on Semantic Domains.* Electronic ed. of the 2nd edition. New York: United Bible societies, 1996, c1989.

MacArthur, John. *The MacArthur New Testament Commentary—Acts 1-12.* Chicago: Moody Press, 1994. WORD*search* CROSS e-book.

MacArthur, John. *The MacArthur New Testament Commentary–Hebrews 11:9,* Chicago: Moody Press, 1983. WORD*search* CROSS e-book.

MacArthur, John. *The MacArthur New Testament Commentary—Revelation 1-11.* Chicago: Moody Press, 1999. WORD*search* CROSS e-book.

MacArthur, John. *The MacArthur New Testament Commentary—Revelation 12-22.* Chicago: Moody Press, 2000. WORD*search* CROSS e-book.

MacArthur, John Jr. *The Book of Revelation.* Audio Series produced by Grace To You, PO Box 4000, Panorama City, CA 91412.

Mangano, Mark, Ph.D. *The College Press NIV Commentary—Esther & Daniel.* Terry Briley & Paul Kissling (Eds.). Joplin, Missouri: College Press Publishing Company, 2001. WORD*search* CROSS e-book.

Marshall, I. Howard (Ed.). *The New Bible Dictionary*, Third Edition Downers Grove, IL: InterVarsity Press, 1996.

Martin, Tony M. & Butler, Trent C. (Eds.). "Chaldea," in *Holman Bible Dictionary.* Nashville, TN: Holman Bible Publishers, 1991. WORD*search* CROSS e-book.

Matoon, Rod. *Mattoon's Treasures—Treasures from Revelation.* Springfield, IL: Lincoln Land Baptist Church, n.d. WORD*search* CROSS e-book.

McGee, J. Vernon *Thru The Bible with J. Vernon McGee.* Nashville, TN: Thomas Nelson, 1983. WORD*search* CROSS e-book.

Merriam-Webster, Inc: *Merriam-Webster's Collegiate Dictionary.* Eleventh ed. Springfield, Mass.: Merriam-Webster, Inc., 2003.

Merriam-Webster, Inc: *Merriam-Webster's Collegiate Thesaurus.* Springfield, Mass.: Merriam-Webster, 1996, c1988.

Merrill, Eugene H. *New American Commentary—Volume 4: Deuteronomy.* Nashville, TN: Broadman & Holman, 1994. WORD*search* CROSS e-book.

Michaels, J. Ramsey. *The IVP New Testament Commentary Series—Revelation.* Grant R. Osborne (Ed.) Downers

Grove, IL: InterVarsity Press, 1997. WORD*search* CROSS e-book.

Morris, Henry M. *The Revelation Record.* Wheaton, IL: Tyndale House Publishers, 1983. WORD*search* CROSS e-book.

Nestle-Aland Greek New Testament, 27th Edition with McReynolds English Interlinear.

Newman, Barclay M. *A Concise Greek-English Dictionary of the New Testament.* Stuttgart: German Bible Society, 1993. WORD*search* CROSS e-book.

Oster, Richard E., Jr., Ph.D. *The College Press NIV Commentary—1 Corinthians.* Jack Cottrell, Ph.D. and Tony Ash, Ph.D. (Eds.) Joplin, Missouri: College Press Publishing Co., 1995. WORD*search* CROSS e-book.

Patzia, Arthur G. and Petrotta, Anthony J. *Pocket Dictionary of Biblical Studies.* Downers Grove, IL: InterVarsity Press, 2002. WORD*search* CROSS e-book.

Peloubet, F.N. *Peloubet's Bible dictionary.* Philadelphia: John E. Winston Co. 1913, 1925, 1947.

Pfeiffer, Charles F. & Harrison, Everett Falconer (Eds.) *The Wycliffe Bible Commentary: New Testament.* Chicago: Moody Press, 1962.

Pfeiffer, Charles F. *The Wycliffe Bible Commentary: Old Testament.* Chicago: Moody Press, 1962,

Philips, John. *The John Phillips Commentary Series—Exploring the Gospel of Matthew: An Expository Commentary.* Grand

Rapids, MI: Kregel Publications, 2005. WORD*search* CROSS e-book.

Poole, Matthew. *Matthew Poole's Commentary on the Holy Bible. (Originally published in 1853.)*

Practical Word Studies in The New Testament. Chattanooga: Leadership Ministries Worldwide, 1998. WORD*search* CROSS e-book.

The Preacher's Outline & Sermon Bible—Ezekiel. Chattanooga: Leadership Ministries Worldwide, 2007. WORD*search* CROSS e-book.

The Preacher's Outline & Sermon Bible—Daniel, Hosea. Chattanooga: Leadership Ministries Worldwide, 2008. WORD*search* CROSS e-book.

The Preacher's Outline and Sermon Bible–Commentary–Ezekiel. Chattanooga: Leadership Ministries Worldwide, 2007. WORD*search* CROSS e-book.

Rand, William Wilberforce (Ed.). *A Dictionary of the Holy Bible.* New York: American Tract Society, 1859. WORD*search* CROSS e-book

Richards, Larry. *The Bible Reader's Companion.* Wheaton, Ill.: Victor Books, 1991.

Robertson, A.T. *Word Pictures in the New Testament.* Oak Harbor: 1997.

Ryken, Leland, Wilhoit, James C. & Longman, Tremper (Eds.). *Dictionary of Biblical Imagery.* Downer's Grove, IL: InterVarsity Press, 1998. WORD*search* CROSS e-book.

Schwandt, John & Collins, C. John. *The* ESV *English–Greek Reverse Interlinear New Testament.* Inc., 2006; 2006. WORD*search* CROSS e-book.

Scott, Walter. *Exposition of the Revelation of Jesus Christ.* London, England: Pickering & Inglis, n.d. WORD*search* CROSS e-book.

Seiss, Joseph A. *The Apocalypse: A Series of Special Lectures on the Revelation of Jesus Christ.* New York: Charles C. Cook, 1901. WORD*search* CROSS e-book.

Soltau, Henry W. *The Holy Vessels and Furniture of the Tabernacle.* London: Yapp and Hawkins, 1860. WORD*search* CROSS e-book.

Spence, H. D. M. & Excell, Joseph S. (Eds.). *The Pulpit Commentary—Volume 12: Ezekiel.* Peabody, MA: Hendrickson, *n.d.* WORD*search* CROSS e-book.

Standard Bible Dictionary. Cincinnati, Ohio: Standard Publishing, 2006. WORD*search* CROSS e-book.

Strauss, Lehman. Lehman Strauss Commentary—The Prophecies of Daniel. WORD*search* CROSS e-book.

Strong, James. *Strong's Greek & Hebrew Dictionary.* 1890. WORD*search* CROSS e-book.

Strong, James: *The Exhaustive Concordance of the Bible: Showing Every Word of the Test of the Common English Version of the Canonical Books, and Every Occurrence of Each Word in Regular Order.* Electronic ed. Ontario: Woodside Bible Fellowship. 1996.

Tan, Paul Lee: *Encyclopedia of 7700 Illustrations: A Treasury of Illustrations, Anecdotes, Facts and Quotations for Pastors, Teachers and Christian Workers*. Garland TX: Bible Communications, 1996, c1979. WORD*search* CROSS e-book.

Today's Best Illustrations—Volume 5. Carol Stream, IL: Christianity Today, 1997. WORD*search* CROSS e-book.

Wiersbe, Warren W. *The Bible Exposition Commentary—New Testament, Volume 1*, (Colorado Springs, CO: Victor, 2001), WORD*search* CROSS e-book

Wiersbe, Warren W.*Wiersbe's Expository Outlines on the New Testament*. Wheaton, Ill.: Victor Books, 1997, c1992, S. 797.

Wiersbe, Warren W. *Be Comforted*. Wheaton, Ill.: Victor Books, 1996, c1992

Wiersbe, Warren W. *Wiersbe's Expository Outlines on the New Testament*. Wheaton, Ill.: Victor Books, 1997, c1992,

Willmington, *Willmington's Guide to the Bible*, (Wheaton, IL: Tyndale House Publishers, 1981), WORD*search* CROSS e-book, 207

Willmington, H. L. *The Complete Book of Bible Lists*, (Wheaton, IL: Tyndale House Publishers, 1987), WORD*search* CROSS e-book, 92.

Willmington, H. L. *Willmington's Bible Handbook*. Wheaton, Ill.: Tyndale House Publishers, 1997, S. 510.

Wilson, Walter L. *A Dictionary of Bible Types*, (Grand Rapids, MI: Wm. B. Eerdmans, 1957; repr., Peabody, MA: Hendrickson, 1999),

Wuest, Kenneth S. Wuest's Word Studies—Volume 2: Word Studies in the Greek New Testament, (Grand Rapids, MI: Wm. B. Eerdmans, 1973), WORDsearch CROSS e-book

Wuest, Kenneth S. Wuest's Word Studies—Volume 2: Word Studies in the Greek New Testament, (Grand Rapids, MI: Wm. B. Eerdmans, 1973), WORD*search* CROSS e-book, 173.

Young, Edward J. *The Book of Isaiah—Volume 3: Chapters 40 to 66*, (Grand Rapids, MI: William B. Eerdmans, 1972), WORD*search* CROSS e-book, 218.

CPSIA information can be obtained
at www.ICGtesting.com
Printed in the USA
FFOW01n0907290916
28028FF